REFLECTIONS ON A MARINE VENUS

*a companion to
the landscape of Rhodes*

by

LAWRENCE DURRELL

With a new introduction by
David Roessel

Marlowe & Company
New York

First Marlowe & Company edition, 1996
Published by
Marlowe & Company
632 Broadway, Seventh Floor
New York, New York 10012

First published in the United States of America by E.P. Dutton 1960

Printed in the United States of America

Library of Congress Catalog Card Number: 96-76839

ISBN 1-56924-791-9

To

SIR WALTER AND LADY SMART

Acknowledgements

I should like to express my thanks to the F.E.R.T. Institute of Rhodes where, through the kindness of Professor G. Morriconi, I was able to study the history of the island, and make use of the invaluable library. I am indebted to the same institution for permission to reproduce the illustrations to this book. I am also grateful to my friend Dr. Raymond Mills for permission to quote from an interesting paper on peasant remedies which he wrote during our stay on Rhodes and to Mrs. Anne Ridler for her help in editing an overgrown MS.

Contents

ABOUT THE AUTHOR

Lawrence Durrell, a British citizen of Irish parentage, was born in the Himalaya region of India. His first ten years were spent in India. After schooling in England, he decided to become a writer. Throughout the 1930's Mr. Durrell devoted most of his talents to his poetry which has won much acclaim. His first novel, *The Black Book,* was published in Paris in 1938; Durrell was cited by T. S. Eliot as being one of the great hopes for modern English fiction. *The Black Book* was published in the United States for the first time in 1960.

World War II temporarily interrupted Mr. Durrell's Literary career. During the war years and for some time thereafter, he served Great Britain in various official and diplomatic capacities in Athens, Cairo, Rhodes and Belgrade.

The publication of *Justine* in 1957, and the subsequent appearance of *Balthazar* (1958), *Mountolive* (1959), and *Clea* (1960) as parts of the same magnificent series called *The Alexandria Quartet* devoted to an examination of the various aspects of love, immediately caused Mr. Durrell to be recognized as one of the greatest and most important writers of modern times.

Reflections on a Marine Venus was first published in 1953.

INTRODUCTION
by David Roessel

"August 27. We set sail from Rhodes for Cyprus on a splendid afternoon. I have turned my eyes upon Rhodes, which sinks at last into the sea. I regret this beautiful island as an apparition one wishes to recall; I could have settled there, if it were less separated from the moving world in which destiny and duty compel us to live!"

These are the words of the French poet Alphonse de Lamartine after two days on the island of Rhodes in 1832. The island was just as alluring when Lawrence Durrell arrived from Egypt over a century later. More fortunate than Lamartine, he stayed for nearly two years instead of two days. *Reflections on a Marine Venus* strives to offer "some sort of effective monument to the charm and grace" of his "sun-washed months" on Rhodes between 1945 and 1947, to describe the effect of a place which has quietly snared the hearts and imaginations of almost every visitor from Lamartine down to the present day.

Durrell had every reason to want to preserve the memory of his stay on Rhodes. The Second World War had brought

exile from his home in Corfu, the breakdown of his first marriage, separation from his young daughter, and the deaths of
friends. For Durrell, as for many others, the war meant the loss
of the world he had known—"in our hearts," he commented
in a manuscript, "we know how much it has aged and poi-
soned us." Rhodes, according to Durrell, provided "our con-
valescence from the war." A major component of his renewed
happiness was Eve Cohen, or "E," as she is called in the text,
whom he brought with him from Alexandria and would marry
on February 26, 1947, in a civil ceremony on Rhodes. Durrell would in later decades write his greatest works, find his
most stable and enduring emotional relationship with his third
wife, Claude, and acquire the financial means to concentrate
on his writing. Yet he may never again have achieved the
peace and serenity of those "dancing summer days passed in
idle friendship and humour by the maned Aegean."

Durrell's volume is subtitled "A Companion to the Landscape of Rhodes," and the nature of the island certainly facil-
itated his recovery. The climate is relatively mild, and in the
heat of summer a breeze always seems to come in from the
western side. It is well-watered, fertile and one of the more
aromatic places in Europe with the scents of lavender, sage,
and styrax hanging almost constantly in the air. The visitor is
not overwhelmed by the monuments of the past, wonderful
as these are in the medieval town of Rhodes or on the ancient
acropolis of Lindos. Rather, as Durrell put it: "the landscape
put her nymph's arms about human habits, beliefs, style of
minds so that imperceptibly they are overgrown by the fine
net of her caresses." The island's "green and gentle self,"
which, according to Durrell, softened the conquering Franks
and Turks, still affects those who venture there.

The geographical position of Rhodes added to Durrell's
sense of tranquillity. It lies 7 miles south of the south-western
tip of the Anatolian peninsula. Until the nineteenth century,

it was a major port of call for ships traveling between Constantinople and Egypt as well as between Italy and the Middle East. But, with the advent of steam-power, ships engaged in trade no longer had to break the journey at Rhodes, and the island grew remote from what Lamartine had called "the moving world" around it. In Durrell's time, with only a daily military mail plane and infrequent caique service, the sense of isolation from the outside world would have been strong. But, unlike the French poet, Durrell had had his fill of duty and destiny during the previous six years, and was quite content to let the outside world pass him by for awhile.

Rhodes provided Durrell with something else he had lacked since he had left the Ionian island of Corfu in 1939—a home of his own. Even though *Prospero's Cell, Reflections on a Marine Venus,* and *Bitter Lemons* are routinely labeled "travel" books, a house stands at the heart of each of them. On Rhodes, it was the "Villa Cleobolus," named after an ancient Greek poet and politician who sometimes appears as one of "the seven sages" of antiquity. After he moved into it, he wrote to his old friend Henry Miller, "I can't tell you what a wonderful peace and quiet it is, having a house of your own after so many years living from suitcases in hotels, or sharing flats with awful people."

Rhodes was in something of a state of political limbo when Durrell disembarked in June of 1945. The other Aegean islands, with the exception of Tenedos and Imbros at the mouth of Dardanelles, had been joined to Greece between the Balkan Wars of 1912–13 and the treaties at the end of World War I. But Rhodes and its sister islands, called collectively the Dodecanese, had been seized by Italy in 1912 after the Italians had invaded Libya during the Italo-Turkish War.[1] The Dode-

---

[1]In Greek, the name means "twelve islands," although there are actually 14 inhabited islands in the group and literally dozens of uninhabited islets which are covered by the term Dodecanese.

canese were still in Italian hands at the beginning of the Second World War, and when they were liberated in 1945, they fell under British Military Administration, until a decision was made as to their fate. Because of Durrell's nearly flawless Greek and his prior knowledge of Greece, he was assigned as Public Information Officer for the entire region. Since the majority of the islanders favored union with their Greek "motherland" and Greece had heroically resisted the Axis powers, the consensus of the victorious powers was that the islands would become part of Greece. Still, in the difficult, often contentious debates about the organization of the world after the war, the Soviet Union withheld approval of such a settlement until June 17, 1946. Durrell had written in a letter to a friend in early June of that year: "How sweet the NO of [Soviet Foreign Minister] Molotov sounds to me." Ironically, by the time the letter was received, Molotov's "no" had changed to a "yes." Even after the islands were earmarked for Greece, the actual transfer was postponed until the final post-war treaty between Italy and the victorious Allies was signed on February 27, 1947. Some two weeks later, on March 7, the islands were officially handed over to Greece and, by that time, Durrell had already begun his journey back to England.

The British Military Administration, while it did laudable service in alleviating the shortage of food and restoring public works, left only one lasting monument of its almost two years on Rhodes—*Reflections on a Marine Venus* by Lawrence Durrell, Public Information Officer and, among other things, official censor. His main duties were to supervise and assist visiting journalists and to oversee the publication of local newspapers in Greek, Italian, and Turkish. Although Durrell lamented in letters to friends about the demands of the job, he was often able to escape from the office. The military mission had provided him with a jeep to travel throughout Rhodes and permission to travel around the Dodecanese on any available naval ship, and he made ample use of these opportunities. He visited the Monastery of St. John on Patmos at least twice, and, the reader will be glad to know, once stayed as a guest of the abbot. On the other hand, for a writer desperately seeking time and leisure to pursue his craft, the distractions of his job must have been quite frustrating. On Rhodes he did not have time to write as he had on Corfu. But his position was hardly as demanding as the work he would find on Cyprus from 1953 to 1956, when he went from exacting hours teaching at the leading high school in Nicosia to the demanding chore of Director of Public Information during a State of Emergency.

Given the post-war problems elsewhere in Europe, especially in Greece, Durrell was doubly fortunate to have landed on a remote sunny island away from the action. Knowing the position on Rhodes was temporary, he made several trips to Athens to see if he could find some sort of employment in the Greek capital. Nothing materialized, but if it had Durrell would have been thrown right into the bitter and bloody political disputes which had already caused one civil war and would soon start another—disputes which are often simplified into a contest between the right and the left but were too complicated and horrible for such easy categorization.[2] Yet as Durrell cheerfully wrote from Rhodes to a correspondent, there were "no party politics here." The reason was simple; all the Greeks on Rhodes and all the political parties in Greece were united in the immediate goal of bringing the islands into Greece. In fact, it was pressure from the Greek communist party which caused the Soviet Union Russians to allow unification to proceed. The one rather light-hearted, even-handed mention of E.A.M., the communist-dominated

---

[2]For an insightful account by an observer at the time, see C. M. Woodhouse's *Apple of Discord: A Survey of Recent Greek Politics in Their International Setting* (London, 1948).

National Unification Front, by the fisherman Manoli in *Reflections on a Marine Venus* is a far cry from the strident partisan rhetoric out of Athens. "They [E.A.M.] come to deliver us from poverty. God knows, we need it. But they will end in enslaving us in other evils. God knows, we don't want that." Durrell only had to contend with the disagreements between British officials and their Greek successors over protocol; these were aggravating but provided material for comedy, not tragedy. Joining the "motherland," two other ethnic groups on the island faced less cheerful prospects. Much of the sizable Italian community, many of whom had lived on the islands for decades, was repatriated to Italy. The larger Turkish population, although they became full citizens of the Greek state, slowly began an exodus across the Aegean to Turkey and only a handful now remain. The Turkish graveyard around Durrell's little house has fallen into neglect and disrepair; vandals have knocked off the tops of the gravestones so that they no longer clearly indicate whether a male or female lies underneath. On my last visit in 1992, a lonely old Turkish woman still cared for the tomb of Murad Reis, the Turkish admiral who helped to conquer Rhodes in 1522, which lies on the other side of the graveyard from the Villa Cleobolus. The call of the muezzin no longer "sounds soft and musical in the dawn-light." Old hatreds and new conflicts, such as in Cyprus, have led to its disappearance from the island.

Durrell marks with regret the departure of the Italians and avoids mention of Turkish apprehension about union with Greece. His sentiment comes through in a line in the poem "The Lost Cities," where, echoing the feelings of the Greek Rhodians, he refers to Rhodes as "Greece which is not yet Greece." Durrell had felt keenly the loss of Greece in 1941 and threw himself into Greek language and folklore when he reached Rhodes. He translated both Greek poetry and prose into English, and, at least on one occasion, wrote an article about ancient Rhodian history in modern Greek for the literary magazine, *Techni*, which he had helped to create. The "Villa Cleobolus," which when last seen was uninhabited and in need of repair, bears a plaque announcing that it was once the home of Lawrence Durrell, "the philhellene." It is a fitting tribute to his attitude and activities on Rhodes.

In *Prospero's Cell*, his book about Corfu, Durrell had cautioned that "[i]t is important when writing about peasants, not to falsify them with sentimental humour." Durrell had difficulty in following his own prescription; his "Greeks" are shot through with sentimental humor. His definition of "the Greek" on Rhodes is a "terrible fellow. Mercuric, noisy, voluble, proud—was there ever such a conjunction of qualities locked in a human breast? Only the Irishman could match him for intractability, for rowdy feckless generosity." Durrell, like D. H. Lawrence, needed a Mediterranean peasantry that was primitive, natural and volcanic as a positive foil for the desiccated, effete, prudish English. Durrell certainly knew well-educated and urbane Greeks—during his visits to Athens he met with the poets George Seferis and Andreas Sikelianos, as well as that master raconteur, George Katsimbalis.[3] They were not voluble, "terrible fellows" from the local coffee-shop, however, so they do not appear in the text. Durrell's attitude can seem condescending, but one must keep in mind that Durrell did not have the superficial perspective of the tourist. He knew the Greek language, people, and customs well, and if in his islands books he chose to portray one class of Greeks rather than another, it was not a choice made out of ignorance of the variety of the Greek world.

In contrast to the colorful Greeks, Durrell had nothing good to say about the other English on Rhodes beyond his

---

[3] A colorful account of Katsimbalis appears in Henry Miller's *The Colossus of Maroussi* (1941).

own small circle of friends. In private letters, he complained quite often about what he called "the largest collection of de-frocked priests, ex-jockeys, haberdashers, and ruined boxers . . . ever to lord it over an innocent and beautiful people; your hair would turn white to see the condescension and rudeness." Perhaps because *Reflections on a Marine Venus* was aimed at an audience including just these same elements, Durrell left such outbursts out of the book.

Durrell began planning a volume about Rhodes shortly after he arrived on the island. In his last months in Egypt, he had completed the book about his life in Corfu from 1935 to 1937. The favorable reviews it received when it appeared in November, 1945, would only have encouraged the idea of an-other such work of Greek landscape. Durrell had another rea-son to want to write and publish several more books quickly; by his own account he needed three to pay for his divorce from his first wife, Nancy. Around half of *Reflections on a Ma-rine Venus* was written during his stay on Rhodes. In fact, one section, the engaging story of his trip to the monastery on Pat-mos and the problems with the abbot's telephone, was pub-lished in the Athenian based journal, *Greek Horizons,* in the summer of 1946. Despite this promising start, progress on the book languished after his departure from Rhodes. Durrell and Eve returned to England, where in late 1947 he obtained an appointment as a lecturer for the British council in Argentina. He left that position after a year, and subsequently became the press attaché in the British Embassy at Belgrade, a post which he held from July 1949 until the end of 1952. During this pe-riod, Durrell struggled to complete *Reflections on a Marine Venus,* which he felt had "gone stale" because of "too many changes of scene and five years of bad postings." It was, iron-ically, from a grim Belgrade under the control of Tito's com-munist party that Durrell sent the completed manuscript about his stay on sunny Rhodes to his publisher in England.

That package contained a volume which was nearly twice as long as the version that was published. Faber and Faber apparently wanted a much smaller book, along the lines of the slender *Prospero's Cell*. Durrell, in the words of long-time friend Alan Thomas, was "loath to perform disagreeable surgery upon a book which embodied so much of his own life," and the task fell to his friend and editor, Anne Ridler. Durrell, not surprisingly, was never completely happy with the excisions, remarking to a friend after *Reflections on a Marine Venus* was published: "Glad the Rhodes book amused you— cut in half as it was—I can't bear it." Despite such comments, Durrell was fortunate to have had such an astute hand in fashioning his book for the public. The *Reflections on a Marine Venus* which Durrell sent to his publisher in 1952 was still very much a post-war book, with many more references to the war and tinged with war-time skepticism and disillusionment. Ridler excised most of the passages and left the descriptions of the landscape and people which continue to delight readers. She oriented the book to sunlight, blue skies, and clear sea.

"History as chronology is misleading," Durrell wrote in *Reflections on a Marine Venus*. So it is not surprising that it is impossible to place events in the book in any proper chronological order. For example, towards the end of the volume, Durrell speaks of pottery which had stood in his house "for two years now." But he did not move into the Villa Cleobolus until July 31, 1946, and actually only lived in the house for seven of the twenty-one months he lived on the island. It hardly matters, however, since the importance of the house, for Durrell and for the book, outweighs the number of days of his residence. And at times the text seems slightly at odds with itself. The appendix entitled "A Short Calendar of Flowers and Saints for Rhodes" comments that on "July 30th there is a huge open-air festival at Soroni to celebrate the arrival of St. Saul who was a fellow-passenger of St. Paul during his ship-wreck at Lindos." It is impossible to reconcile this entry with the climactic chapter in which the festival of the same St. Saul, or Soulas, occurs on the very day that Durrell received his orders to leave the island in two weeks—a directive which had actually arrived in mid-February of 1947. How does July become February? "Only by a strict submission to the laws of inconsequence can one ever write about an island," a sentence that makes perfect sense in the world of islomania.

The assiduous archivist or die-hard Durrell lover would have even more trouble tracking down information about the irrepressible Gideon, with his glass eye on one side and his clear glass monocle on the other. He, is it seems, half-fictional creation and half-Lawrence Durrell (Gideon's literary interests, such as the translation of the elegy by Cleobolus and the translation of the Greek novel *Pope Joan,* were both projects of Durrell's). In a footnote, this same character is said to have been "accidentally killed in crossing an unmarked minefield" leaving "a gap in our lives that could never be filled." Even when one discovers that Gideon only existed in Durrell's pages, that gap seems no less real.

In December, 1952, Durrell resigned his position with the foreign service with the intention of recreating the happy past with Eve on the island of Cyprus. But Eve suffered a nervous break-down just before the move was to be made, and Durrell went on alone with his small daughter, Sappho. Eve came out almost a year later, but the marriage failed and by the middle of 1955 both Eve and Sappho had left for England. And Durrell's good fortune at missing the bitter political struggles in post-war Athens ran out when, in the mid-1950s, the Greek Cypriots began calling in earnest for their own union with the Greek motherland. Durrell, who became the Director of Public Information for the Colonial Government in August of 1954, was in no position to call Cyprus "Greece which is not yet Greece." It led to bad feelings on both sides, and when

Durrell finally left the island in 1956 the close bond that he had with the Greeks, while not broken, would never be the same. At around the same time, the great work which had been brewing in his mind for well over a decade began to appear in print. The four novels of *The Alexandria Quartet* would establish Durrell as one of the leading writers of his day, and ensure that he could devote the rest of his life to his work, including his last great series, *The Avignon Quintet,* in his new home in southern France.

Reflections on a Marine Venus and *Prospero's Cell,* along with Henry Miller's *The Colossus of Maroussi,* were all written in the shadow of a war when travel to Greece was nearly non-existent. Yet those books changed the nature of travel writing about Greece, signaled by the fact that when Patrick Leigh Fermor, who went on to become the best interpreter of Greece in the next decade with *Mani* and *Roumeli,* first read *Prospero's Cell* on Corfu in the summer of 1946, he went almost immediately to Rhodes to visit Lawrence Durrell. The Greece we see in our minds, the Greece filled with what Henry Miller called "antinomian spots," was introduced to us by Durrell and Miller. They prepared the way for the favorable reception of the first English translation of Kazantzakis' great novel, *Zorba the Greek,* which appeared in 1953. Whether we carry *Reflections on a Marine Venus* to the Greek islands for both actual and imaginary voyages, it still goes with us. So it is better simply to have the text at hand, and to sit back and let the pages, like the days on Rhodes "drop as softly as fruit from the trees."

The author would like to acknowledge with appreciation the generosity of Yiannis and Jean Moschovakis, in whose home this introduction was written.

CHAPTER I

Of Paradise Terrestre

Alvarez fled; and after him the doom
Of exile was sent out; he, as report
Was bold to voice, retired himself to Rhodes
  MIDDLETON: *The Spanish Gipsy*

S omewhere among the note-books of Gideon I once found a
list of diseases as yet unclassified by medical science, and among
these there occurred the word *Islomania,* which was described as
a rare but by no means unknown affliction of spirit. There are
people, Gideon used to say, by way of explanation, who find islands
somehow irresistible. The mere knowledge that they are on an
island, a little world surrounded by the sea, fills them with an indescribable intoxication. These born 'islomanes', he used to add, are
the direct descendants of the Atlanteans, and it is towards the lost
Atlantis that their subconscious yearns throughout their island life. . . .
I forget the other details. But like all Gideon's theories it was an
ingenious one. I recall how bitterly it was debated by candle-light
in the Villa Cleobolus until the moon went down on the debate, and
until Gideon's contentions were muffled in his yawns: until Hoyle
began to tap his spectacles upon the thumbnail of his left hand, which
was his way of starting to say goodnight: until Mehmet Bay, in the
house across the oleander-grove, banged his shutters together as a protest against the lateness of the hour. Yet the word stuck; and though
Hoyle refused its application to any but Aegean islands, while Sand
could not bring himself to look a theory so irrational in the eye, we
all of us, by tacit admission, knew ourselves to be 'islomanes'.

This book is by intention a sort of anatomy of islomania, with all its formal defects of inconsequence and shapelessness: of conversations begun and left hanging in the air: of journeys planned and never undertaken: of notes and studies put together against books unwritten.... It is to be dedicated to the resident goddess of a Greek island—Rhodes. I should like, if possible, to recall some part of those golden years, whose ghosts still rise up and afflict me whenever I catch sight of a letter with a Greek stamp on it, or whenever, in some remote port of the world, I happen upon a derelict tanker flying the Aegean blue-and-white.

In Rhodes the days drop as softly as fruit from trees. Some belong to the dazzling ages of Cleobolus and the tyrants, some to the gloomy Tiberius, some to the Crusaders. They follow each other in scales and modes too quickly almost to be captured in the nets of form. Only by a strict submission to the laws of inconsequence can one ever write about an island—as an islomane, that is. And then who could ever hope to pin down, to circumscribe, the charms of a resident Goddess? I have not attempted to cut down below the surface of my subjects' poses. I have attempted to illumine a single man by a single phrase, and to leave him where he sits embedded in the slow flux of Grecian days, undisturbed by literary artifice—as a good host should.... Gideon with his monocle screwed in sitting soberly before a bottle of *mastika*; Hoyle winding his enormous watch; Mills talking; Sand sucking his pipe; Egon Huber walking the deserted beaches hunting for scraps of wood to carve; and the dark-eyed E, whose shadow is somehow spread over all these—a familiar, a critic, a lover—E putting on a flowered frock in the studio mirror with her black hair ruffled. I have tried not to disturb them in the little eternities of their island life, where somehow their spirits mingle and join that of the Marine Venus standing in her little stone cell at the Museum like a challenge from a life infinitely more remote. If I have sacrificed form it is for something better, sifting into the material now some old notes from a forgotten scrap-book, now a letter: all the quotidian stuff which might give a common reader the feeling of life lived in a historic present.

That spring afternoon of 1945 when the order to embark came through to us in Alexandria, my first glimpse of Gideon, I remember, was not reassuring. We were to be fellow-passengers aboard a military HDML—a vessel whose sleek and powerful lines suggested to my innocent eyes speedy and comfortable travel. We were promised an early morning landfall in Rhodes. In a few hours, then, I should find myself, after some four years of exile, on a Greek island once more.

Gideon stood among a cluster of engineers and seamen, abstractedly reading a book. I recall thinking to myself that he looked the personification of orthodoxy: the monocle, the clipped silver hair, the polished boots. . . . (An Indian Army regular whose knowledge of routine has placed him at the head of a sub-department devoted to sanitation or supply?) If I were to spend twenty-four hours in his company, I thought, I should undoubtedly spend them in politely deferring to judgements based on popular prejudice, or the *naif* self-regard of a regular soldier who has come to regard his regimental mess as the whole wide world. His rather obvious glass eye regarded the world from time to time with what seemed to me to be a somewhat boorish indifference—an impression which was strengthened when I saw him accept without thanks a comfortable chair and a cushion. The rest of us lay about his feet upon cushions improvised out of our kit. He was followed by a little black and white terrier, obviously very well trained.

On one point, however, my mind was soon set at rest. The panting of the great engines as they drove us storming across the oily waters of Alexandria towards the open sea made it quite clear that conversation would be an impossibility. We were each of us to be sealed up in the great throbbing privacy of sound. I cannot say I was unhappy. There was so much to think about, so much to hope for, in the idea of seeing Greece again. I thought of all the letters I had received in recent months—letters with an obituary flavour. 'You will find it completely changed' said one. 'The old life has gone forever' said another. 'Go to America' urged a third. Tomorrow I should see for myself whether the old Greek ambience had survived the war, whether it was still a reality based in the landscape and the people— or whether we had simply invented it for ourselves in the old days, living comfortably on foreign exchange, patronising reality with our fancies and making bad literature from them. Tomorrow I should know whether I must relegate my feelings about Greece to the dusty corners of memory along with so many other mad vagaries of the heart.

As we rounded the old fort I turned back to catch a last glimpse of E standing and waving to me from the corner of the esplanade before the mist began to settle and the whole scimitar-like sweep of minarets and belfries of the upper town dissolved in soft pearl and gold. Egypt and Greece—for a moment the conflicting loyalties of love and habit assailed me. But E was following me to Rhodes after an interval of weeks: and she was my only tie with Egypt. I saw her enter the old office car, and watched it move slowly off in the murk. The journey had begun!

Ten miles off Alexandria we were still carving up a solid brown trench in the waters of the open sea—waters polluted by the dense Nilotic silt—when a solitary dolphin struck surface and galloped alongside us for a moment; my heart rose at the augury, for the fish is a bringer of fair weather and luck. I leaned to follow it with my eye when, with the suddenness of an axe falling, we hit the pure Mediterranean blueness of the true Aegean: a sea with depth and tone, that swallowed and gave back the sky; a sea that belonged to the waterless islands and grey windmills, to the olive-trees and the statues. At long last we had burst through the misty curtain of atmosphere that lies forever over Mareotis.

The sun was slowly setting, lumbering down into the Underworld. My fellow-passengers had, for the greater part, fallen asleep. Gideon alone sat awake over his book, tapping away an occasional yawn with a long index finger and caressing his dog. The crew came up and distributed mugs of service tea. If you leaned to the rail now and stared down into the water you had the impression that we were flying; the flared bows of the HSL were lifted high as she drove her coarse furrow through the still sea. The snarling of the great engines wrapped us all in a deaf silence—a marvellous brutal music of vibrating steel and wood. Behind us we left great stains of oily heat upon the waters and a white cicatrice which slowly healed again. The warmth of the coarse sweet tea was delightful; it reminded one that night was falling, and that the cold was slowly settling in from the west. Presently I too lay down and drifted into a shallow sleep from which all this noise seemed to be like the placid roaring in some coloured sea-shell picked up on the warm beaches of Corfu or Delos in those happy years before the war. It was as if my longing to be back in Greece had all but exhausted itself in fulfilment. I was numbed. Forgotten scenes came into my mind, without form or coherence, yet bathed in the sunny lambency of the Greek past, and even in my sleep I felt something like the absurd disposition to tears with which I last saw the shores of Crete fade into the mists of 1941.

The storm which caught us some eighty miles off Alexandria had been described in the weather report as 'a slight squall'. It seemed nothing so negligible. Indeed the first impact suggested something like the eruption of a volcano. The HDML hit the first wave with a prodigious slap that jolted every bone in our bodies. Such weather would have been bad enough in an island *caieque,* but in a craft which could not throttle down to less than fifteen knots without making leeway, its effect was indescribable. I awoke to see the Aegean heaped up around us in glossy valleys, lit by the yellowish glare of the ship's lamps. The even snarling of the engines was now punctuated by a regular series of sobs and grunts and by the horrible grinding of the screws as they were lifted clear of purchase.

In later days Gideon was used to say (when asked how first we had met) that we had been thrown together. He enjoyed the literal as well as the figurative aspects of the phrase far more, I am sure, than either of us enjoyed the storm which first introduced us to each other. But thrown together we certainly were. At the first impact of wind and water the ship began the butting, goring motion we were to learn so well. The noise of the screws before they buried themselves in the sea once more suggested the noise of a giant grinding his teeth. Hurled into a corner, I found Gideon's head in my lap, and my legs round the neck of a soldier. We lip-read each others' apologies and disengaged as gracefully as we could—only to be flung down once more in a heap. It was impossible to stand upright; it was rather more than difficult to manage to stay in one place. Throttled down as far as she would go the HDML skidded along the surface of the sea with the waves breaking over her in a series of stabbing white concussions. We braced our feet firmly and listened to the dull whacking of the hull against the water, and the dismal sound of crockery being smashed in the galley. From this time forward we lived on all-fours, crouching like apes whenever we wished to move about the ship. Sleep became an impossibility. The terrific slap of every wave was like a punch to the solar plexus. The little dog retreated with a world-weary air to the furthest end of an empty kit-bag where it curled up and slept.

Several people began to be picturesquely sick. Gideon and I retreated in opposite corners like spiders and contemplated this weakness on the part of our fellow-passengers with a disgust so identical that we were forced to smile, catching each other's eye. I saw that he had smashed his monocle. Unbuttoning his jacket he pulled out a cigar-case containing, as far as I could judge, some twenty replacements, and inserted one.

The dawn came up as thick as glue; westward the sky had taken on the colour of oiled steel. The storm had passed over us, leaving behind it only a heavy sea propped up in an endless succession of watery slabs. The prow of the HDML still buried itself in the waves with feverish crunchings and tremblings. Some of us slept, and later by the watery beams of the early sun, were able to extend the limits of our visibility as far as a horizon dipping and swelling—but offering as yet no trace of land.

The passengers lay about upon piles of disordered kit, for all the world like corpses on pyres, waiting for torches to set them alight. As the daylight advanced a few of the hardier souls took courage and stuck out their pallid and unshaven faces to ask questions of the crew. Where were we? When would we arrive? The army showed a disinclination to discuss the question. Indeed it looked as if they knew as little as we did. We had been blown off our course. Speculation which at first seemed academic, began to be ever so slightly tinged with alarm, as we caught sight of the captain poring over a chart of the Eastern Mediterranean. The cook distributed mugs of cocoa over which the problem was discussed from every angle. Gideon, I discovered, was reading an account of Aegean travel published in the eighties of the last century by an eccentric divine, the Rev. Fanshawe Tozer, whose writings were to amuse and delight us so much afterwards. He passed me this work with the opening paragraph heavily scored by his thumbnail, and made a grimace as he did so. I took it and read: '*There is an element of excitement attending a voyage to Rhodes arising from the uncertainty which exists with regard to reaching that island.*' The Rev. Tozer then had shared many of our present misgivings in the early eighties. I hoped sincerely that this passage was not to prove an augury. It seemed a positively ominous quotation to stumble upon at this time and place.

Later we shared some mouldy rounds of sandwich and a bottle of Cyprus cognac which I had had the forethought to bring with me; and finally, inspired by the warmth of the sun and a calmer patch of weather we left the dumb-show in which our politeness had been so far continued (the wind and rain plus the noise of the engines precluding any more civilized exchange) and fell to words: single words carefully shouted across the intervening space to form sentences.

'We'll probably touch Cyprus tonight.'

'Cyprus? Surely not.'

'What will you bet?'

'It's hundreds of miles away.'

'Bah! These Army people never do anything right.'

An officer who happened to be crawling past with that peculiar air of devout forbearance that seamen affect when they are carrying unwelcome passengers, glared at Gideon. He seemed about to say something rather forcible, but my companion had already retreated behind his book. He emerged to wrinkle his nose at the retreating back.

'Mark me,' he said, 'They could land us in Beirut without turning a hair.'

It did not seem wise to continue a conversation any further along these lines. I fell into a doze and the morning passed in a series of watery sunshines punctuated by squalls and the threshings of the sea. In the late afternoon the weather brought us its omens of approaching land—two spring turtle-doves, blown off their course, no doubt. They swerved over us and were gone in the direction of Africa.

The problem of our position had not been clarified by any official pronouncement beyond the bare admission that we were off our course. Speculation still made pretty free with place-names. Dusk closed down in a series of thin, misty rainstorms, which reduced visibility to a few hundred yards; and darkness had barely followed dusk when there was a shout which turned every head in the direction of the lighted cockpit where, above the great illuminated dials of the dashboard the rubber windscreen-wipers bored circles of clarity in the pervading murk of that sottish dusk. Someone had spotted land—the merest etching of darkness upon darkness—and for an hour we thundered along a black and rocky coast, catching fitful glimpses of its capes and cliffs through the shifting packets of mist. To add to the rising emotions of optimism and relief came the pleasant sensation of a calmer sea. We began to reassemble our dispersed possessions and comb our sticky hair. I could taste the sharp brine which had dried on the unshaven stubble of my lips. Gideon traced the parting of his silver hair with something like complacence, and then examined the cavities in his teeth. He seemed to approve of what he saw. Then he offered me his comb. 'You see,' he said, 'it will turn out to be Cyprus.'

It turned out to be Rhodes. We rounded several more headlands before an officer came aft and told us so. As if endowed with powers of human understanding Gideon's little dog (its name turned out to be Homer) emerged from its hideout and began to tidy itself up. 'That's the stuff' said its master.

Vague lights now appeared and the note of the engines mellowed and sank in tone. Dark slabs of harbour masonry wallowed and glittered against the street-lights as we nosed slowly in. All that could be seen of the famous harbour was a small area of some fifty square yards lighted by some makeshift method to guide shipping. The rest was blackness which swallowed up the cracked masonry, the steel pickets and the rusty barbed wire which covered the whole of the waterfront. Absolute blackness otherwise.

The silence that now fell with the extinguishing of the great engines was almost greater in volume than the sound to which we had accustomed ourselves for so long. People still shouted deafly at one another. Space had swollen again to its customary dimensions. We landed in the murk. The yawing and pitching of the ship had given us all a trembling muscular reflex movement of thigh and shoulder—so that we walked like old salts in a musical comedy. Our passes were collected by a tired-looking naval officer who motioned us with a vague gesture of his arm towards the outer darkness. Shouldering our packs we stumbled off towards the transit hotel down a dark street lined with rustling trees. I broke a leaf off and crumpled it in my fingers to inhale the sweet odour of eucalyptus oil. At the end of the long corridor of darkness two tall gates rose up, and behind them the once famous *Albergo della Rosa,* showing here and there a point of light, weak and diffuse. The steps seemed endless—it was like climbing into the sky. . . .

But already as I write the weariness of that late arrival begins to melt the clear outlines of the detail. I vaguely remember the vast entrance hall littered with shed equipment, the buzz of conversation from the dining-hall which served as a mess, the smashed marquetry panels of the lounge, and the timid Italians who serviced the hotel. I remember too the draughts of pure sea air that stole in from the terrace, bearing with them the scent of spring flowers, and the desire for sleep which struggled against the urge to walk into the garden and smell the darkness which stretched away across the straits to Anatolia. But it was no good: the journey had been too much for us.

We lay upon adjacent sofas in the gaunt lounge with its foggy mirrors, waiting for our rooms to be prepared by a sleepy maid with a hare-lip. I remember Gideon lying there, his monocle almost touching the floor—it had rolled out of his eye to the end of its cord: his feet clad in a pair of much-darned socks: his whole body slack and unstrung: snoring.

So we slept.

Much later we were awoken, and blind with sleep followed the clerk to our rooms. The open windows gave directly on to the sea whose melodious sighing was the perfect accompaniment to a landfall as felicitous as a Greek island: to a sleep as blankly anonymous as that which welled up around us.

I speak for myself. Some centuries later (or was it back: had one travelled backwards into sleep like history?) I woke to feel the warm early sun in my eyes, reflecting the running dazzle of water from the white roof of the room. Gideon was already standing on the balcony, clad only in a monocle and a towel, doing his exercises with the rapt devotion of a yogi, watched by his little dog.

Presently we scrambled across the garden, and still half drugged with sleep, burst into the Aegean water, clear and cold as wine.

Before us across the straits the Anatolian mountains glowed, each one a precious stone. Icy though the water was we stayed awhile in it, speechless with gratitude—rubbed by the salt until our skins felt as cold and smooth as the pebbles which tesselated the shining floors of that magnificent beach.

To the memory of that first bathe I should add the memory of that first breakfast (mere bully beef and dry biscuit) eaten in the company of our fellows at the long trestle-tables which filled the once fashionable dining-room. Both were commonplaces no doubt—but translated into miracles by the feeling that, after all, we had arrived. The morning fairly danced and sparkled. Outside the hotel (whose desolate corridors, chipped marquetry, smashed fittings and marble cornices suggested nothing so much as a carnival which had ended in an earthquake)—outside, the blue race of the sea swirled round the stone lighthouse and deployed crisply across what must be one of the finest shingle beaches in the world. The sunlight freckled the foreground of things with blue and gold, while the gaunt backcloth of Caria, only tipped as yet with sunshine, seemed to be softly sifting itself through a spectrum. Utter peace.

'Heavens, I feel well,' said Gideon. We had carried our third cup of tea out on to the terrace, and were full of the warmth and well-being of that spring sunshine.

Idling there upon that terrace we first began our exploration of each other. My own task here was prosaic enough. I had been accredited to the occupying forces as an Information Officer. Gideon's own business was more obscure; he made several mumbling attempts to describe it. Finally he squared his shoulders and produced a crumpled movement order which he handed me to read. I could see nothing very strange about it. It informed me that Captain A. Gideon was proceeding to Palermo via Rhodes on duty. 'You don't see anything odd about it?' he said with a chuckle, and with a touch of fatuous if innocent pride. 'Neither did the provost-marshal.' He beamed at me and explained. He had long ago noticed that the legend 'will proceed from X to Y' on a movement order was sufficiently well-spaced to allow him to insert the word 'via' followed by the name of any little corner of the globe that he might wish to visit. He had spent a good part of the war travelling unwillingly *from X to Y*—but always *'via'* somewhere or other where he really wanted to go. 'It's my form of revolt' he said coyly. 'For Godsake don't tell a soul.' I promised gravely. 'You've no idea what a difference it makes to go from one hellish place to another when you can go and spend a few days "in transit" in a place you really like.' Rhodes, I gathered from subsequent conversation, was an old love, first visited before 1914 war; more than that, Gideon was hoping to find himself a billet in the administration which would enable him to escape from an O.C. he detested in Palermo. He seemed quite confident that a few days of lobbying in Rhodes would produce something suitable. Behind the idea of a transfer, too, lay another—more deeply cherished: he intended to settle in Rhodes after demobilisation. This was interesting. We were, it seemed, both islomanes.

It was in this context that we began to share reminiscences of the pre-war world and unearth common friends. Gideon too had been a tramp in the Eastern Mediterranean before the war: had lived in Athens and Alexandria.

His figure was undergoing a transformation in my eyes. It was to suffer many others, but none so radical as this first one, from that of the average sightless soldier to the man of culture and comparatively wide reading. One element only was missing from the picture. I supply it from subsequent experiences. I had no idea what an old rogue he was. I was taken in by that air of benevolence, of courtly gentleness. I was tempted to shake my head sadly over the innocence of a man who imagined he could cadge himself a job after a few days in Rhodes. How wrong I was! I realised it a month later when I glanced at a circular which named him the newly-arrived director of —Agriculture, of all things. But none of this could I have foreseen that spring morning as we walked down to the harbour to pay our respects to the military rulers of the twelve islands. I was not to foresee Gideon's numberless state visits in his broken-down old car— visits undertaken with the greatest urgency to consult me upon a Point of Style, or an infinitive that had somehow split like a string-bean in the heat of composition. Nor could I foresee how much pleasure I was to derive 'putting some style' into those fatuous concoctions titled PROGRESS REPORT ON BEET or THE WATERCRESS OUTLOOK FOR NEXT YEAR. We lavished the combined treasure of our

25

not inconsiderable intellects on those reports. To read Gideon on Beet was a new literary experience. Everyone was pleased except the Brigadier, who pronounced Gideon's style abominable and refused to grant him his majority until he had read and studied Swift.

That morning however we made our first sortie into Rhodes town, Gideon 'en pèlerinage', as he expressed it, and I very much on duty—for I had to locate the printing-plant which was to be the greatest part of my inheritance from the Army. Rumour had it that the linotypes were buried somewhere in the castle and accordingly we set off along the sparkling water-front in the direction of the Street of the Knights, Gideon talking discursively on everything under the sun, and exclaiming with pleasure at every new sight and sound.

Taken in by the uncritical eye of a visitor the town looked lovely that morning despite the infernal wreckage of war—and there was plenty of it. Transcribed from a letter which remained unposted in the back of an old writing pad, these few lines give an impressionist view of Rhodes as I found it, 'Absolute chaos still reigns. The esplanade along Mandraccio, the ancient harbour, is studded with pill-boxes and long rows of iron staples from which grave Indian infantrymen are unwinding the barbed wire. Groups of German prisoners, still whey-coloured from starvation, are busy filling in the bomb-craters in the asphalt, dressed for the most part in shorts and forage-caps only.We have thousands of them on our hands. Clouds of violet smoke hang over Monte Smith from some disposal squad's morning offering to the Gods—exploded enemy mines. I have not had time to look at the medieval town as yet, but it looks fearfully disappointing from the harbour with its spattered administrative buildings and truncated statuary: the old walled town looks like a wedding-cake with all the icing chipped and cracked. A deserted market-place. An empty mosque. A very few white-faced civilians picking over garbage-tins for food. Most of the population has fled to the islands of Symi and Casos. The streets are empty of all but troops and forage-gangs of German prisoners.'

Less impressionistic, but as factually relevant to this first view of the island which I was to come to love so much, were extracts from a report which no doubt still lies mouldering somewhere among the archives of a department in Cairo, whose representative I was then. 'The position in the capital is very far from normal. Most of the population has fled leaving behind them shattered buildings and a gutted market. Those who remain have suffered from the prevailing starvation. Malnutrition cases are coming in at the rate of sixty a day. All public services are at a standstill; the buses were put out of order by the Germans, the post-office deserted, and only the little news-sheets issued by the Army Propaganda Executive in two languages maintains a tenuous local distribution. The engineers have nearly completed their work, however, and it is hoped that the electric light plant will be functioning again this week. The island is stiff with mines which await the attention of the Sappers. . . .'

Civic order was indeed to be a long time coming; the restoration of postal services with the outside world, the establishment of news-papers, the patching up of shattered dwellings—upon all these was 'order' in its twentieth-century sense conditional. It is only if one has seen a town reduced by siege that one can get any feeling of how much our sense of community is founded in these small amenities. I was nearer, I realise, to Demetrius Polyorcites that June morning than I shall ever be again; I was near, I mean, to seeing something like the historic Rhodes as it must have been after the great siege, after the attack by Mithridates, after Cassius had gutted it; a Rhodes dispersed into a million fragments, waiting to be built up again.

Mandraccio Harbour ('The Sheepfold' of the Ancient Greeks) presented some odd contrasts; fully half of its surface was covered by wrecked boats and skiffs, huddled together, as if against fear of bombing—or perhaps blown gradually together by the force of frequent bombardments. In a clearer anchorage, under the fort of St Nicholas lay a number of island *caieques* in good repair—visitors no doubt which had been ferrying back refugees. They floated languidly in the sticky mirror of the harbour-water which was now viscid with oil from a German launch which lay on its side, its tanks squashed by a bomb, deep in the sludge. The whole length of the waterfront was picketed and wired with a thoroughness that left one in no doubt as to the original determination of the enemy; stakes driven into the rocky bases of the piers trailed underwater wires, while the shallows bristled with concrete blocks and underwater

defences. Shrapnel had peppered the buildings and snipped off fragments from the maudlin row of bronze Caesars with which the
Italians had thought to dignify the port area.

We sat for a while upon a cracked slab of masonry and contemplated
all this desolation as we listened to the innocent lapping of the water
along the harbour wall. Then we pursued our way across the deserted
market-place and entered the old walled town of the Crusaders,
passing by the lovely and undamaged gothic tower of St Paul. At the
spur of a gentle incline we turned into the famous Street of the
Knights at the top of which lay the Castello—that monument to bad
taste executed by the latest Italian governor. By now the hideous
archness of the restoration work was becoming fully apparent.
Gideon, who had seen the island under a kindlier dispensation, became plaintive and fretful. 'This will never do' he said reproachfully.
But there was worse to come. The Castello, perched on the marvellous spur where once the temple of Helios stood, commanding the
whole shallow spade-like tongue of land below, was in the most tasteless of traditions. Sergeant Croker led us round it, a little puzzled no
doubt by our behaviour. I do not think that the most liberal of con-
ventions would allow me to transcribe half the oaths that Gideon
shed as we walked from room to garish room, from chapel to chapel,
corridor to corridor; wherever you turned you were greeted with
ugly statuary, tasteless hangings and tapestries, and the kind of
marquetry work that suggested the lounges of passenger steamers.
The sweep of Gideon's rage took in the Italian governor, the archi-
tects, the stonemasons, and the decorators who had shared in the
ignoble deed. He spitted them with every thrust of his outraged
forefinger. He had them dragged apart by wild horses. He pursued
their ancestors back as far as the fourth century B.C. and beyond.
Croker, the duty-sergeant, was a trifle annoyed; he had bothered to
memorise a few items about the history of the place and was anxious
to act as guide. But Gideon would not hear a word of his patter.
'My dear man,' he said testily, 'it is no good you rambling on about
it. The thing is horrible. A design for a Neapolitan ice perhaps.'

'Very good, sir.'

'Anyone who thinks it's beautiful is an idiot.'

'Very good, sir.'

'And stop repeating "Very good, sir" like a parrot.'

'Yes, sir.'

Homer followed us everywhere with a sage, judicial and disapproving air. He obviously shared Gideon's views.

Yet the views from the slitted windows, and from the parapet of the roof, were superb. The town lay below us, splashed with sunshine. Swallows and martins dipped and swerved in the warm spaces of the gardens. The tangerine-laden trees of the foreground dappled the landscape with dancing points of fire. The air was charged with all the sulphurous odours of spring. The sea was calm again and blue —bluer than any metaphor could express. 'Well, I don't know,' said Gideon propping his elbows on the warm stones and wrinkling his nose to taste that tangerine-scented wind. 'If you wanted a thesis about totalitarian art, why here it is.' The duty-sergeant looked reproachfully at the back of his head; he was a north countryman with a long sandy lugubrious face and pent-up cheek. His hair grew like a mastiff's and was trained down across a pale forehead into a sort of quiff. He kept his horny thumbs strictly in line with the seams of his trousers, his shoulders square. It was obvious that he thought us a couple of frightful highbrows.

It was in one of the cellars that we at last ran my printing-presses to earth. In an atmosphere whirling with lead fumes and dense with the noise of clacking linotypes the daily news-sheets were being put to bed under the eyes of a watchful young R.A.F. officer. Here I transacted my business as briefly as possible, chatted to the compositors in order to try and assess their professional abilities, and scribbled a few notes. I learned with relief that the presses were to be moved back to their pre-war establishment; their present gloomy location in this crypt had been a measure taken against fear of bombardment. The semi-darkness here made proof-reading and layout as exacting as invisible mending.

Later the three of us walked down the hill into the old town to try and find a glass of wine. Among the loopholes and fents of the medieval town we finally discovered a little tavern called *The Helen of Troy* where we found a glass of inferior Chianti with the distinct flavour of paraffin. As a drink it was disappointing; nevertheless it must have contained some of the right ingredients, for in the corner

of the tavern two Greek soldiers, very drunk, danced quietly together to the monotonous squibbling of a clarinet played by an old
man in a greasy turban who lay, half asleep, upon a bundle of boxes
in the corner of the shop.

We were to separate, if I remember, about our various business,
but it was here, at the Helen of Troy, that we met once more at
sunset—one of those fantastic Rhodian sunsets which have, since
medieval times, made the island so justly famed according to the
accounts of Aegean travellers. The whole *Street of the Knights* was on
fire. The houses had begun to curl up at the edges, like burning
paper, and with each sink of the sun upon the dark hill above us, the
tones of pink and yellow curdled and ran from corner to corner,
from gable to gable, until for a moment the darkening minarets of
the mosques glowed into blue ignition, like the light glancing along
a sheet of carbon paper. No longer susceptible to a beauty become
familiar, the dark shades of the refugees moved among their bombed
houses, their voices clear and shrill as they lit lamps, or disposed
their tattered furniture against the evening, shrilly chaffering. Gideon
was holding a glass of some rosy wine up to the red light of the sky,
as if he were trying to imprison the last rays of the sunset within it.
'Where by association' he said 'would Homer get an adjective like
rosy-fingered from—unless he had experienced a Rhodian sunset?
Look!' And indeed in that weird light his fingers, seen through the
wine, trembled pink as coral against the lambent sky. 'I no longer
doubt that Rhodes was Homer's birthplace,' he added gravely. I
could see that he was a trifle drunk. He motioned me impressively
to sit and imitate him, and for a while we examined our own
fingers through our glasses before solemnly drinking a toast to
Homer. ('Not you, you fool' he said to the dog.) For one moment
now the whole street trembled with the unearthly light of a stage
fiction, and then the darkness slid down from the hill. 'A stained-
glass window shattered by a grenade.'

We walked arm in arm down those narrow unlit streets, losing our
way once or twice, until we stumbled upon the squat gate of St Paul,
and sneaked through its shadow into the twentieth century. A few
sporadic points of light shone in the new town, but the street-lighting
had not yet been restored and we walked in a deep calm darkness as

the first stars began to take shape upon the evening sky. It was now, I remember, that we stumbled upon the little garden which encircles the Mosque of Murad Reis—a garden at whose heart I was later to find the Villa Cleobolus; and here we sat for a while perched upon Turkish tombstones, smoking and enjoying the darkness which had now (spring was advanced) an almost touchable smoothness, the silkiness of old velours. And here, I realise, we were very close to the spirit of old Hoyle—for later it was in this garden that he took the deepest pleasure, lying out on the star-scattered grass to smoke his cigars, or dozing away the long golden afternoons in a deck-chair. Hoyle has not put in an appearance as yet, though it is high time he was introduced, for seen across the false perspectives of memory it seems as if somehow we had already met him. Gideon, it is true, had known him years before; they were of the same generation. But his arrival in Rhodes post-dated this first week of Rhodian exploration by something like a month. He had been British Consul in Rhodes and was coming back. Apart from the printing equipment bequeathed to me by the administration there were a number of other articles which were reputed to belong to the late consul—a series of musty consular tables and code-books, together with some old tin trunks. These we had carefully stacked in the cellar which held our stocks of captured newsprint, where they were a perpetual obstruction to everyone. We were always bruising our shins on them. We had fallen into the habit of kicking the trunks viciously whenever we had any work in this particular cellar, and Hoyle became by extension in our imagination as tedious and obstructive an individual as his personal possessions were to the staff of the newspaper. It was with relief, then, that I heard of his arrival one morning. He was, they told me, even at that moment examining his jettisoned possessions in the cellar. I hastened to present myself to him, and there ensued a meeting for which he, I think, was as little prepared as I. He was standing in the cellar clad in fragments of his consular uniform, an ancient dress hat on his head, gazing with myopic disgust through the wrong end of an ancient telescope. The floor was piled ankle-deep with fantastic objects, both consular and personal. I remember a string of signal-flags, numberless cipher-keys, volumes of birth-certificates, a top-hat, a bird-cage, the remains of a consular uniform, detective stories, a sextant, a film projector, several tennis racquets, and heaven only knows what else. Hoyle looked for all the world like a startled puppy. He dropped the telescope and sheepishly removed the hat. 'Extra-ordinary', he said, 'the sort of junk a grown man can collect around him'. I agreed. We introduced ourselves with a certain constraint. For my part I was dying to laugh, and Hoyle looked a trifle sheepish. He picked up a fencing foil and fell to making idle passes in the air as we talked.

Hoyle was small and rotund, with a large head and luminous eye. His manner at first suggested affectation because he had a curious slurring way of talking, and a way of varying the register of his voice from treble to bass, which gave one the impression that he was being swung back and forth in a see-saw as he talked. To this he added a mannerism which strengthened the impression—that of sawing the air with the index finger of his right hand, and marking the periods of his sentences with full stops, poked, as it were, in the air. Later I was to discover that his conversation was manufactured for him by a mind which valued exactitude above all things, and a heart which had never outgrown some of the delightful shyness of childhood. But one might easily have been deceived by his slowness of utterance into thinking that it implied slowness of thought. Quite the contrary. Ideas came so fast to Hoyle that his eyes were suddenly irradiated with light; it was the mechanism of exact expression that caused him to halt to grope for the right word, and never to be satisfied with it. Coupled with this slowness of speech was a slowness of gait which also took some time to interpret. Hoyle walked with such exaggerated slowness, with such a sleepy air, that one might have been forgiven the sin of describing him as a slothful man. Here again one would be wrong. A weak heart which needed constant care was the reason for this octogenarian's gait. But what was remarkable was the manner in which his intellect had used this physical defect for its own use. A man who cannot walk fifty yards without a rest might be forgiven if he were fretful of his infirmity. Hoyle was as equable and unruffled as a child; but since he must pause and rest after every little exertion, he had developed an eye for the minutiae of life which all of us lacked. Forced to stand for ten seconds until his heart slowed down, Hoyle would notice a particular flower growing by the road, an inscription hidden in some doorway which had escaped us, a slight architectural deviation from accepted style. Life for him was delightful in its anomalies, and no walk was possible with Hoyle without a thousand such observations which none of us could have made for ourselves. Gideon was always fond of explaining that he took a 'bird's-eye' view of life; by the same token one might describe Hoyle's eye as being microscopic in its attention to particularities. 'I wonder,' he would say, 'why the Mufti's shoes are too small? I saw him limping today.' Or 'I wonder why in Rhodes they tie up their cats with string. I saw one attached to a front door-knob this morning'.[1] Gideon used to explode with mock-exasperation at the preposterous frivolity of such observations. 'Really Hoyle,' he would say, 'I don't know where you get it all from.' Hoyle's answer never varied in tone or content. 'I was standing having one of my little rests,' he would say, 'and I distinctly noticed him limping.' Admirable Hoyle!

Among his other qualities was the gift of tongues. In the course of his long consular career he had mastered some nine languages, and the greater part of his life was spent in studying comparative linguistics with the nine fat dictionaries he carried about with him in a tin despatch case. Gideon had an imitation of Hoyle which Hoyle himself very much enjoyed hearing. It turned upon this point, for when a conversation began in Greek or Turkish it was not long before Hoyle's eye lit with professional zeal, and he exclaimed: 'Yes, now that's an odd word, when you think of it. It very much resembles the Turkish "*duff*" the Arabic "*fluff*" and, come to think of it, the Persian "*huff, puff* or *snuff*".' And out would come his pencil and his notebook. Whether the mountain of notes which Hoyle carried about with him all over the world will ever be refined and pruned into a thesis is another question. My own feeling is that it has become too much of a life-passion. What would Hoyle do if he had no great bundle of MSS to play with: to add to, to subtract from, to rearrange, to reconsider, to prune, to shape? He would probably die. Nor, for that matter do I ever hope to see printed his great prose anthology

---

[1] During the siege nearly all the cats of Rhodes were eaten by the starving, and this was later to result in a plague of rats which was only conquered by the import of cat-reinforcements from Cyprus. At this time pets who were valued were carefully tied up.

compiled from the writings of consuls and entitled 'A Home From Home', which contains much good material—the fruit of unhurried choice, of considered opinion ripened in the smoke of many a fine cigar; material from writers so dissimilar as Sir Richard Burton and James Elroy Flecker.

But here I shall permit myself a further digression in time from that hulk of Turkish masonry upon which Gideon and I sat together during that early nightfall: a digression from that garden-graveyard whose guardian, the Mufti, we were soon to meet. I should mention Mills, the young doctor who was later to be placed in charge of the medical service on the island. I do not remember how first we met— it was simply as if he had always been there. I do, however, remember an early occasion in our association when Gideon, for some reason best known to himself, decided that he was developing appendicitis and telephoned for him. (I was later to discover that excessive self-indulgence in food or drink always produced in my friend a form of guilty stomach-ache which lent itself to diagnosis as appendicitis.)

Mills drove about his vast parish in an absurd little Italian sports car with enormous exhaust-pipes and a bonnet held down by straps of prodigious size. He was in build short: in character voluble: in colouring blond as a kingcup. His medical equipment, loosely rolled in a piece of oilcloth that looked as if it had once held wrenches and spanners, bulged in the pocket of the blue seaman's pea-jacket which he wore when he was on duty. It would be difficult to think of any-one who seemed to be such a walking certificate for good health; it simply oozed from him, from his candid face, fresh complexion, sensitive fingers. It took him a very short time to discover little beyond an overworked liver wrong with Gideon. 'Old man,' he said, 'You have been flogging your liver. I shall send you a bottle of castor oil and a lemon.' Gideon's face showed a mixture of feelings; relief that his malaise was not serious combined with annoyance that it did not merit sufficient attention. 'You've hardly examined me yet' he said rather testily. Mills drank a glass of wine and regarded his subject with a steady and equable humour. 'What can I tell you that you don't know?' he said at last. 'Smoking and drinking are your two diseases. Cut them out and you'll live forever.' 'Thank you' said Gideon stiffly, struggling into his bush-jacket. 'No trouble at all,' said

Mills. He rolled his stethoscope up into the oilskin pouch, finished his wine. 'Well,' he said, 'we shall meet again': and he was gone.

Hoyle once said: 'Mills switches himself on and off like a light'—and this was an apt enough description of him, for I have never known him spend more than two minutes in one place, nor five minutes with the same patient. Yet somehow he escaped the charge of carelessness or thoughtlessness, for Mills conveyed a feeling of perception and penetration which remained with his patients long after he himself had vanished down the road in his small car, swerving about like a drunken hornet. His diagnosis of disease seemed somehow to be a criticism, not of the functioning of one specific organ, but of the whole man. Like all born healers he had realised, without formulating the idea, that disease has its roots in a faulty metaphysic, in a way of life. And the patient who took him a cyst to lance or a wheezing lung to think about, was always disturbed by the deliberate careful scrutiny of those clear blue eyes. One felt slightly ashamed of being ill in the presence of Mills. It was as if, staring at you as you stood there, he were waiting for you to justify your illness, to deliver yourself in some way of the hidden causes of it. But over and above his skill, the breadth of his intellectual curiosity and humanity were qualities which added richness and colour to our island society. He was by upbringing a Quaker. He had married a delightful Greek girl who had been his chief nurse in the U.N.R.A. unit to which he had been attached before joining the civil administration. They lived in a small flat upon the seashore, whose rooms were crowded with miscellaneous material for all the studies Mills intended to make of people and things outside the immediate limits of his own skill. Once inside the ever-open front door one stumbled over boxes full of geological specimens, of ancient pottery, of sea-shells. Every time a window opened manuscripts of essays on poetry, on sex, on biochemistry, on Elizabethan music were scattered in the air. His wife found him a delightful trial. I still hear her grumbling musical tones protesting: '*Mais voyons, chéri*,' as he proposed some new field of study—such as the guitar, or the clarinet. '*Ça, alors*,' his wife would groan. '*Soyez raisonnable*.' But Mills did not believe in reducing his enthusiasm to normal proportions; there was so much energy to be got rid of, life was so short. . . . I can hear him protesting in his fluent

French and Greek. And when he had left the room to bring you his microscope slides to see, Chloe would shrug her shoulders and allow herself to smile as she said: '*Comme il est bizarre, lui. Mais dites-moi—est-ce qu'il est un vrai Anglais?*' Like all Mediterraneans she had been brought up to believe that the hall-mark of the true Englishman is an unfathomable reserve. Mills seemed more like an Italian in his bursts of enthusiasm. And listening to him sing his Greek folk-songs to the guitar she would shake her head and sigh—for surely Englishmen didn't sing in foreign languages with so much feeling? And certainly no true Englishman lost his temper, as Mills sometimes did, and threw himself with gusto into a domestic row? This, then, was Mills, and he was part of it all: indeed from points of view this is more his book than mine, since it is he who decreed the shape of it. I remember him sitting in the Villa Cleobolus one dark winter evening, roasting chestnuts before the fire, while Chloe (after her fifth attempt to make him take her home) had kicked off her shoes and gone to sleep on the sofa—I remember him repeating in his clear voice: 'I do so hope you'll write a book about the island sometime when you feel like it. I don't feel Gideon's history will ever get written somehow, nor Hoyle's study of the dialect: but it needs a book. Not history or myth —but landscape and atmosphere somehow. "A companion" is the sort of idea. You ought to try for the landscape—and even these queer months of transition from desolation to normality.' I do not remember what I answered. I realise now that he was pleading for some sort of effective monument to all the charm and grace of our stay there in Rhodes; the golden sun-washed months which only Hoyle has been left there to enjoy while the rest of us have been scattered about the earth by our several professions and that conspicuous ill-luck which, as Gideon used to say, always afflicts islomanes when they have discovered the island of their heart's desire. In the pauses of the conversation the sea roared upon the deserted beach and the wind whistled in the pines and oleanders of the garden. 'Above all,' Mills is saying, as the chestnuts burst in a series of muffled explosions on their bed of soft wood-ash, 'Above all, introduce your main characters right away. Give the reader a chance to see if he likes them. It's only fair. So he can close the book if he doesn't. That's how you should begin.'

There is only one portrait I shrink from—that of the Marine Venus. If the reader should ever visit her in her little cell he would know why. The presiding genius of a place or an epoch may be named, but she may not be properly described. Yet the Venus, when she was raised that sunny morning from the damp crypt in which she had lain hidden; when the packing-case which held her had been broken open: when the pulleys finally raised her out of the darkness, slowly twisting on the end of her cable—why, which of us could fail to recognise the presiding genius of the place? ('A statue of a woman: period uncertain: found at the bottom of Rhodes harbour: damaged by sea-water.') I can still see the faces of my friends as they surrounded the dark trap-door out of which she rose so gravely into the sunlight. Hoyle and Gideon sitting astride a plank; Egon Huber, who had helped to bury her, smiling with pleasure to see her undamaged: while Mills and Sergeant Croker and a collection of barefoot urchins grunted and groaned on the ropes which were raising her.

She rose as if foamborn, turning that elegant body slowly from side to side, as if bowing to her audience. The sea-water had sucked at her for centuries till she was like some white stone jujube, with hardly a feature sharp as the burin must originally have left it. Yet such was the grace of her composition—the slender neck and breasts on that richly modelled torso, the supple line of arm and thigh—that the absence of firm outline only lent her a soft and confusing grace. Instead of sharp classical features she had been given something infinitely more adolescent, unformed. The ripeness of her body was offset by the face, not of a Greek matron, but of a young girl. We carried her, swaddled in sacking, down the Museum corridors, up a staircase, to the little room in which you will find her today. It is an ugly enough stone cabin—and chosen for her by a man who had some silly theory that she was too damaged to look beautiful except from certain angles; hence the theatrical north light which plays up the fine modelling of her back and throws those innocent features into dark relief. But in a little while your eyes will have accustomed themselves to the consuming darkness of the room, and you will be able to trace them with your finger, the cold lip and eyebrow, the stone tresses. It is as if she were made of wax: had been passed very rapidly across a flame intense enough to blunt her features, yet not materially to alter them; she has surrendered her original maturity for a rediscovered youth.

The fishermen dragged her up one afternoon in their nets. It seemed to them to be a rich catch; but it was only a heavy marble figure of a Marine Venus, tangled in weeds, and with a few startled fish leaping like silver coins about her placid white countenance with its sightless eyes.

She sits in the Museum of the island now, focused intently upon her own inner life, gravely meditating upon the works of time. So long as we are in this place we shall not be free from her; it is as if our thoughts must be forever stained by some of her own dark illumination—the preoccupation of a stone woman inherited from a past whose greatest hopes and ideals fell to ruins. Behind and through her the whole idea of Greece glows sadly, like some broken capital, like the shattered pieces of a graceful jar, like the torso of a statue to hope.

CHAPTER II

Orientations in Sunlight

From the windows of my office I can overlook some of the twisted streets and warrens of the old town. It is an admirable point
of vantage from which to look down unobserved upon the
conversations and quarrels of the Greeks. At mid-day I caught sight
of a small procession consisting of a mother and father followed by
two little children and a miscellaneous body of relations. The father
walked at the head, carrying an ikon of the Virgin from which hung
down a little lighted lamp. They were moving house, it seemed. The
man walked with calm circumspection, shielding the flame of the
lamp with his right hand lest a gust of wind should put it out and thus
prejudice the luck of the new house. Slowly and anxiously the little
procession turned a corner and was gone. Watching the serious faces
of the children I found myself hoping that the family ikon would
arrive safely at the doorway of the new house, and that the happy
augury would help them build their luck confidently next year
against the bitter trials of the world to come. Surely, I thought,
history as chronology is woefully misleading; for the history of a
place, dispersed by time, lives on in fable, gesture, intonation, raw
habit. No text-book can capture it fully. Here in Rhodes, for example, one runs across songs left behind by the Crusaders, living
on side by side with a belief in a fresh-water Goddess whose antiquity
stretches back beyond Plato.

The Aegean is still waiting for its painter—waiting with all the
unselfconscious purity of its lights and forms for someone to go
really mad over it with a loaded paint-brush. Looking down upon it
from the sentinel's tower at Castello, from the ancient temple at

Lindos, you begin to paint it for yourself in words. Cerulean sky touched with white cirrus—such fleece as grows between the horns of nine-day goatlets, or on the cocoons of silkworms; viridian to peacock-tail green where the sea threshes itself out against the cliffs. Prismatic explosion of waves against the blue sky, crushing out their shivering packets of colour, and then the hissing black intake of the water going back. The billiard-green patch edged with violet that splashes the sea below Lindos. The strange nacreous bones of cliff at Castello. But to paint Greece one would have to do more than play with a few colours. Other problems: how to convey the chalky whiteness of the limestone, the chalk-dust that comes off the columns on to one's fingers, the soft pollen-like bloom on the ancient vases which makes so many of them seen like great plums of pure light. And when you had done all this you would still have to master the queer putty-mauve, putty-grey tones of the island rock—rock that seems to be slowly cooling lava. An impossible task when all is said and done. It is pleasanter not to try, but to lie dozing in the shade and watch Gideon working away on squared paper with his little child's paintbox. He stops whistling only to swear and shake his fist at Anatolia which is manifestly eluding him. 'I nearly had it in this one' he says. The paint-box was a present intended for his daughter; but one day, cooped up in a transit-camp he decided to try the colours out. He has graduated via railway-trains and one-dimensional drawings of houses and cows to sedate little water-colours of the landscapes he has visited. Some are quite good; but though I offer to buy them he refuses. 'This is my diary,' he says.

My patrimony has finally been decided upon. I am to inherit three linotypes, a mass of assorted hand-type, and all the greasy junk that goes with a printing house; apart, I mean, from the thirty or so devils who keep the machinery running. Later a Government printer is to be appointed who will take over the staff work and leave me free to be simply and solely an editor. But for the time I am playing the part of peacemaker, lawgiver and minor oracle to this large mixed staff. Italians, Greeks and Turks must be made to work amicably together. Did I say amicably? The rows we have sweep the whole building like thunderstorms. It is, however, the ideal laboratory for a study of national character. The Turk one very soon begins to know; slow,

shy, mole-like and very suspicious he goes about his work with circumspection, doing it grain by grain. In our Italians one sees at once
the large florid feminine sense of decoration, the innate taste, the
desire to please. But the Greek is a terrible fellow. Mercuric, noisy,
voluble and proud—was there ever such a conjunction of qualities
locked in a human breast? Only the Irishman could match him for
intractability, for rowdy feckless generosity.

My terms of reference do not make it any easier. We are to produce
three daily papers: Greek, Italian, and Turkish.[1] The Greek editorial
staff is locked away in a room of its own where its ardours and disagreements cannot be heard. Muffled by the heavy doors I hear them
blasting and bombinating all morning through. One can almost hear
their fingers flying as they argue. And all morning long there comes a
stream of visitors trying to get free advertising or to bribe the editor
to print material full of political bias. It is going to be tiresome work.

By one every day my newspapers are made up, however, and I walk
across the old town to collect Gideon from his office on the water-
front before walking home.

Now at long last E has arrived from Egypt with the rest of the
office staff and enough domestic luggage to enable me to start thinking in terms of a house. It hardly seems fair when she will have to stay
on in the great hotel herself; but the air and the scenery of the island
are enough to compensate her for the prospect of six months in a bed
sitting-room. For years now I have been trying to describe Aegean
scenery to her, but I have always been aware of a suspicious look in
her eye as she listened. It was obvious that she suspected me of poetic
licence. Now she is speechless with it all, and like a woman she says:
'But why didn't you tell me it was so marvellous?' 'I tried to. You
wouldn't believe me.' Sitting under the great plane-tree on the walls
of the fort we dawdle away our afternoons watching the windmills
turning against the blue sky and listening to thin bored cries of the
fruit-vendors in the market stretched out at our feet.

The little Swedish tanker on which she travelled ran into bad
weather and was forced to lie up in Carpathos for a week. She could
not have had a happier introduction to Aegean Greece, for Carpathos
is as pure in contour as a primitive sculpture. The little *pointilliste*

[1] *Chronos,* the Greek daily still exists.

harbour with its vivid houses is later work—Seurat plus abandon. After Egypt with its swarming vermin, its population of Apes in nightgowns, its dirt, disease, and truncated beggars on trolleys, Carpathos must have seemed preciously close to Paradise in this spring weather. She spent her days bathing, and lying in an almond-grove near the sea where the village children gathered round her and sang her their songs. Being an Alexandrian she speaks fairly good Greek, and so found herself at home. She has brought with her a couple of Carpathos songs which Mills will soon be singing. One has a delightful chorus:

'O sweet lemon tree, with lemons up
When will you lean and lemon me?'

Lemons are identified with breasts in the popular literature, and this is supposed to be sung by a young girl. By the same token 'olive' in poetry stands as a symbol for the mole upon the dark face or arm of a girl.

This morning the blazing sunlight gives a promise of the coming summer; but a promise which could only take in those to whom the calendar means nothing. E swears that in the plane-tree she heard the first tentative strokes of the cicada; but by lunch-time the sirocco had started up and the clouds were pouring down over the islands and piling up upon the Anatolian hills. Night came tearfully on through a rainbow of watered silk touching Smyrna at the further end. The peasants say of rainbows, that when one crosses over a carob-tree it dries it: and that the wood of the tree becomes deep-scented and pleasant. They put, adds the tale, this wood into their clothes-chests to make them smell nice and to keep the moths away.

I am told by Hoyle that in some parts of the island a rainbow is known as 'Helen's Cord' because, say the peasants, a great queen hung herself with a rainbow from a tree. Is this perhaps one of those curi-ous survivals which delight him so much to unearth? According to one ancient source when Troy fell Helen was driven out by her step-sons and took refuge in Rhodes where Polyxo hanged her from a tree to avenge the death of Tlepolemos in the Trojan War. Torr has already noted the tree-cult of Helen Dendritis in Rhodes during ancient times. The reader must draw his own conclusions. Yet the line of descent seems clear enough. As for Tlepolemos, he enjoyed the posthumous honours of a hero, but there is no record which tells us where his temple stood.

Our circle of acquaintance has widened to include Sand, the newly arrived director of antiquities, and Egon Huber, an Austrian potter who has lived here for some fifteen years and has been responsible for much of the lovely Icarus pottery turned out during the Italian dispensation. Sand is dour and Scotch, with a gibbous face, and the pleasantest turn of humour imaginable. Huber, by contrast, is a born solitary, tall, fair-haired, and living in a state of perpetual and melancholy detachment from this world of wars and conquests. Fourteen years ago he was washed up in Rhodes during a storm. He had been trying to travel from Venice to Alexandria in a canoe. The island pleased him and he stayed, while the Italian governor, who had been appealing to Rome for an expert in pottery for years past, suddenly heard that God had answered his prayers, and had provided him with a penniless and talented Austrian needing some form of subsistence beyond the ikons he was doing for the churches. Huber lives now in a little Martello tower much ruined by damp and neglect. How he avoided having to join the German Army is a miracle—yet he did it, on a series of ridiculous technicalities which only a long Levantine experience could have helped him to think up. He works in desultory fashion at the ruined workshop outside the town where in the past his world-famous pottery brought him tourists in their thousands and where shortage of clay has reduced him to poverty. No word of complaint ever passes his lips, however, for he is one of the aristocrats of the spirit—the poor artist who wishes for nothing but a chance to create.

Gradually the town-characters have begun to assert themselves, to fill out with detail the idiosyncrasies of their various personalities. Emerging to the notice first as people encountered daily in the street, the outlines of character and habit follow. From thence it is only a step to the essential details—for everyone knows them: the subject is married or unmarried, has collaborated or has not, is rich or poor. So, gradually Rhodes becomes people by living people: Mehmet Bey, Manoli the net-maker, Baron Baedeker, and Christ. Characters in the order of their appearance, as they say.

43

Mehmet is my neighbour. He lives across the oleander grove, beyond the tombs, in a little house of his own. Every morning he salutes the dawn by flinging wide his wooden shutters and expectorating with marvellous precision upon one or other of the white Leghorns which run about the wired enclosure outside the house. Then he creaks down the stairs, growling at his wife for being a slowcoach, and emerges languidly into the sunshine to stretch and light a cigarette. He is a tall, heavily built man with a pale skin and the lazy dark eyes which betray his Turkish ancestry. He wears the blue skirt and high boots of the Cretan mountaineers, but it is as if his courage (or his resources) had failed him at this point, for he tops off the costume with a white shirt and a soiled handkerchief knotted at his throat. His general manner accords with this appearance of lackadaisical piracy. He wanders round the town on a series of small errands, shambling like an unhorsed gaucho, to emerge in the garden towards noon carrying a pair of trussed chickens, a wire box of quail, a handful of parsley, a honeycomb—or some other such item of domestic concern. It is always a bargain, and he gives the impression of having made no effort to achieve his triumph. It is as if, on awakening in the morning, a sixth sense told him immediately into which quarter of the town he must plunge to secure the day's meal. Twice a week he slaughters a chicken with hideous expertness on a block, standing with the bloodstained chopper in his hand, and a cigarette in the corner of his mouth, to watch the headless corpse run bubbling and coughing round the yard until it falls in a heap.

Once a month Mehmet disappears on what is a technically forbidden journey—to Turkey. Nobody knows how he goes or how he returns; but after an absence of some ten days he returns with a cargo of contraband which he distributes to agents in the town at something like the speed of light.

The theory is that he runs his cargo ashore somewhere near Trianda and loads it on to mules. He then joins the dawn caravan of mules which bring the country produce into the markets of the town. I hear him softly crunching along the gravel paths to his house in the early morning; he taps at the door and calls hoarsely. Sometimes he is dragging something heavy along the ground. I shall be sorry if he is caught, as the fines are enormous for smuggling.

But Mehmet is remarkable for other things; in the town he is regarded with reverence as a man who, born very rich, dissipated three fortunes by sheer joyful improvidence. He was also the last Turk on Rhodes to have a harem, says rumour. '*Complètement épuisé, ce type-là*,' said the Baron Baedeker the other day, setting down his 'expresso' to jerk a thumb in the direction of Mehmet, who was shambling gravely across the square, led by that unerring sixth sense, towards a sucking-pig or a goose.

Sirocco again—a huge white-capped sea racing away for Anatolia, to dash itself in pieces on the headlands, buried in smoke. 'All poetry,' says V, 'partakes of the epitaph. Even the Epithalamium participates in the death of joy.' It is perhaps a gloomy view. I think of an epitaph scrawled in charcoal above a niche in the catacombs of Rome: a niche containing the bones of a Christian martyr. *Clementia tortured, dead sleeps: will arise.* Ah! Give us the same power of compression, to resume life and death in poems of not more than six words!

The question of origins. . . . Gideon and I have been doing some reading in the little archaeological library which Sand has put at our disposal. I have been ploughing through the lush verbiage of Bileotti and Cottret (to whom Gideon has given the collective name of 'the Abbé Cutlet') while he has been chuckling over the primness of Torr, whose two volume account of Rhodes is perhaps the best history of them all.

Helios was the great God of Rhodes; of all the ancient names for the island, Heliousa, the Sun-friend, is perhaps the one most worth recording, for it is the Sun-God's portrait, more than any other, which emerges from the welter of myth and classical conjecture. The first inhabitants of Rhodes were his children, the Heliades. To his favourite, the nymph Rhodon, was the island bequeathed as a place to live in. The festival of Helios was yearly in September. His priest gave the name to the year. The Colossos was built in his likeness, and the coinage of the realm bore his image, while in the great yearly festival which honoured his name white or tawny lambs, white rams, white horses and red honey were offered as a sacrifice; and the wrestlers, boxers and charioteers contended for a wreath of white poplar. So famous were the festivals of Helios that neighbouring States

sent both their best athletes as competitors and their diplomatic envoys.
A team of four horses was sacrificed to him by casting them into the
sea. This celebrated in symbolic form his daily journey across the
sky, from the great submarine palace where he lived to the western
darkness of Oceanus. His temple stood where now De Vecci's[1] card-
board fortress stands, and within its precincts was the famous statue of
the Sun-God standing up in a chariot drawn by four steeds. Before
the town of Rhodes was founded in 408 B.C. the Rhodians, who
claimed Argos for their parent state, lived for the most part in the
three glittering cities, named after the heroes Lindos, Ialysos, and
Camiros, grandsons of Helios. There were other great towns on the
island—and every year fresh evidence of forgotten sites comes to
light—but these three cities alone governed the island and its colonies.
With Cos and Cnidos they formed a religious league and shared a
common temple on the Triopian Cape. What induced them to band
together and found a fourth town more beautiful than any of the
others, to which they surrendered the government of the island?
Some suggest an earthquake which shattered the three cities. Was
there some feeling perhaps that the site of the new town, on the
spatulate north-eastern tip of the island, would offer them both the
strategic use of three admirably situated harbours and an immunity
against the volcanic disturbances which from ancient time have been
the curse of the Sporades? We shall never know. The modern
peasant version of the foundation of Rhodes is worth translating
from one of the pamphlets of Vronty. 'After the great plague of
horse-flies which bit everyone and died there came a great earthquake on the feast-day of St Demetrius. In the earthquake the three
cities fell down so they built the new city in a better place where it
would not be affected by such things.'

White bread is the great novelty of the day. The Rhodians have
become positively snobbish about it, and the meanest beggar would
refuse a piece of brown if it were offered to him. 'English bread' they
call it. Today I saw a small gesture which pleased me and reminded
me once more how deeply significant, almost biblical, is the Greek

[1] The latest Fascist governor of the island whose florid and tasteless rebuilding
of monuments has all but ruined the splendid thoughtful work of Mario Largo who
devoted half a lifetime to governing and beautifying Rhodes.

attitude to bread. A family party under a tree in some forlorn, bombed back-yard in the city. Grandfather, grandmother and three small noisy children were eating bread and garlic. As I passed them a piece of bread fell to the ground. The old man picked it up, saying in the kind of voice one would use to a child: 'Come up with you, little English breadlet, then,' and kissed it before he put it back into the grubby hand of his grandson. The staff of life!

It is inevitable that we should, in the course of our reading and arguing, rub up against the question of the rose of Rhodes. Is it a rose? Egon Huber has taken some clay squeezes of the device with which the Rhodian manufacturer, in ancient times, sealed and guaranteed his little flasks of oil, wine or scent. In many cases the flower is a pomegranate-blossom. Huber himself is of the opinion that the true 'rose' of Rhodes is a hibiscus. A German archaeologist who visited him during the war told him so. Certainly the hibiscus is everywhere: the three prevailing notes are the reds of the oleander and hibiscus, and the raw massive purple of the bougainvillaea with which the Italians have drenched the modern part of the town. Nearly all the cottage gardens of the peasants, however, are picked out with the scarlet stabs of the hibiscus. Yet Cottret and Biliotti have decided upon the wild rose—somehow too modest a flower I think to symbolise an island as powerful as Rhodes was in ancient times.

In summer, says the naval handbook which Gideon has stolen from somewhere, the Etesian wind springs up to cool the edge of the heat. It hardly marks the sea, yet one will feel it, cool on the forehead and breast, dispersing the afternoon *accidie* which sets in with the noise of the cicadas. This will be called the *meltemi,* unless I am mistaken— Graeco-Turkish hybrid which chimes with 'mellow' 'melon' 'melting' and the Greek for honey, which is *meli.* That should give you a taste of its quality, for it is one of the treasures of the Aegean. In Rhodes, adds Tozer, its younger sister is a shore-wind, eagerly waited for by those who wish to cross the straits. This blows inshore till noon and then offshore until dusk. This is called the *imbat.* 'The whole region from Rhodes and Eastern Crete to Samos and Ikaria' adds the book 'continues the geological structure and configurations of South-West Anatolia'. The poetry of precise observation! We are, then, only part of the rim of a volcano, the Aegean. 'Much of the foothills have been submerged, leaving only the mountains above water. Great heights and depths are thus produced. The sea is 10,600 feet deep east of Rhodes, with Mount Atabyron rising 4,069 feet in height above sea level.' The naval geographer who produced the handbook was no doubt unconscious of any lyrical impulse. 'The old crystalline rocks, schists and marbles, are converted by exposure into a light sandy soil. . . . The massive limestones are very pure in quality. . . . Volcanic soils are represented by the craters of Nisiros and Patmos and the pumice gravels of Kalymnos. These usually break up easily into rich red and black soils.'

Writing poetry educates one into the nature of the game—which is humanity's profoundest activity. In their star-dances the savages try to unite their lives to those of the heavenly bodies—to mix their quotidian rhythms into those great currents which keep the wheels of the universe turning. Poetry attempts to provide much the same sort of link between the muddled inner man with his temporal pre-occupations and the uniform flow of the universe outside. Of course everyone is conscious of these impulses; but poets are the only people who do not drive them off.

Poems, like water-colours, should be left to dry properly before you alter them—six months or six hours according to the paints you use.

These reflections are the fruit of an afternoon spent alone, reading under a cypress tree on Mount Phileremo. The valley of Maritsa lay below, its soft creamy limestone carved in a million places by the winter torrents, and overgrown with shrubs until each fissure looked like a mouth half covered in a golden beard. The gaunt burnt-out skeleton of the airdrome beneath with its charred aircraft was a reminder that one was, after all, in the world; for the air of Phileremo is so rare that one might be forgiven for imagining oneself in some more successful dimension where the hero had finally mastered himself, and where the act had somehow become connected once more with the concept of love. The Hellenic fountain breathed quietly, half asleep.

Manoli sits on the sunny wharf all morning working at the tattered seines upon which he depends for a livelihood. His hands are like battered horns, blunt and dirty, yet the evolutions they perform among the heavy swathes of net are as finished and delicate as those of a lace-maker. He sings as he works, in a voice of gravel, his lips pursed about the sail-maker's needle. He is clad in sailcloth breeches and a coarse woollen shirt. His tangle of silver hair has been pushed under a dirty cloth cap to which his daughter has fastened a rose with a pin. No morning would be complete without a chat with this fragrant old ruffian who carries in his voice, gesture, intonation, the whole flavour of the Aegean. Manoli's feet are swollen by salt-water, and have obviously never been cramped by shoes. He holds his spare needles and wax between his toes. His finger-joints, too, have been stretched and blown-up by rheumatism until they look like sausages.

His sixty-year old body reminds me of some ancient boat, cankered and swollen at the seams from years of sea-work; yet his heart is in repair still, and with it that marvellous natural intelligence which is only to be found among the semi-literate. His daughter reads the newspaper to him. His interest in world-politics is a consuming passion and it is wonderful how clearly he reads between the lines of a conference or a speech to deduce at once its failure or success, its truth or intrinsic falsity. He is a much keener judge of affairs than his counterpart in England would be; yet a poorer judge of Greek matter than any child—domestic Rhodian affairs, that is.

'Finland is waking up,' he says oracularly.

'Do you think they will give in to Russia?'

'Naturally.'

'I don't.'

'You are English. They never see things before they happen. The English are very slow.'

'And what about the Greeks?'

'The Greeks are fast . . . piff . . . paff. . . . They decide.'

'But each one decides differently.'

'That is individualism.'

'But it leads to chaos.'

'We like chaos.'

'Manoli, what do you most like doing?'

'Sitting about, drinking.'

'What would you do if you became dictator of the world?'

49

'I should say to everybody: "*Stop. At once. We will change every-thing.*"'

'And if they did not stop?'

'Then I should cause a revolution.'

He laughs harshly at the hopelessness of the situation—the human no less than his own personal situation as a dictator. And, since he is Greek, his immediate reaction is typical. 'If I thought it hopeless I should take all the money I could steal from the Government and retire into private life.'

'And then?'

'And then the world would be exactly where it is now. At least I would not have made it any worse.'

His laughter has no cynicism in it. But he has seen enough not to nourish delusive hopes. He is not at odds with his experience; he has been forced, so to speak, to swallow it, this great weight of bitterness, to accommodate and digest it; and the process of acceptance has given him a kind of joy—a water-tight happiness which plays about his face and gestures, investing them with a strange kinetic beauty. Speaking of the E.A.M., for example, he said yesterday: 'They come to deliver us from poverty. God knows, we need that. But they will end in enslaving us with other evils. God knows, we do not want that.' His style of expression is always gravitating towards the proverb—the only literary form with which he is familiar. 'Take away my poverty but can you give me the happiness which I have in here?' touching that shaggy chest with his fist.

No. His happiness is his own work, cultivated like the tiny pot of basil in the window of his house, by patience and the bitter harmony of experience. 'But to remove poverty is something,' I say. He nods. 'It is very much. But there are many selfish people in the world. Whichever donkey it is, they will always reach the saddle.' 'But you could reach the saddle with better education, book-learning.' Manoli lights a cigarette and exhales a long voluptuous streamer into the blue. He hops about like a crow among the nets for a moment. Then he takes off his cap, sniffs the rose, and replaces it. 'Who can say what I should gain—and what I should lose?'

Who indeed?

How often have I not been into the little churchyard behind the

Mosque of Murad Reis? Then how is it that only today I saw the house which I would like to live in? It is buried in overhanging trees, and hidden in a triple circle of oleanders and rhododendrons: it consists of a tiny studio, bedroom and bathroom. That is all. A coloured table built round the trunk of a baobab-tree makes a shady dining-room. Outside the shrubbery the Turkish tomb-stones lie with the yellowish sickle-shaped eucalyptus leaves drifting over them. I stand listening to my own breathing in all that silence. The green foliage seems to blot out all the sound of passers-by upon the main-road which is quite near. It is simply a match-box of a house, but its situation is more beautiful than anything I could have imagined possible so near to the ugly hotel. It is untenanted too, for its owner has been repatriated to Italy.

'Rising Jupiter means luck in Springtime' says the horoscope which the great astrologer Moricand once cast for me in Paris. I know this is true now, for Martin, the lively and goodnatured South African major who is responsible for Rhodes, has told me that I can have the house provided the Mufti does not object to a Christian living on the edge of the Turkish churchyard. I call upon the dignitary one morn-ing on my way to work, and find him in his little courtyard paved with white and grey sea-pebbles, sipping coffee and—miracle of miracles—talking to Hoyle in Turkish. 'I did not know you knew each other' I say. Hoyle introduces me. The Mufti is a meek-mannered man dressed in elastic-sided boots, who smokes his cigarette in an ebony cigarette-holder. Typically enough he speaks not a word of Greek. I say 'typically enough' because it seems to be a characteristic of Turkish communities outside Turkey. As a nation they are the most withdrawn and the most secretive of any I have met. This does not imply either lack of spontaneity or of goodwill—they have a great measure of both. But the centuries of religious difference have given each Moslem Turk the look of a walled city. In Rhodes they live like moles behind barred windows, inside walled gardens, full of orange trees; as a community they are not divided internally as the Greeks are by petty jealousies and schisms, nor externally by a multiplicity of political interests. If you wish to know what the Turkish community thinks on any given subject you have only to ask the Mufti—for it is he who thinks for them. Yet to judge by his

face as he sits now, listening to Hoyle pleading for me in his best
K.C.'s manner, you would think he had the greatest difficulty in
holding an idea in his head for two consecutive minutes. He wrinkles
his face and pushes back his turban with the index finger of his right
hand as the argument proceeds with its succession of single syllable
puffs and grunts. As far as I can see Hoyle's oratorical methods are
flawless. At any rate the Mufti cannot think of a single objection to
his new tenant. We shake hands warmly and I make him a little
speech in Greek to which he replies in Turkish. Neither of us
understands the other, but we are both prompted by a sense of
social propriety in the matter of compliments. Our agreement is
cemented by a visit to the grave of Hascmet, the Turkish satirical
poet, who lies buried in a small walled enclosure in one corner
of the courtyard. The tomb is chipped and stained by rain. A
goat munches and scratches round it, tethered to a dwarf eucalyptus
by the wall. I put my hand to the gravestone and feel the warmth of
the sun upon it. Who was Hascmet,[1] and how did he come to be
exiled here, to this forgotten graveyard full of the sedate tombs of
Turkish civil servants? It is an after dinner problem for Gideon to
solve. But meanwhile the house is mine.

We walk back now, the three of us, across the melancholy but
beautiful churchyard, pausing from time to time in the shade of the
tall flowing trees as Hoyle deciphers the lettering on a tomb, or
offers the Mufti a chocolate from the little silver box he always
carries about with him in his pocket. Our feet crunch the crisp sickles
of eucalyptus-leaf underfoot as we walk. The graveyard is in a sad state
of disrepair. Many of the tombs have fallen to pieces, and in places
the loose drift of leaves has half obscured others. The majority of
those who lie buried here are Turkish civil servants. A few are political exiles. The gravestone records the sex of its tenant: with a heavy
marble turban surmounting it, in the case of a man, and with a sort
of marble pine-apple in the case of a woman. The greater dignitaries
have a small vault to themselves—a sort of stone sentry-box with a
domed roof and barred windows. But now with wind and weather
many of the stone turbans have been blown off and lie about in the
pathways like heads blown from statues. We skirt the final row of

[1] He was banished for a satirical poem.

tombs and plunge into the dense thicket of oleander which hides the house. A path suddenly appears, and following it we come upon the Villa Cleobolus with its beds of tiger-lilies and the great baobab-tree which rubs its outer wall. Hoyle too has noticed the peculiar density of the silence here for he says: 'Listen', and raises his hand. We stand and listen to our own breathing. Remote, beyond the curtain of silence, the noise of quotidian traffic sounds from the road beyond. But so dense is the green that it is as if the house and garden were under a glass bell. The Mufti nods his head, as if in agreement, and blows the smoking dottle from his cigarette-holder on to the path. 'He says you will be happy here' says Hoyle.

St Constantine's Day is a day of coronation for the fig and the pomegranate; the owner of the trees pays them a special visit and crowns them with wreaths of oleander and wild marjoram. The peasants call this 'getting engaged', and the object of the ceremony is to make the trees bear. If, adds the story, the owner omits this cere-mony and does not visit his trees, they imagine him to have died and from sadness do not bear. Contemporary beliefs suggest that aspho-dels should not be picked, as this hinders the orchards from bearing.

Four little Turkish children walking hand-in-hand. The eldest, a fat-faced boy of perhaps nine, is smoking a cigarette and laying down the law. They do not see us in the shade of the olive-tree until we are practically face to face. Then they halt in confusion and turn tail. We greet them in Greek but they do not reply. We are infidels. The smallest turns her head and spits as she runs. In a moment all the horrors of Egypt rise to mind: the suffocating beastliness of Islam and all it stands for, bigotry, cruelty and ignorance. Yet here all the jagged edges of the faith have been filed away; the minarets rise above the market-place with slender grace, the call of the muezzin sounds soft and musical in the dawn-light. The patriarchal face of the Mufti in his scarlet fez and elastic-sided boots, moodily smoking a cigarette in the courtyard of the mosque and greeting the faithful. Rhodes has converted Islam and made it part of the island's green and gentle self.

Whitewash, some coloured pottery, and a few pieces of bright curtain-material have transformed the little Villa Cleobolus into as delightful a studio as one could wish for. For the last week E has been busy, diving into the Turkish quarter to buy these commodities as cheaply as possible. Now the work is done and I am at last allowed to see it. Bed, table and bookcase have been borrowed from the Custodian of Enemy Property. The pottery is a laral gift from Egon Huber. The curtains, the bright peasant rug, and the Turkish bedspread which depicts a billowy princess with eyebrows like watercolour brushes playing a lute under a pee-pul tree cost us in all ten pounds. I am absolutely speechless with happiness. So much so indeed that E thinks for a moment that I do not like it. 'Is there something wrong?' she asks. No, there is nothing wrong. But the feeling of privacy and space round one after so many years of living from suitcases and sharing flats is something one will have to get used to again; we stretch out our arms in that tiny room—as if they were antennae, exploring the free space around ourselves, turning about: sitting now in this chair, now in that. Space, light and solitude will have to be rediscovered again here, in all their ramifications. The silence seems saturated with a thousand forgotten essences: contained and held, somehow, in the bright peasant carpet, the crude warm pottery of Rhodes on which Huber has traced so lovingly these dancing figures, this silver-green olive tree, this donkey trotting along a dusty road. It is much the same feeling as comes over one when a poem forms in the mind, its outlines misty, inchoate: until the white paper on which you have scribbled a dozen words and crossed them out, blazes in your face like a searchlight and paralyses you by the multiplicity of possibilities it presents, by the silence it opposes to your inner tension.

While we are still walking about the little room the door bursts open to admit Gideon and Hoyle and a cask of red wine with which, they say, they propose to 'inaugurate' the house. It is a happy thought. We retire to the little clearing which is to be our dining-room, and set ourselves down at the coloured table which has been built around the baobab-tree. This is to be the first of many such evenings I hope— evenings spent in idle gossip and content, until the night falls and the candles are lit, and in the rosy pool they have scooped from the darkness I can see the faces of my friends: Gideon protesting so violently that his monocle falls out, Hoyle smiling his preoccupied little smiles, Mills managing to talk and laugh all in the same breath, and E with her splendid dark head propped on her arm listening to them and smiling.

Later, when they have gone, I walk about the churchyard for a while, listening to rustle of falling leaves among the tombs, and watching the moon rise slowly from the sea.

'I should have knocked perhaps; but coming silently into the darkened room of the Villa Cleobolus (the room you had taken so much trouble to furnish) I found you sleeping on the divan, one arm behind your head, your warm cheek pressed to the painted face of the Turkish lovers on the counterpane. You had been crying in your sleep, for I saw a tear on your dark lashes. It could only have been with happiness to have escaped to this island. Beside you on the bed-side table lay the unfinished letter to your parents. A sad childhood is a poor preparation for unexpected happiness. Cheer up, you have escaped. By the time you wake and read this I shall be swimming. Come and bathe before tea.'

Among the more singular inhabitants of the town is the man whom Hoyle has christened 'The Baron Baedeker'. He is to be seen wherever there is a function, a display, a procession of any kind, darting in and out of the crowd, his coat-tails flying. Over his shoulder he carries the kind of short step-ladder that shoe-salesmen use to reach their more inaccessible wares. From time to time he pauses, grounds his ladder, and climbing to the top of it leans over with a camera between his hands to take a photograph.

The Baron is a tall and finely built man, whose silver hair is cut strictly *en brosse* over his large and sheep-like head. He wears clothes reminiscent of a German diplomat of the old school—a faded frock coat, dark trousers, and a black tie knotted round a celluloid collar. His glasses are very powerful and his grey eyes swim in the pear-shaped lenses with a sweet and reproachful mildness. Whatever the crowd and whatever its size, the Baron's figure may be seen emerging from various parts of it like some strange flower, to hang for a moment by his elbows as he takes a photograph. He is festooned with cameras of different sizes. He palpitates with earnestness.

During the first few weeks of the occupation the Baron succeeded in utterly demoralising the Brigadier who was a bad public speaker. 'Every time I make a speech,' he told Gideon, 'I have only to look up and I see that obscene tulip of a man leering at me off a ladder and aiming something at me. Find out who he is and why he looks so like an U.F.A. spy, will you?'

The bulge in the Baron's hip-pocket is not, as the Brigadier surmised, caused by a gun but by a Bible. So much I discovered when he came to visit me yesterday in order to persuade me to buy some prints from him for use in the newspaper.

He is Greek, born in Asia Minor, and his real name is Panagiotis Kalopodas. He is so devout as almost to be angelic. He has practised photography for fifteen years in Rhodes and for the last ten has been the representative of the Foreign Bible Society—which perhaps accounts for the sobriety of his dress. 'I am known in Rhodes as an honourable man,' he observed once during the course of our talk, with a simplicity that was most disarming. 'Even the Germans, sir, treated me with respect.' In those clothes who could help it?

His photograph albums constitute a unique history of the island which he guards most jealously. 'One evening I shall show you them all,' he says. 'I have recorded everything—even the visit of Goebbels.'

As for the Nereids—they are the presiding spirits of these islands; almost every spring is haunted by them, and everywhere in the long verdant valleys beyond Monte Smith you will find dells and glades where the circles of daisies mark their dancing floors. They are benign spirits, fond of running water and shade; though not all their manifestations are harmless, and the superstitious fear them. All the half-witted children are supposed to have been bewitched by Nereids and woe to the man who unwittingly intrudes upon one of their dances, for they will force him to join in and dance till he drop. Once upon a time near Aphando, where the dates were supposed once to grow, and where now the fig-trees stand in their solid lowering stances, like crocodiles, heavy with fruit; in Aphando there was a shepherdess who had lately borne a child. She was on her way up the hill to her sheepfold when she came upon a group of Nereids dancing. She began to run, but they overtook her; but on her back, in her little bag, she carried the swaddling-clothes of the child, and when the Nereids touched her they recoiled, crying: 'It burns. It burns.' A Nereid could only bear a changeling.

Rodd has a chapter on Nereids which is worth reading. I understand now why the whole countryside folds up like a flower during the midday hours; why the self-respecting husbandman and townee alike prefers a carefully shuttered room to the intensity, the silence and brilliance of the southern afternoons. It is a weird time of day when everything seems to succumb to the silence—everything except the tireless cicada. It is the hour, says Rodd, when Pan takes his rest and he quotes the swain in Theocritus:

> O Shepherd, not at noon, we may not pipe at noon,
> For Pan we dread, who then comes from the chase
> Weary and takes his rest . . .

Hence the haunting fear of the tree's shade; no labourer will sleep under the shade of an old tree, or one that is supposed to have grown a spirit. For it is here in the shadows of trees, at cross-roads, by running water, that Pan's assistants, the contemporary Nereids, lie in waiting. Flash of naked bodies between the trees of Siana and the noise of the spring interrupted by the sound of drinking! Sweep of skirts as the dancers line out on the daisy-clad slopes by St Nicholas!

Christ is one of the bears. There are only six all told who merit this wonderful old printer's appellation—I suppose because the ceaseless walking back and forth, picking up and examining type, which are part and parcel of the handsetter's work, are reminiscent of a bear's movements in a cage. He is the youngest of them, but by far the quickest. A pale youth of some twenty odd years, he is dying of phthisis which has given his eyes a preternatural brilliance. He has long periods of illness, but such is his grace and charm that none of his fellows complains at the extra work his absence involves. This year he has by far exceeded the sick-leave allowance stipulated by his contract. and I have been forced to turn a blind eye to it, because Christ is supporting his mother and two younger children by his work.

But the most interesting thing about the boy is that last week he discovered himself to be a writer. The air-bag was delayed and we were short of material. I do not know how it happened, but some say the ebullient Manoli suggested scornfully that the paper would be better if the printers wrote it and the editorial staff printed it. Christ pulled out a sheef of loose galley and in ten minutes had written a column on this theme which reduced his fellow type-setters to tears. Enquiring what all the noise was about, Kostas, my Greek editor emerged from the printing-house with Christ's work which he read to me with delighted giggles. 'Good,' I said, 'Set it up.' Kostas was aghast. 'Print it?'

'We've always needed a live columnist on this moribund sheet,' I said. 'Open up a column on the left hand side of the second page. Call it 'Ο κοσμακις (a delightful expression which may be translated 'The little Man's World') Tell Christ he must fill it four times a week on any topic he likes except politics. We will pay him thirty drachmae a line.'

Kostas took this news down to the typesetting room. A pregnant hush fell. Earnest debate took place in low voices throughout the morning. It was as if the news had shocked everyone.

That afternoon work took me back to the office in time to see the first pulls come off the machine. It was a feast day, and according to custom CHRONOS was made up with a coloured head. It looked very handsome. In a dark corner by the machine stood Christ with a copy of the paper held in his trembling hands. He was speechless with pleasure. He hung his head with shame when he caught sight of me. Kostas was proof-reading the final page before roaring 'Fire' through the hatch into the machine-room.

Below us in the darkness Christ was waiting at his station (it was his duty-afternoon) to throw the switch and set the great machine in action. 'That boy has been in a dream all morning,' said Kostas. He finished vetting the last page and threw back the hatch into the printing room. 'Okay,' he said, and gave my arm a sympathetic squeeze before shouting 'Fire'.

The great grunting and swishing began below. Christ unbolted the outer door and let in the horde of urchins who were to collect and distribute the paper for us. The newborn writer stood with hanging head beside the machine, smiling to himself. He still looked dazed.

By next morning his fame had spread throughout the poor quarter in which he lived. On his way to work, Kostas told me, at least a dozen people came up to congratulate him on his article. His fellow printers receive him with the same jokes and jibes now, but there is a touch of apprehension, of respect in their attitude. There is nothing like cold print for commanding the respect of the ordinary. Christ has entered the most impoverished aristocracy in the world.

CHAPTER III

The Little Summer of Saint Demetrius

Tomorrow I am to visit my parish for the first time. On the great ordnance map which hangs above my desk I have traced and retraced the outlines of my islands until I know the distinctive shape of each of them. Rhodes might be a flint arrowhead: Cos a sperm whale: Leros an octopus: Patmos a seahorse: Symi an expended meteor rubbed smooth with air: Kalymnos a mussel.

Of their products, their climates and their inhabitants I already know a good deal, thanks to a brief but intensive period of study with the Army in Cairo. Even the tables of industrial statistics which fill the little army source-books seem to hold some undertones of magic for me with their cold hints of sponge, emery, currants and white cherries. Now I am to marry my theoretical knowledge to that of an eye-witness.

I have chosen the Little Summer of St Demetrius for the journey, counting upon its last fine days to enable me to travel as far as Leros and back on equable seas.

Symi

Moving northwards through this marvellous Aegean landscape lit by the intense white light of the sun, I feel the kick and plunge of the little island caieque as she aims for Cos. The mountains sweep down into the sea, planted here like the feet of petrified elephants, to revolve slowly as we pass them, as if on some great hairy turntable. On the way to Cos you come across whole hillsides littered with debris from Maillol's studio—half-finished ankles and heads, breasts and toes. Dawn had not broken when we entered the great cobweb of stone which is Symi, so I have no clear picture of it—only a series of impressions. It lies there like a black rusk upon the water—but rock so pitted and perforated by the tongues of sea thrown out by Anatolia that you would think of it as most like some black stone lung. Everywhere the sighing and blubbering of blowholes, the sound of water breathing and snuffling in that black honeycomb. On this unpromising foundation a town was built, by an idle youngster in coloured bricks. It started up the mountain but soon tired of the gradient and dissolved into a scrabble of ruined plaster and heaps of stone which nobody will use now. A human voice launched across the noise of the water and the wind from the open sea sounds small, ant-like—as if you were to scratch upon a rubber bladder with the point of a pin. '*Kalo Taxidi*—a good journey to you. . . .'

Kalymnos

In Kalymnos the infant's paint-box has been at work again on the milky slopes of the mountain. Carefully, laboriously it has squared in a churchyard, a monastery, and lower down repeated the motif: a church, a monastery, a town; then, simply for the sake of appropriateness, a harbour with a shelf of bright craft at anchor, and the most brilliant, the most devastatingly brilliant houses. Never has one seen anything like it—the harbour revolving slowly round one as one comes in. Plane after stiff cubistic plane of pure colour. The mind runs up and down the web of vocabulary looking for a word which will do justice to it. In vain. Under the church the half-finished caieques stand upon a slip—huge coops of raw wood looking for all the world like the skeletons of dismembered whales.

Three little girls in crimson dresses stand arm in arm and watch us. The harbour liquefies under the keel as we throttle down and move towards the port, our engines now puffy and subdued, yet quickened like our heartbeats as we sit and watch the island. The echo of our passage—the hard *plam-plam-plam* of the exhaust—bounces gravely off the rusted iron hull of a steamer which lies on its side in the shallows, its funnels sticking up like nostrils, but all the rest of it submerged in water as clear as the purest white gin. This is Kalymnos.

High up, under the walls of the Church of the Golden Hand a woman is singing, slowly, emphatically, while from the wharves across the way a man in a blue overall is hammering at a coffin. Uncanny isolation of sound and object, each dissimilar, each entire to itself. Detached from the temporal frame. A song and a hammering which exist together but never mix or muddle the hard outlines of each other.

Cos

Cos is the spoiled child of the group. You know it at once, without even going ashore. It is green, luxuriant and a little dishevelled. An island that does not bother to comb its hair. Hard by the port the famous tree of Hippocrates (to which Mills has promised himself a sentimental pilgrimage) stands, in a little arbour of greenery, like some Nubian women stricken with elephantiasis. Whole trees have burst out of it in all directions, and with no reference whatsoever to gravity or proportion. The kindly worshippers have propped, here an arm, there a thigh, with votive pillars of bricks or stone. Somehow the whole improbable structure still stands—indeed its luxuriant foliage covers a whole courtyard like a tent. The children play wonderful games among the branches. 'A stranger,' they cry, 'a stranger.' I must be the first foreign civilian they have seen for some time. We exchange oranges against sweets and discuss life in Cos. Everywhere it is the same—conversation revolves about food. They look ragged and thin but not actually starving. We climb the Frankish castle with its mounds of rubble and shattered ravelins. Once more one comes upon mounds of twisted and rusting steel—machine-gun ammunition and shells and empty petrol tins. There is no time to see the Aesculapium on this visit, as it lies some way outside the town, and the captain of the caieque is anxious to make Leros while the good weather holds. Our journeys must still be made in swept channels, as the whole sea hereabouts is mined, and I think he fears that bad weather might push us into one of these fields. . . .

Leros

In Leros one always seems to be weather-bound, according to the captain. It is a beastly island without any character, despite its rather noble Frankish castle and picturesque village. There is, however, no pastoral or agricultural land worth the name. Simply gigantic port installations now crumpled with bombing, and rotting away in the damp—prodigious jumbles of copper, steel and brass. The harbour is choked with sunk craft, and the little town has been very badly bombed. A miasmic gloom hangs over everything. God help those born here, one mutters, those who live here, and those who come here to die. The water is brackish—like the wits of its inhabitants. As far as I am concerned I am wholeheartedly on the side of the poet Phoclydes who used the name of Leros to throw mud at an enemy of his unlucky enough to be born here. An early example of literary mud-slinging! And 'Leros' still means dirt today. Yet weather-bound or not, there has been time to think, time to jot down some notes about poetry in the little black note-book E bought me, which is now stained with salt water and brandy. Major France, who presides over the officers' mess, is a delightful eccentric, an ex-commando who has spent many years of his life, in peace and war, travelling among these islands; in pre-war years he carried cargo in a small tramp-steamer belonging to himself, while during the war he exchanged his role for that of secret agent. Clad in rubber boots with soles a span thick, and armed with the most fearful assortment of cutlery the mind of man can devise, he travelled about cutting throats, piloting one of the tiny caiques belonging to the Sea Raiding Forces. Now he sits at the head of a hospitable table, covered in campaign medals as thick as confetti, and pines for the rigours of the Burma campaign.

In the smoky tavern whose frail walls quiver at each blast of rain and wind I spend half a day transacting business with the agent who is to handle distribution for me in Patmos and the other small islands. He is a little man whose appearance is one of extreme indigence, and of a cast of feature so terribly pessimistic that it is obvious one can hope for nothing in the way of efficient island distribution. While the Greeks have kept their language, only a very few can write it, and fewer still read it, he tells me. But that is not to say that they will not subscribe to a paper. No. He swigs tot after tot of burning mastika, settling his neck more deeply after each emergence into the collar of his ragged overcoat. People will buy the newspaper all right, but he cannot guarantee readers. Owing to the great shortage of wrapping paper, he says, almost *any* paper is welcome to the inhabitants of the island. They need it for wrapping fish in, or eggs. They need it for parcels and packages. So that my sales will be safe-guarded by this great shortage in a way that even full literacy and the keenest interest in the affairs of the world could not achieve for me. It is one of the anomalies of war that the daily newspaper which we issue at a penny is worth twopence as wrapping paper, and already in Rhodes our receipts for scrapped issues are greater than our receipts on current sales. It puts journalism in its right perspective somehow. Meanwhile I am delighted to think of the inhabitants of these atolls subscribing faithfully to my newspaper simply in order to wrap fish in it. The agent does not smile. He is beyond that. As we part he depresses his cheeks into a sort of deathmask of a smile and says: 'At any rate you know the truth now.'

The evening comes down, smudged with rain, from a sky of dirty wool. We stand at the great bay window and watch the skirls and eddies roar into the landlocked harbour and dance like maniacs in the riggings of the caieques. A loose foresail cracks and cracks like pistol shots. Above us the shattered Frankish castle stands its ground as it has done for centuries; but each year a few more bricks are pried loose and come rumbling down the hill into the main street, a few more shreds are blown off the towers. As it gets darker the sheet-lightning starts and France tries to take a photograph of us all sitting round the table playing pontoon by its blank staring stabs. By dawn, he says, it will have blown itself out and we shall be able to start for Patmos, the last island on my visiting list, and the one I most want to see.

Patmos

Just before dawn there were one or two flashes of lightning and I woke to see the hunchback standing in the dark hall, with a telephone in one hand and a lighted candle in the other. 'Hullo', he was calling in his cracked voice across the miles of water, 'Hullo there Patmos!' A thin crackling came back across the German field-telephone from the island, like the leaky discharge of a low electric current. The lightning flashed twice again—milky throbs of whiteness behind the

63

dense clouds that covered Leros. 'The storm has lifted a little,' shouted the hunchback, grimacing with the effort of maintaining that tenuous contact. 'We are sending them over.'

Outside, I thought I could still hear the roaring of the sea and the whack-whack of the wind in the palm tree up the hill. The hunchback entered the room and placed the lighted candle beside me with the cup of tea. 'The sea is calm,' he said, and as if in sympathy with it, his own voice lost its harshness and became calm too. 'They will be here in a little while to take you.' For four days we had been marooned in Leros by the weather. I said nothing, drinking my tea and exploring the warm corners of the bed with my feet. He stood looking down at me for a moment, and then taking his squat pipe from his pocket, lighted it at the candle. 'Get up,' he said, and marched off in his creaking black boots to the kitchen.

I lay and watched the whiteness of the daylight slowly leak into the sky, outlining the black paw of cloud that lay across the town and shrouded the top of the castle. The air in the room smelt stale and used up. The high cracked ceiling, the odd-shaped windows above which hung the pelmets of mouldering brocade disturbed one by their associations: a Venetian etching. Lying here I felt that I was breathing in the desiccated air of another century; and the candle with its rosy pool of light added to the illusion. A room, you would say, in the house of an exiled Prime Minister in the reign of King Otto. The assassins entered by the window. In the far corner, where the wallpaper has faded, stood the sofa on which they laid him. . . .

The faithful E was awake, combing her dark head by the light of a candle and yawning. I sat and watched her dress eating some bread and butter, talking in whispers so as not to wake the others, who lay in odd corners of the old house, peacefully snoring. 'Do you think we can make it?' she asked from time to time, dreading heavy sea as much as I did. 'It's only three hours,' I said. 'It will be rough of course.'

I was wrong as it turned out. We heard the rapid imperative note of voices in the hall, and tip-toed down the cracking staircase, packs on our shoulders, to where they stood waiting for us. We left the house like thieves.

Beneath the darkness of the cloud the immediate foreground was wrapped in a dense ground-mist, raw and chilling. It was not raining, however, and the boatman grunted his satisfaction at the fact. 'The sea is calm,' he said, 'too calm.' We walked down the avenue of chestnuts together towards the town, listening to the chilling noise of torrents which had swollen with the rains. A flash of lightning showed us the main street which the storm had turned into a swirling black stream; then the darkness came down, ominous and complete —the darkness that comes with the closing of a camera's shutter. It is difficult to explain: for behind it, at the edges of the sky, the light advanced in degrees of dirty white. It was as if all one saw was the silhouette of the darkness itself.

We splashed through the narrow warrens of the port and emerged at last on the quay-side where the caieque lay, its crew stuck fast, it seemed, in attitude of complete apathy, awaiting us. The captain hung from a rope, leaning his body out at an angle, staring down at the water. The boy and the man sat, submerged in themselves at the tiller, their splayed bare feet among the twists of rope. They shook themselves as we whistled.

She was called 'Forgetfulness': a powerful little caieque built to the shallow-bosomed shape which the fisherfolk call 'Racers' because they are judged speedier than the normal deep-hulled models. The sea-raiding people had put a tank-engine in her which gave her about twelve knots. You felt the power at once as she fanned away from the stone-quay and out into the harbour, edging towards the black buoys which, the captain said, marked mine-fields. Huddled in our coats we watched the black, uninviting headland of rock paying out past us like a rapidly diminishing rope, drawing us nearer to the proper sea. Across the waters, from the direction of Turkey, the light had broken through in one place; a drop of red had leaked between the interstices of sea and sky, and was running round the rim of the horizon like the knife that slips along the rim of the oyster to let the light in with it. The red mingled with the black and turned it purple; the meniscus of the sea copied the tone: strengthened it: turned it green, and an edge of the sun shone for a second across the waste of waters and islands, hideous, like a head with one eye. Then the darkness again and the steady throb of the engines. The boy was posted at the prow. He strained through the mist and guided the helmsman with shouts and gestures.

'So we'll get to Patmos after all,' said E, unpacking the sandwiches and the little bottle of cognac.

Patmos, I thought, was more an idea than a place, more a symbol than an Island.

Yet to the boy crouching at the prow, his eyes fixed upon the mist-darkened territory ahead, it had no doubt become a name like any other, marking only a brief stony point in an oft-repeated routine, distinguished at the most by a special tavern where the wine was resinous or a house where the conversation seemed the better for a beautiful elder daughter. From time to time as he peered, he saw the shapes of islands come up on us like battleships, and with a brief wild cry—as of some trapped seabird—shook his arm to right or left, guiding us to the safety of the deeper channel. A few yards away the wet fangs of rock would emerge and slide back into their unearthly vagueness, and the note of the propeller deepen in the deeper sounding as the vellum of a drum when the player alters its tensity. Once the mist drew back for an instant and we saw, tinkling upon a scrubby headland, a swarm of sheep like gold bugs, loitering among arbutus, while on a rock commanding the prospect stood a motionless hooded figure like a janitor. Their bells were softly dumbed out in the mist, losing volume but not their richness.

The sun had somehow swindled us and climbed into heaven without once shining directly upon the water. Through a cloud-surface with a thick yellow nap like a carpet it allowed its beams to diffuse themselves over everything with a dense coppery hue, turning the water to lead beneath us. It increased our range of sight, however, and with it our speed. From where he sat at the tiller the captain made a chopping motion with his hand to indicate, in Greek fashion, the fact that we were making better time. The boy came aft and sat for a while to make conversation. Points of water glistened in his beard and hair. 'Patmos', he said, 'you will like it. All foreigners like it. They have good fruit and water.' Then raising himself the better to cup his hands about a box of English matches as he lit a cigarette he added, with a touch of medieval wonder: 'And there is a telephone. The Abbot speaks to it every day.'

'Have you ever used it?' I asked him.

'I? What for?'

The sense of blindness had now given place to a sense of headache. The atmosphere had become warmer, but the clouds still lay between us and the sun, which burned with a bilious humid intensity upon the sea. The last of the islands that lined the corridor between Leros and Patmos like ancestral totems, was kicking in our wake. Presently we should see our objective through the trembling curtain of the mist.

The captain handed over the tiller and came forward to the prow; hanging outwards he stared long and intently towards the vapourized horizon, and then came aft to consult a watch—not without a touch of pride, for it looked like German booty. We had been going two hours.

'In the channel it is often rough', said the old man. 'Praise God, it is all right. But tonight there will be more storm.'

We informed him that we had determined to return to Leros that night, and he nodded once or twice in a protective manner as he puffed his cigarette. 'And if you can't,' he said, 'there is no need to worry. There is the telephone.'

Our attention was caught by a cry from the boy who had returned to the prow. Away to the northward the mist had shifted and beyond it, gleaming in a single pencil of sunlight was a white cape—lifted like the wing of an albatross upon the very place where sky and sea met. For an instant this snowy apparition paused, and then the beam moved slowly along the mass to pick out a turret, a battlement, the cupola of a chapel. 'The monastery,' said the captain. 'Patmos.'

W stood for a long time now watching the lights playing upon the island, now touching up a dazzling pane of glass in the monastery, now extinguishing the whole seascape to the tones of a black and white drawing. The sun was trying to find a way through the clouds.

'In another half hour,' said the old captain, as if he were trying to instil patience into himself. 'In another half hour we shall be there.'

'Come,' said E, 'we should eat now.'

We had neither of us had much appetite before, but now with the still straits before us and the island in sight, we turned with real hunger to the cognac and the sandwiches. The boy boiled a kettle of water and I saw with some surprise that the whole crew had developed the habit of drinking British Army Tea, brewed sweet and strong— surely the most disgusting drink ever invented. This was a legacy of the sea-raiding days no doubt, as was the expertness of wrist with which the captain opened a tin of bully beef.

We finished eating just as the caieque fanned into the little harbour of Patmos, free from cloud at that moment, and blazing like a diamond among the hillocks.

'Welcome,' cried the figures on the quay as we tied up, and at once we felt grateful to be back in the traditional type of Greek island after the rather spurious Italianate atmosphere of Rhodes. They were all there in that little whitewashed port; you could see at a glance the representatives of the six or seven types which have furnished Greek islands since the beginning of history. The old sea-captain with his knotted hands and shaggy whiskers, the village schoolmaster in his dignity and European clothes, the mad boy who plays the violin outside the tavern door—the island poet whose wits, says tradition, have been turned by the Nereids. Their clear eyes and lovely brown skins proclaimed them islanders, born in this clear blue air; and the pleasure and warmth with which they cried 'Welcome'—and uttered among themselves the sacred word 'Strangers'—proved them as Greek as one could wish. We declined in rapid succession, a donkey, a bunch of flowers, and a conversation about how old we were, where we had come from, and what our business was. The tavern-keeper swept us a disappointed bow from the door of the tavern in the shadowy interior of which the familiar Homeric group sat round a table playing cards. We walked through the narrow main street between the smiling faces of the women, past the old date palm tree—last of many palms which earned for Patmos the name of Palmosa among the Venetians—and addressed ourselves to the bare hill whose brown rocks were still wet with the rain and noisy with overflowing torrents.

Before us, balanced against a cloud, stood the monastery, its odd arrangement of machicolated turrets and belfries reminding one of a medieval castle—such as one only sees in Russian films. The great gate stood open. One expected to see a troop of Tartar horsemen swing out of it suddenly, waving their lances and hide bucklers, uttering shrill cries; but nothing passed through the door save some small children singing an island song in tiny cracked voices, perfectly reproduced by the blue atmosphere despite the distance.

Halfway up we met a shepherd, sitting on the stone parapet crook in hand, talking to his daughter, and occasionally uttering barbaric whoops at his flock. We sat down and rested beside him, for the going was steep and hard. In exchange for the piece of bread he shyly offered us we took his photograph, while he showed a hospitable annoyance with the Patmos weather for not favouring our visit more conclusively. The ominous wrack of cloud still stretched away to the east and west of the island; while everything lay, enchanted by sunlight, in an oasis of midsummer. Even the bees in the little white hives by the monastery were duped by it.

'Are they expecting you?' asked the shepherd.

'We telephoned to the Abbot.'

'Then you will eat well,' he said comfortingly; the monastery lay about a quarter of an hour off, along the great sill of red-brown stone. The smaller monastery of St John, where the Apocalypse was written, lay beneath us with its cave of the illumination and musty banners. The three ruined windmills glimmered on the ultimate crags.

'We'll be going', I said.

'God be with you,' he responded, reluctantly, for conversation with strangers is a rare pleasure among islanders who have known each other from childhood. 'God be with you,' repeated his daughter, enchanted by her own grownupness.

We entered the great gate and found ourselves immediately in a warren of cobbled streets, each just wide enough for the passage of a loaded mule, and thrown down upon each other in a sort of labyrinth. We followed them up stairways, down alleys, round corners, doubling back upon ourselves at different levels until we found the great door of the monastery. It also stood ajar. From every nook now the prospect began to shine out, the brilliant bay and the further seas, set in the green and grey.

In the courtyard the hush was intense. The faces on the painted wooden screens glowed softly. Then from the gloom of the chapel came the thin scribbling noise of Byzantine Greek, lifted in prayer. Another voice began a humming twanging response. 'There's a service going on,' said E. Several voices now attacked the silence as if heard through a comb and paper. The faint chink of censers, the faintest whiff of incense leaked out of the darkness. I eased the heavy pack off my back and coughed twice. Immediately a servant came out of the recess under the staircase and told me my name, showing no surprise when I did not disagree. 'At once,' he said in a low, urgent voice, 'at once.' He sprang into the dark chapel like a diver into a pool and re-emerged holding the Abbot by the hand. We began our greetings, seasoning them with apologies for the interruption. The Abbot smiled in his beard and waved the latter away. 'Come,' he cried with a spontaneous good-nature, 'we have nearly finished. Come with us.' And led us by the hand into the little darkness where by now the very anna livia plurabelle of a service was going on.

They looked for all the world like benign tree-bears which had burrowed into the trunk of an old tree for honey. The deacon was humming and yawing from a muscle-bound byzantine evangel which he held against his chest. The Abbot subsided into his place, and we each fitted ourselves into those uncomfortable pews where you hang by the elbows like a bat. It was an admirable introduction, for while the utterances and responses rose and fell in the darkness, I was able to rest and let my eyes wander over the rich altar-screen with its ornaments and paintings. The only light came in through a foggy piece of glass in the dome. The darkness was restful, and I found myself inclined to doze, as the monks trotted backwards and forwards to various points of the darkness, shouting and twanging out of various books, or swinging the censers and spinning round upon themselves with predetermined smartness. One had a sense of infinite remoteness—these voices rising, it seemed, from the bottom of the sea, muffled by the mushroom-shaped dome of the monastery, muffled by the darkness, by the dense gloom.

Presently the service came to an end; facing the altar one of the deacons lifted his mouth and blew out a candle; and at once we were among friends. Six large priests, with luxurious curling beards and expressive hands. 'Praise be to God,' the Abbot said, 'at last some English we can talk to.' Later he doubtless revised his opinion of my lame Greek. But E chimed in, and under her interest and delight everybody came alight, falling naturally into that generous full-bodied loquacious amiability which is so truly Greek, as we streamed out once more into the courtyard to have the painted wood screens explained to us, and the intricacies of the corridors exhibited. In a little dark magazine behind the altar we were shown the treasures of the monastery—richly embroidered copes and stoles, a dozen different kinds of pyx, diamond-studded bindings for books.

By now the weariness of our journey was upon us, and we asked leave to rest; but this was not to be. There was the whole rambling architecture of the place to see; and then there was the fatal bait of the camera which I carried slung from my shoulder. I could see several pairs of dark eyes fixed meditatively upon it, and several pairs of dark hands beginning with an anticipatory combing-out of beards, the adjustment of black stove-pipe hats. Presently we should have to take everyone's picture.

The monastery of St John was itself as much a treasure as any of its heavily priced treasures in silk or ivory or vellum; it was a wilderness of chimneys, cupolas, belfries, turrets and dazzling white walks. Connecting battlements complement each other so you can walk from the eastern side where the island lies and study the shapes of other islands, faint as a wash drawing on the smooth surface of the sky. Leros, Icaria, Amorgos, Samos. The clouds had turned them down like wicks, but there they lay stubbornly insisting on their identity against the darkness of the horizon. 'Bad weather,' said the Abbot, learning that we intended to start back that afternoon. 'You should have stayed for a month with us.' This gave him a chance to show us the commodious quarters for guests, eight lovely whitewashed rooms, with angle-windows looking out on to the sea. I would have liked to stay for the rest of my life, but did not wish to seem fulsome in expressing so a thought which must have sprung to so many minds. 'Are you not lonely?' said E to the Abbot. The old man repeated the word once or twice, looking from one to the other of us, holding it, as it were, so far away from himself as possible, the better to see the concept which it represented. He did not answer directly. A few drops of rain fell loudly on the terrace. The rent in the cloud-scape was rapidly closing once more. Below us the harbour with its viridian borders and the pearly tones of the hill beyond, began to dissolve and fade, as the thunder opened up in the west. He led us into the library and showed us the famous manuscripts, writhing painted bestiaries and ancient scripts, pressing our shrinking fingers to the thick vellum to feel its weight and quality. When we had exhausted these treasures he allowed us to photograph him leaning in the narrow window-sill, conscious of the elegance of his beard and beautiful hands. Outside a rain of thistles had begun to descend blotting out all perspectives, and turning the whole monastery in a moment from dazzling white to soaking neutral grey. The rain stood for a moment in great drops on the lips of the bell and then ran down to the courtyard, seeking the already swollen gutters. 'We shall never get away tonight,' I muttered.

In the refectory, whose windows were lit by yellow stabs of lightning, we watched the storm slowly wheeling the clouds into formation. The islands had vanished. Strange manoeuvres were going on in the dark sky beyond which the sun still shone. We ran from window to window calling to each other to look. Through holes in the cloud long shafts of yellow light played down on the leaden sea like searchlights, circling slowly, or running the whole length of the horizon before going out. Such tense needles of light as one saw piercing the gloom of those old oil-engravings to the shilling Bible, on which the dove descended as upon a scaling ladder.

An old woman had laid out supper for three, and presently the Abbot joined us to pour out the heavy red wine into the glasses and serve us portions of the delicious chicken with lemon-rice. He seemed obscurely troubled and looked up nervously as each heartbeat of lightning lit up his bearded face. For a while we attempted a desultory conversation which could compete with the storm. Drops of water climbed down the windows. Somewhere a shutter banged again.

'It was you who telephoned?', asked the old man.

'Yes, from Leros. Major F's servant spoke to you.'

He nodded twice with something like impatience and ate another mouthful of chicken. 'So many people ring up and say they are coming,' he said. 'Some do. Others never seem to arrive.' He issued some impatient orders over his shoulder to the aged woman and began to tell us of the war. The monastery was forced to play the role of philanthropic neutral to three nations. A smile lit up his face as he told us how three separate units, Italian, German and English, had been sheltering in the monastery at the same time. 'Two of the three might have shot us,' he said. 'What could we do? An Italian signal section on the top floor, a wounded German officer whose life I saved in the granary, and six British commandos in the cellar which was their H.Q.'

It had been as difficult and dangerous a time as any he cared to remember. Naturally they were pro-British—but a monastery is a monastery. 'We could not leave the German to die outside on the hill. As for the Italians. . . .' He shrugged his shoulders.

Suddenly he turned round and said: 'And this man Anthony— why did he not come with you from Leros?' We looked at each other. 'An English Major who also rang up.' To the best of our knowledge there had been no one else in Leros intending to make the crossing; had there been he would certainly have had to ask the permission of Major F, our host. We should certainly have known. 'That's what I mean,' said the Abbot in a distressed tone. 'People are always ringing up.'

The storm had travelled over the peak and was now thrashing the palm tree in the valley. We finished the excellent chicken, and the Abbot led us slowly from room to room of the monastery, down winding corridors, up and down stairs. This was where the brothers lived. This was a reception room. This was where the conclave met to discuss ecclesiastical problems, or those connected with the admin-istration of the monastery. In one of these large echoing rooms stood the German field-telephone, a replica of the one at the mess in Leros—an ugly bakelite box with a handle and a small receiver. As the Abbot looked at it I saw an expression of disgust and anger cross his face. 'This is the telephone,' he said. The rain was pouring in at an open window, stirring the dust on the floor, and shaking the heavy red hangings by the dias. I closed the window, and we went down the corridors in single file. As we emerged upon the penultimate balcony overlooking the courtyard we heard the sound of voices. Looking over, I could see the soaked figure of our captain standing in the great door with a piece of sacking over his head. In half an hour, he shouted up at us, there would be a lull in the storm. If we chose to take advantage of it we could be back in Leros by dinner time. If not. . . .

'We have not spoken of St John,' said the Abbot. 'Of his wonderful book. You must see his church. Stay with us.' His tone changed to one of hospitable coaxing. It was very difficult to explain that, if we missed the motor-launch which was due to start for Rhodes at dawn the next day we should be stranded for a week over schedule—delightful as the idea seemed. He was sad. He had intended an exposition of the Apocalypse.

However, he helped us pack our belongings, and one by one the brothers came out of the various rooms to shake our hands and bid us goodbye. 'Come again,' they cried, 'come and stay with us. We are on the telephone, you know. You can always ring up and say you are coming. Just come any time, and stay with us as long as you like.'

We passed out through the great doorway into a blinding drizzle that thinned off as we neared the harbour; the little caieque was standing off with her engine going. It had all been timed to a second. With hardly a moment to say a breathless goodbye to the friendly loafers in the tavern we were aboard, and drawing free of the harbour towards a sea that looked foully disturbed, with whitecaps flicking the horizon.

Darkness fell before we had cleared the rough straits but we were making good time. The caieque rode superbly, her round canoe-shaped nose chopping down the head-sea. By seven, the black shapes of rocks gleamed wetly at us from either bow, and we slackened speed. Leros hung against the sky, a part of the darkness and yet separable from it if one looked carefully enough; but the middle distance was blotted out by skirls of rain. One could taste the dry salt on one's lips, feel its powdery dryness upon the throat and ear. Soon we crossed the bar and the few dim lights of the harbour bulged greasily at us. It was still raining as we disembarked and crossed the wet deserted streets towards the mess. The rain rattled like shot among the chestnuts.

In the dark hall we stood for a moment, peeling off our clothes and shouting for the hunchback, who came from the kitchen at last, bringing with him a great bar of light and the gleam of an oven.

Upstairs, the two officers were finishing dinner. It was good to sink into one of the luxurious armchairs with which the German commander of Leros had furnished his mess and sip a drink while our baths were heated up. We gave an account of our trip to our host and thanked him suitably for the use of his caieque. As we were talking the telephone in the hall began to ring. 'The damned thing,' said the young officer running downstairs to answer it. 'It's been out of order all day.' In a moment he returned and said: 'It's the Abbot. Wants to know if you are safe. Would you like to go down and do your stuff?' I picked my way down to the dark hall and picked up the ugly little receiver. Damp crepitations echoed inside the earpiece. 'Hullo,' I called, and for a moment I heard, as if in a sea-shell, nothing but the sibilance of sea-water lashing those stony promontories, boiling among the shapes of volcanic stones, among the deserted quays of Patmos harbour.

'Hullo'. The Abbot's voice emerged from a criss-cross of scratchings and whirrings, as if from some old prewar gramophone disc. 'Your Beatitude,' I said, giving him, for good measure, what was really a patriarch's due. 'We arrived safely, thank you.' And I added compliments suitable for the occasion. The young officer came downstairs and stood beside me as I spoke, putting a cigarette between my lips and lighting it. 'After you,' he said. The Abbot sounded squeaky and alarmed. No doubt he was unused to telephones. 'This man, Major Anthony,' I said, 'who is he? The old boy wants to know whether to prepare food for him or what.' The officer took the phone from me and began a bantering conversation with the island. 'No such person, Abbot,' he said. 'Your imagination again. No. You won't be disturbed for some time now.'

Together we walked upstairs to the lighted room where the cards had been laid out upon the table and where a sleepy E was already beginning to put her things in order against packing. Tomorrow, at dawn, the naval launch would take us back to Rhodes. Much later, when I was already in bed, listening to the whacking of the palm tree up the hill, the young officer came to say goodnight standing at the open door with a candle in his hand. We should not see him before we left. 'Is the Abbot often mistaken about visitors who ring up?' I asked on a sudden impulse.

'It's just one of those things,' he answered indifferently. 'Beastly things, these German phones.' Then he added: 'It's curious. The

Abbot always seems to be getting phone calls from this Anthony chap. I wonder who he could have been—if at all, I mean. . . . Well, goodnight.' I wondered, too. Lying in bed, tasting the luxury of the sleep which was moving toward me across the noises of the house, and the deep hushing of the wind and the rain, I suddenly thought to myself that perhaps this was a ghost which for some reason or other was destined forever to long for Patmos (which is after all a symbol of something for which we all keep a place in our hearts).

On the way home, another storm is brewing. Heading for the harbour we pass a poor wretch in a leaky boat, half-naked, setting out lobster pots. He does not even turn to watch us as our wash sets him bouncing. Through those patched rags I see the lean muscles of his arm tighten as he struggles for purchase in that crazy cockle-shell. Yet he does not even turn to curse us—and in a flash I see the Greece I love again: the naked poverty that brings joy without humiliation, the chastity and fine manners of the islanders, the schisms and treacheries of the townsmen, the thrift and jealousy of the small-holders. I see the taverns with their laurel wreaths, the lambs turning on the spit at Easter, the bearded heroes, the shattered marble statues. Eastward now lies Anatolia, its sunburnt mountains brooding under the eagles where the shepherd treads all day among myrtle and arbutus stabbed scarlet with berries. Some day I shall find the right way of dealing with it in words. . . .

The run is perfectly timed; behind us, the wrack of the coming storm, before us a dead calm bathed in afternoon sunlight. From this angle Rhodes looks unbelievably romantic. It is this entry into the harbour which I thought of when I wrote:

'If you should have the luck to approach it, as perhaps one should, through the soft yellowish tones of a June nightfall, you would undoubtedly imagine it to be some great sea-animal asleep in the water. The eastern spit of sand upon which both ancient and modern town were built shelves slowly down into the channel from the slopes of Monte Smith, so called because Sir Sidney Smith once set up his battle headquarters there. This would constitute the hump of your whale. Eastward loom the weather-worn Carian Mountains, casting shadows so dense that the sea is stained saffron by the last rays of the sun. Nestling in the natural amphitheatre where once stood the white buildings and temples of the ancient town, the Crusader fortress with its encircling walls and crumbling turrets looks for all the world like a town in pen and ink, situated upon the margins of some illuminated manuscript: the medieval dream of a fortress called Rhodes which the mist has invented for you, and which will dissolve again as you enter the little harbour of Mandraccio to anchor under the fort of St Nicholas where once, it is suggested, the Colossus stood.'

This is the entry that Gideon and I should have chosen for ourselves when we set out for Alexandria.

In Rhodes things are moving. The portentous soldiery has entrenched itself securely in the rococo building which once housed De Vecci's staff. A martial hauteur may be remarked upon many faces. Gideon has been making a few friends and many enemies—the usual proportion, as he says. 'I never could get on with haberdashers in pips and crowns,' he adds sourly. However, there are compensations. The lighting-unit for the town has been fixed, and the whole harbour cleared of enemy equipment in record time. The post office has started to work, and has been inundated with remittances from Dodecanesians all over the world. One street lamp in ten has been persuaded to light after dark. These are not small things—they are part of that unknown quantity, civilization—for the street lamp brings order, and the post office confidence. Nevertheless, Gideon says that he smells the odour of garrison life creeping over the town. This is because he hates the British Officers' Club and yet the cheapness of whisky there forces him to have his evening drink there. He is making a list of conversational gambits overheard within those august precincts. Some of them, I fear, have the air of being manufactured. We amuse ourselves in trying to guess the speaker in the cases of phrases like: 'O Fuzzy-wuzzy is a jolly decent chap when you get to know him,' and 'I found the Swahili a perfect gentleman', and 'The Greeks are perfectly bloody don't you think?'

A passage from a letter which reached Gideon yesterday from G:

'So you are in Rhodes? We landed there briefly among the first few units. I was shocked. It was simply a shell of what it had once been. Walking on the shattered sea-front in the dark I tried to reconstruct a pre-war incident whose flavour has never quite left me.

I was walking here in 1939 at that indeterminate twilight hour, after dark but before the lamps had been lit. I collided in the darkness with the soft figure of a woman. She stood before me without speaking. 'Who is it?' I said. She did not answer but softly placed a hand upon my arm, and I understood. We stood thus for a moment by the harbour wall.

'I fumbled for a box of matches and struck one, saying as I did so: "All right, if you are beautiful." The match-flame copied itself into two dark eyes: a face much older than itself—serious, beguiling, and most world-weary. We climbed the slopes of Monte Smith and lay down together in one of those rock-tombs, still warm.

'She was lean and half-starved and her clothes tasted of sea-salt. Her poverty was poignant in a way that no one who has not experienced the Mediterranean can understand. In her I tasted the whole of Greece, its sunburnt airs, dazzling bony islands, and the chaste and honourable poverty which the people has converted into a golden generosity. Her name was Aphrodite—I know! I know! She walked all day by the sea gathering firewood and sea-coal. Her husband had been a prosperous fisherman but he was now in the last stages of consumption. She made a little money as a casual. Everything that might have seemed ugly or dirty was transformed somehow by the human experience which underlay her actions; she knew the full measure of them, so to speak. It would have been unworthy of me to regret or criticise either of us. Life had been too big for her; by accepting she was conquering it. It may sound silly to philosophise over a casual encounter with a prostitute but there are lessons to be learnt from her. She had a rock-rose fastened to her shawl with a pin. When we parted she detached it and handed it to me with a magnificent friendliness. I had an inkling then that the Greeks were still the natural poets of the Levant. They understand, you know, that hunger is not proud and that the Tenth Muse is really Poverty.'

'Poverty,' mused Gideon. 'Well, I wonder.' He added that what he respected in G was his readiness to *make a place* for new experiences. 'Most of us simply cannot squeeze in a new sensation which does not conform to the established prejudices with which we have been paced. I should have been horrified—or should I?'

Hoyle lit a cigar. 'You know,' he said, 'on such a high literary level the whole incident was probably invented. Though of course that would not invalidate its essential truth.'

'Nevertheless,' said Gideon, 'I think it is true. This last passage convinces me, where he says: "Here I am, a writer, thirty-one, who cannot bring his equipment to bear upon material of this sort without running the risk of sentimentalising something which was as clear as a glass of water. If I touch it I damage it. What a dilemma." '

CHAPTER IV

The Sunny Colossus

I have profited by the absence of Hoyle and Gideon in another island of the group to assemble a few hasty notes upon the Colossus—in the manner of a man talking to himself. Mills is away also in the south of the island upon some errand of mercy. And while I miss my companions I have taken the precaution of borrowing their works of reference on Rhodes. Thus I have time at last to tackle history—that vast complex of analogies—without getting lost among the shoals and quicksands of argument and polemic. For no companion to Rhodes would be complete without a reference to the island Colossus; and yet the subject cannot be touched upon without some reference to the siege out of which it was born, and to commemorate which it was designed.

The siege itself was a colossus in kind—so that to write of the statue of the Sun-God is to write of a colossus born of a colossus: of a peace born of a war.

Demetrius (surnamed Polyorcites or 'Besieger' after this epic attempt) was the direct author of the battles and the indirect author of the statue which commemorated them. The coins, Gideon tells me, show a fleshy face and a long sensitive nose, expressing clearly the mixture of coarseness and sensibility which one reads into his character as Diodorus described it. If the motto of Cleobolus was 'nothing in excess' that of Demetrius must certainly have been 'excess in everything'; as a general he was considered a candidate for the honours of a second Alexander. He excelled in two qualities: science and lubricity. The inventive side of his genius came to full flower in the giant Helepolis—a third colossus—which so nearly overpowered the defences of the Rhodians. By the time he arrived off Rhodes in 305 B.C. he was already at the height of his powers as a soldier. He had thrashed Ptolemy and Cassander in summary fashion, and was a claimant for the empire which Alexander had left to fall to pieces after his death—an empire disintegrating under the attacks of many claimants like a jelly-fish stranded on the beaches of Time.

The causes of the war were as follows: Antigonus, the father of Demetrius, had solicited an alliance with Rhodes against the Egyptian Ptolemy; this had been refused by the Rhodians on perfectly logical grounds. Their trade with Alexandria played too large a part in the economy of the island to be surrendered at the whim of a predatory old tyrant.

Rhodes, at this time, could afford to decide for herself. Her history, like that of England, might have been summed up in the words sea-power, gold and neutrality. Both by geography and temperament Rhodes lay just ouside the storm-centres of trouble, and at every turn in her ancient history she took advantage of the fact. Where possible she reserved judgment and trusted in a fleet so powerful and skilful that it was famous in ancient times as the mythical colossus is in modern. The Rhodian sailor was famous for his courage and daring. "Ημεῖς δέκα 'Ρόδιοι δέκα νῆες they said of themselves—'Ten Rhodians, ten ships'. For a great trading-station lying upon the main routes of the Aegean there was no other course. But here and there this enviable neutrality was broken. A choice was forced upon the peaceable Rhodians. Always they chose with an eye to the main chance: their one objective was to retain their independence. They did not always manage to do so: Artemisia, Cassius, are fateful names among those who broke the spell, and there were others. . . . So that the news of Demetrius' arrival off the coast of Rhodes must have been received with mixed feelings. The Rhodians had sought no quarrel with him; indeed they continued to treat for peace right up to the moment of embarkation, and even voted a public statue to Antigonus in the hope that flattery would do what policy had failed to do; but it was in vain. Demetrius had been sent to teach them a lesson, and there is nothing to show that he was loth to add yet another victory to those already to his credit.

The general was a thorough man; whether it was a question of debauchery or of scientific invention he gave himself wholly to it with admirable singleness of mind. His preparations for the siege left nothing to chance. Transported laboriously across those miles of sea his infantry numbered some 40,000 men. This figure excludes cavalry, sailors and engineers. The 170 troopships were convoyed by some 200 men-of-war of different sizes—some perhaps the fifteen-bench galleys designed by Demetrius himself which struck such terror into the defenders of the coastal forts who watched them advance to the attack. This great fleet, as it rolled across the blue carpet of the straits, under the Carian mountains, was followed, say the chroniclers, by countless ships of provision, and a horde of smaller vessels—vulture-boats—manned by itinerant adventurers who had followed the conqueror in the hope of chance spoil. Standing on the flat roof-top of his house, with the whole dazzling panorama of the town glittering in its marble amphitheatre below him, the Rhodian sentry who first caught a glimpse of this armada might be forgiven a momentary pang of fear as he watched it, contrasting the peaceful temples and colonnades of his capital below with that minatory horde of vessels forming up for an attack on the harbours. Across the still waters of the gulf he must have heard the creaking of tackle, the neighing of horses, and the hoarse voice commanding; the shrill squeaking of bosuns' pipes and the crunch of oars as the galleys moved up the channel.

Yet to do the Rhodians justice their preparations were complete, and if their military leaders awaited the onslaught with comparative calm it was because they knew how powerful the defences of the town were. Six thousand citizens and a thousand aliens within the city had been marshalled and armed; all who refused to bear arms had been expelled. The very slaves had been armed for the siege. Torr suggests that they alone must have added some 16,000 men to the standing garrison. Later there came reinforcements from Crete and from Egypt, for throughout the siege the superior naval skill of the Rhodians enabled them to keep the sea-routes open to the south and west. A sympathetic Crete pushed a reinforcement of 150 men into the town, while Egypt sent 2,000 to help her ally. It was a case of some twenty-five thousand men besieged by roughly twice that number. If Demetrius was a thorough man the Rhodians showed themselves no less so; their defences were strengthened as much as possible, the armed slaves were promised citizenship if they fought well, and the fleet was ordered to stand by for action. Meanwhile such citizens as were not standing to arms were busied in the construction of catapults and balistas to mount along the parapets of the town-wall. While Demetrius' scouts worked their way slowly round the walls, cutting down trees to make palisades and destroying any suburban houses they came across, the Rhodian fleet made a sudden sortie against some provision-ships which had arrived for Demetrius. These they captured and brought into harbour together with a number of captives from them. This was a rich gain in ransoms.

Demetrius, however, was taking his time. He had decided upon an assault to be launched against the main harbour—indeed there were no other anchorages of any use to him along the shovel-shaped end of the island; and if he failed to take the port he would be unable to refit and refuel his forces. He had built two great tortoises—floating pent-houses strong enough to carry assault-crews, archers, and a great armament of catapults—and these he proposed to float into the mouth of the harbour. He had also constructed two great towers of wood which would enable him to overshoot and enfilade the towers guarding the moles. These were also contrived upon a float. The whole of this uncouth equipment was assembled and the signal to engage had been given when a storm sprang up, and the whole battle-order was disturbed. During the day the sea lashed the siege-craft of Demetrius until it seemed that he would lose everything; but as night fell a calm came over everything. It was an opportune moment for an attack, and he took advantage of it, with qualified success. Four hundred men got ashore and captured a small eminence about 500 paces from the wall, where they dug themselves in. Early next morning the rams were brought up and the signal for the general attack was given to the sound of trumpets. A series of violent exchanges began which were to last the whole of that day. Several breaches were opened in the wall which guarded the mole, but the Rhodians resisted with tenacity and held the enemy off. At nightfall Demetrius withdrew his main forces for refitting, and while he was doing so the Rhodian fleet, under cover of darkness, tried to float fire-ships amongst the enemy units. At first they were unsuccessful, but later they did him considerable damage with their sudden sallies from the port. But the major action of the siege was yet to be fought. Demetrius tried several times to force the harbour; a series of skilful and exhausting actions were fought in the breaches of the mole. Giant catapults mounted on the hillock he had captured pounded the city-wall until it rocked under the great bullets of stone. It should be remembered that the missile engines of these early times had been developed into formidable instruments of offence and defence. They could throw from seventy pounds up to six hundred pounds of stones; or launch darts from six to twelve feet long. Archimedes at the siege of Syracuse constructed some which could lift and throw no less than eighteen hundred pounds of stone. The ranges offered considerable variation according to the size of the machine, but for the larger ones six hundred yards was the average for direct fire and a thousand yards for curving fire.

But to return to Demetrius, his picked infantry tried escalade after escalade only to be forced back from the parapet by the defenders. It became obvious that an attack on the harbour would fail; it became obvious moreover that a blockade was impossible in view of the Rhodian naval superiority. Demetrius withdrew temporarily and refitted his fleet for yet another attempt on the harbour; he wanted to be quite sure that it was impregnable before adopting other methods or objectives. His second assault met with the same fate—due once more to weather and to the Rhodian navy, which made a sally when it was least expected and damaged many of his ships. There seemed to be nothing for it but to construct a Helepolis and let it loose upon the Rhodians. Once more the forces of Demetrius were stood easy while the general indulged his scientific turn in supervising this colossus among siege-engines. Meanwhile the Rhodians had recovered some of their usual fire; their nimble fleet harassed his communications, and in one sortie carried off a number of rich presents, pictures, and a letter from Demetrius' wife Phila— the whole of which, including the letter, they sent to Ptolemy of Egypt: an act which infuriated Demetrius beyond endurance. To add to his troubles Rhodian infantry made sorties during the night and set fire to some of his batteries. Meanwhile, however, the giant Helepolis was well under way. Diodorus describes it lovingly—almost rubbing his hands along its massive sides. It must have been an awe-inspiring machine to look at.

The Helepolis was a moving tower on wheels of oak. The base of it was square and the sides sloped inwards. There has been some argument about the original size of it. Diodorus says it was 150 feet high by 75 feet broad. Much later Vitruvius calculated its weight at 125 tons but this may have been an academic exercise in mathematics only. Nine stories high, it towered above the Rhodian walls. It was replete with catapults, grappling irons, and drawbridges which could disgorge its infantry upon the parapets they had not succeeded in scaling. It groaned and creaked as it moved, but it worked—and what is more astonishing, it took an operational crew of three thousand four hundred men to propel it. In common with most of the siege-weapons of the day it was given a tough outer skin of plaited osiers or hides. The top floor was a nest for archers, but the floor beneath carried tanks of water serviced by force pumps with hoses made from the intestines of cattle. On either side of the Helepolis were built supporting tortoises with rams, and covered gallery for the sappers to work in. It is not hard to imagine what the Rhodians felt as they saw this great siege-piece assembled and dragged within assault-distance from their walls. They must have seen the engineers testing the monster, testing its great battering rams and drawbridges before it was dragged towards the walls of the city. Indeed they had made frantic attempts to impede the work of construction, but in vain. Desultory sorties had not been undertaken in sufficient force; burning arrows had been quenched by the sappers; while industrious mine-works had been met with counter-mines which advanced the ends of neither party. Hopes had been raised by the arrival of a Cnidian embassy to Demetrius which had been sent to offer mediation. Demetrius however refused to countenance any further talk. The Helepolis was his answer. He had it moved into position for the assault, noting with his professional eye how little effect the hail of stone-shot had upon it. Certainly the Rhodians showed no weakening of resolve. Their morale was high. Abundant food supplies had reached them from their allies. The first victory had been theirs—a good augury; while Demetrius had failed by sea twice, and had recently failed to buy his victory with a bribe. His agents had approached Athenagoras, the captain of the Rhodian guard, with the offer of a vast sum of money in exchange for his complicity; the offer was promptly announced to the Rhodians, who voted Athenagoras a gold chaplet and five talents for his honesty. Since he himself was not a Rhodian but of Miletos, and in command of Egyptian mercenaries, the augury was a good one. To bind the resolve of the besieged still more firmly the Rhodians announced that those citizens who fell in action would be buried at public cost, their parents and dependents maintained out of treasury funds, and their daughters dowered by the state when they married. Their sons, added the decree, would be crowned in full armour in the Theatre at the Festival of Dionysos, when they had reached manhood. It was a sound stroke of policy. Emboldend by these announcements no less than by the sudden arrival of supplies, the Rhodians manned their walls and prepared to defend them or die.

It was perhaps during this part of the siege that the attacking forces broke through a part of the wall and took back with them the news that there, in a walled garden, they had seen the painter Protogenes painting away with perfect calm in all the din of assault and counter-assault. His famous painting of Ialyssos as a hunter was occupying his mind to the exclusion of anything else. A deputation of Rhodian citizens had already pleaded with Demetrius to respect this work and guarantee its safety. According to Pliny's anecdote, Demetrius asked Protogenes to present himself at his headquarters, and when he did so he asked him how he could work away at his painting while the fate of the town hung in the balance. The painter replied: 'I am aware that you are making war upon people and not upon the arts.' There is just the faintest flavour of flattery about it; enough at any rate to win over Demetrius, who assigned the painter a special body-guard and ordered that he was not to be molested.

At the first rush the great Helepolis knocked down a tower and carried away a vital section of wall. Troops poured into the breach like ants and a ferocious mêlée took place across the gap. For a time the pendulum seemed to swing towards the attackers, but the Rhodian line held, though it was strained to cracking point. The battle lasted all day, and when night fell Demetrius saw that his troops had not managed to force an entry into the town. Worse still, the Helepolis was damaged, and would need to be repaired. Once more he was obliged to call a halt. Diodorus does not record the language the general used as he surveyed the stricken engine, mounted upon the rubble of the blood-stained wall it had breached, choked with dead bodies and ammunition. Whatever he had to say must have been sultry in the extreme. Meanwhile the Rhodians were hard at work, taking advantage of the lull to dig in behind the great half-moon of the fallen wall. Siege-pieces were renewed and refitted. A scratch crew went up and towed back the Helepolis to a place of safety where the engineers could work on it untroubled by the whistle of arrows and pointed shot from the walls which still swarmed with defenders. It was beginning to develop into an ugly stalemate. No doubt the Athenian embassy which arrived at this juncture took occasion to point this out; yet even their offers of mediation fell upon deaf ears. Both parties stood firm. The Helepolis was repaired and moved slowly back into position opposite that tantalising breach in the city-wall. Demetrius was like some great cat hypnotised by a mouse-hole too small to admit more than a single paw. The faded arguments of the ambassadors hardly grazed his intolerable restless resolve to attack and conquer the city.

Now for a delightful piece of Greek jobbery. Some time before the siege a certain Callias of Arados had arrived in Rhodes and set himself up as an engineer specialising in siege-pieces. One of his designs captured the popular imagination. He proposed to mount a crane on the walls which, he said, would be strong enough to pick up a common Helepolis in its grab and lift it over into the city at one blow. The idea was charming though mechanically unsound. Yet one can see why it should have made him so popular. . . . A Helepolis suddenly lifted into the air, with its infantry tossed out like weevils from a broken biscuit, its drawbridges flapping loose, its water-tanks pouring. . . . Such a crane as Callias could design would be an even more remarkable machine than the Helepolis itself: so at least they told one another. Callias was delighted at the warm reception the Rhodians gave his idea. He accepted without hesitation the the post of state architect to Rhodes, a post then held by one

Diognetus. The crane was built according to specifications and mounted. But alas, it was quite incapable of fulfilling the demands Callias made upon it; not only did it not drag the Helepolis over the wall. It failed even to lift it. The crash of the falling wall, and the cloud of dust which hung in the air where once the tower stood as a strong-point must have brought the truth of the matter home rather forcibly to all concerned. The Rhodian fathers went hotfoot to the house of Diognetus. They wanted him back as state architect. But Diognetus was in a huff—one of those unfathomable Greek huffs which have been handed down unchanged into modern times, and which every traveller must learn, sooner or later, to deal with. Deeply wounded in his pride, burning with that all-suffusing resentment which today lights up his descendants whenever their slightest whim is not gratified, he refused to consider the requests of his fellow-citizens. He shrugged away the tears and entreaties of the greybeards. He ate fruit and raised his eyebrows to indicate with absolute finality that he had long ago washed his hands of the whole business. People foolish enough to trust charlatans, etc. . . . The pattern of the conversation is perfectly clear. It is a conversation which takes place daily in Greece today. Nothing less than a full-scale procession of ingenuous youths and maidens, bearing branches, would soothe an amour-propre so deeply wounded. *Diognetus wanted the Rhodians to ask nicely.* Thus in the midst of the siege a procession was organised, led by moaning priests from the temples, and followed up by wailing choirs of maidens and youths bearing branches of laurel. 'Help us' they cried; and Diognetus watching the extent of the procession and hearing the heart-felt wails of the suppliants, condescended to accept his former post once more. A wave of relief swept over everyone. Diognetus was back at work. The procession had finally won him over. The vindicated state-architect made his way back to the walls and gazed out across the shattered suburbs of the city to where the great machine stood, waiting for the signal to be given before it advanced toward the breach. Rhodian infantry were still busy digging in around the half-moon of fallen masonry. A sickening suspense—thick as the white clouds of dust from broken statuary and crumbling walls that eddied in the still summer air—hung over everything. The enemy had re-formed. Fifteen hundred picked men were to force the breach by night and effect an entry; while the signal for the general assault was given they were to establish themselves inside the city, based upon the theatre, and there to hold out until the Helepolis widened the breach, and the rest of the infantry could be pushed in to reinforce them. The plan appeared to work. The entry was made, the theatre taken, and for a while the garrison was thrown into a panic by the knowledge that the enemy had gained a foothold inside the walls. But the Rhodians recovered their resolution far more quickly than Demetrius had imagined possible; the area round the theatre was sealed off by the best of the Rhodian infantry and the Egyptian mercenaries were thrown into the battle against the enemy. Fires raged all night long, and fierce hand to hand combats took place. Meanwhile the lumbering Helepolis had met with a second and final disaster, thanks to the intelligence of Diognetus. There are two versions of the story, of which the latter is by far the prettier. The first states that a long mine-shaft was opened along the projected line of advance of the Helepolis; the second states that Diognetus skilfully diverted the sewage of the town into the path of the monster, and that it stuck, ankle-deep, in the quag and could not be budged. This was most disheartening. It ruined Demetrius' chances of pushing his infantry into the town to support the shock-troops. The latter by this time were much reduced by the Rhodian attack, and by the middle of next day, were forced to surrender. It was the end of the attack.

But while the battle was at its height Demetrius had received the most urgent message from his father ordering him to conclude a truce with the Rhodians as soon as possible and to return. Antigonus had other problems on his mind. At the same moment—most opportunely this time, for their arrival enabled Demetrius to save his face—came a deputation from the Aetolians, asking permission to mediate. Demetrius accepted the offer on condition that the terms were acceptable—and ambassadors were despatched to the city to arrange them. The Rhodians, too, by this time were disposed to treat; the latest battle had been for them an extremely narrow escape from defeat—and it had brought home most forcibly the penalties of war which a truce might prevent them from suffering. They were anxious to accept the terms of the treaty—and indeed its articles were not politically unfavourable to the future of Rhodes. In exchange for an alliance with Antigonus against any enemy save Ptolemy they were allowed to keep their freedom. A hundred hostages were to be held by Demetrius against this assurance. Once the articles were accepted the besiegers would decamp and not trouble the island more. It was an honourable enough compromise, and the Rhodians rejoiced in it; Diognetus enjoyed his share of the honours, while the Helepolis was dragged into the city and dedicated to the people.

Walking over the ruined suburbs of the great city with the little knot of treaty-makers Demetrius found himself wondering what he could do with all the useless, half-smashed equipment which littered the ground. Magnanimity was not entirely foreign to his nature. He admired the stubborn way the Rhodians had defended themselves against him. Was there nothing he could do to set a seal upon this contagious goodwill which, now the siege was ended, infected everyone, friend and enemy alike? On an impulse he handed over all the equipment he had brought with him to the Rhodian people; he asked that they should sell it, and from the proceeds of the sale erect a statue to commemorate a siege so notable in the history of their times. It was a gesture quite in keeping with his character, and was accepted in that spirit. So it was that the statue of the Sun God was born. Only a colossus could adequately bear witness to the greatness of the siege, the size of the engines used, the heroism of both sides— and the odd impulses of generosity which sometimes stir the hearts of tyrants.

The statue was undertaken by Chares of Lindos, a pupil of Lysippus. It cost three hundred talents (£72,000) which resulted from the sale of the siege-train which Demetrius had left behind him in the spring of 30 B.C. Moreover it cost the sculptor twelve years of his life to cast and mount. Its height is variously given but was most likely 105 feet. A prodigious statue, one would think, to work and mount with the available equipment of the day. Pliny does not state how large a staff of pupils and workmen was retained by the sculptor, nor what sort of scaffolding and machinery was necessary to set the statue up. He does say, however, that even when it had fallen down and become a total wreck it was still a prodigy. Its very finger was larger than many of the statues in that city of colossi. The gaping rents in it, the cavities and fractures, revealed the masses of rock and iron which had gone to building an armature heavy enough to support the great construction.

Pliny's account is the most circumstantial. Writing three hundred years after the earthquake which overthrew the statue, he was still in time to see the ruins as they lay upon the ground. For those who enjoy scholastic ambiguity and polemic however there is an inscription attributed to a certain Simonides which claims the work as executed by Laches of Lindos. The portly Sextus Empiricus has offered us an intellectual compromise on this burning question by producing a not unlikely story that Chares, the designer of the statue, having offered his estimates for the work, was told to double its size; this he did, but as he had already spent the money given him he took his own life, and left Laches to carry on the work. The statue, then, took twelve years to build, and enjoyed a life of fifty-six years before the earthquake of 227 overturned it.

The site of the Colossus has never been determined with any accuracy, nor has the pose been described for us by reliable eye-witnesses. Argument over possible sites and poses is likely to go on until the next earthquake, in which presumably the whole island of Rhodes will sink into the sea and leave behind it legends as tenuous as those which make up the myth of Atlantis. At any rate the story that it stood straddling the harbour with its huge legs is a medieval confection. And here it must be confessed that the greater part of the Colossus' fame dates from the Middle Ages. 'In ancient times it attracted little notice; it did not rank among the masterpieces of Greek sculpture, and in size it was rivalled by earlier and surpassed by later statues.' It was, it is true, placed in the catalogue of the Seven Wonders—and to this, no doubt, it owed its great celebrity during the Middle Ages.

For fifty-six years the Colossus stood as a tribute to the magnitude of the siege, and then came one of those sudden earthquakes to which much of the Aegean area is still subject. The town was shaken to its foundations. The temples, the arches, the statues—in the space of a day they had been swallowed up. And in the forest of falling statuary the Colossus was only one of a number of casualties sustained on that memorable day in 227 B.C. An inscription recently unearthed by Sand positively forbids the Rhodians to add another statue to the temple of Aesculapius. The earthquake must have more than regulated such questions of votive overcrowding; the echo of tumbling statues and falling public buildings reached every corner of the civilized world. For nine centuries the figure of the Sun-God was to lie prostrate in the town it had adorned. It was not until the VIIth century that the shattered remains of the piece were knocked down to a Jew from Syria and transported in camel-loads to the Middle East for boiling down. Presumably the statue was formed once more into the implements for a fresh war. This is the kind of inverted poetry by which we live. At any rate the amount of the successful bid has not been recorded; the Jew probably got it cheap; the story goes that it took him 900 camels to load and carry it off. 'The twenty tons of metal,' says Torr coldly, 'would not, however, load more than 90 camels.'

It says something for the veneration and love with which Rhodes was regarded in the ancient world that though the city was razed to the ground the island's allies at once began to send presents of money and food. Ptolemy, that perspicacious hunter of fine books, was deeply moved by the disaster, while the Kings of many other neighbouring states bestirred themselves to help the Rhodians. Treasure flowed in—the greater part of which, no doubt, was intended to help with the restitution of the Sun-God. The Rhodians themselves were anxious to set up the great statue once more, but a curious fact prevented them from doing so. The Oracle of Delphi pronounced against the idea. Worse evils might follow, it said, if the Sun-God were to be set up again. The Rhodians, recalling that *hubris* always carries its ugly reward, desisted.

A good deal of ink has been shed in an attempt to elucidate the problem. Why should the oracle of Delphi, the centre of Apollo-worship, transmit so unfavourable an omen to stricken Rhodes? Insinuating tongues have suggested that the Rhodians found better uses for the donations of neighbouring states, and even that they came to some underground arrangement with the priests of the oracle in order to provoke such an announcement and be free from the irksome necessity of rebuilding the Colossus. It is also hinted . . .

but here again the evidence becomes, in Torr's phrase, 'flimsy,' and in Gideon's 'rather thin on top.' I must leave the reader to worry his own way through the alleys and loop-holes of the argument. As for ourselves, we have spent days arguing about it; afternoons diving in the harbour for fragments of it (in pursuit of some mad theory of Gideon's that it was situated upon the easterly mole, and that some of its shattered fragments must surely have fallen into the water): and now the historical impact of its name is mixed with memories of this pure sunlight, these dancing summer days passed in idle friendship and humour by the maned Aegean. Who could ask for better?

CHAPTER V

In the Garden of the Villa Cleobolus

It is difficult to convey the extraordinary silence of this garden, for it is true that the main road runs along the length of it, and that the noises of motors can be heard; but so dense is the packing of oleanders and small pines and so heavy the shadow in which the house is set that sound itself becomes blurred and mingles with the hushing of the sea along the beaches to the eastward. Here in the evenings we gather for drinks and gossip, sitting in cane chairs around the little painted table, hearing through the dusk the shallow strains of some forgotten fugue wafted to us from the old horngramophone which is the Mufti's special pride. Here Gideon and Hoyle play out those interminable games of chess, which always end in a wrangle (and the discovery that Gideon has been cheating). Here, sitting on the ground, the grave detached Huber is whittling at the hull of a ship or the bowl of a pipe.

Presently the servant comes swaying down the dark path with a rosy branch of candles shielded in the coarse red coral of her hand: to sweep up the ash-tray and discarded books and set our supper-places. The little dog shakes itself, yawns and stands up to sniff the premonitory odours of the kitchen. And Mills, dripping wet from the sea, comes panting down the path to change for dinner—from a wet bathing-costume into a dry one.

Gideon has unearthed a peasant legend which purports to explain why the juice of the oleander is so bitter. The Virgin, says the tale, was walking towards Golgotha distracted by her grief when the hem of her dress was caught by an oleander; impatiently she cursed the tree saying: 'May you harbour forever the bitterness I feel today.' Immediately the sap of the plant turned acid. Today the peasant uses it as a styptic for cuts—when he cannot find a cobweb.[1]

Gideon's preoccupation with his livestock is assuming the proportions of a mania. 'Every time a cow coughs on the island,' says Mills bitterly, 'I receive a signal from this bloody old agricultural fool and have to motor forty miles to see what has happened. It won't do, Gideon. I shall complain to the Brigadier.'

Gideon sighs and gazes round him for sympathy. 'Unamiable fellow,' he says mildly. 'I am being inspected next week by the G.O.C. Cows. As it is half my damned cattle can't stand up. You don't want me to lose my job, do you?'

'Yes,' says Mills, 'I do.'

'Come,' says Gideon reproachfully, 'Take the larger view, old boy. Don't let your horizons be limited by a petty outlook. Expand. Be generous. Be large. . . .'

'And as for that milk. . . .'

'My dear fellow, an administrative oversight. . . .'

'Wasted in pig-swill.'

'Be just.'

A large consignment of powdered milk, long and anxiously awaited by the maternity hospital which Mills runs, disappeared last week from the quay. An officer, whose signature on the bill of lading was quite undecipherable, had carried off the consignment in a truck. Careful enquiry proved it to have been Gideon; but by the time Mills caught up with him he was forty miles to the south of Rhodes, where the precious consignment had been mixed into the swill of a dozen 'host pigs' imported from Cyprus.

'Like Cellini,' Gideon explains, 'I threw everything into the furnace. The battle against undernourishment must go on. My job must be kept at all costs.'

The forthcoming inspection of his department has certainly been preying on his mind. His cherished 'host-pigs' were suffering from sea-sickness. What was one to do?

'I should pour your whisky ration into them,' says Mills bitterly, hovering between genuine fury and laughter.

[1] A few peasant remedies are given in an appendix.

Gideon adjusts his monocle with an air and says:

'What an uncommonly good idea. I never thought of that. I shall do it.'[1]

Three afternoons a week we invite the monk Demetrius to teach us modern Greek. He is a delightful character with an immense beard and a beguiling repertoire of stories—not all of them in the best taste. After a few desultory attempts to find a set book on which to work Gideon has selected 'Pope Joan',[2] that delightful albeit rather salacious novel which we translate together, amid shrieks of laughter from Demetrius. Hoyle, whose Greek is too perfect to need the same attention as ours, enjoys taking part in the conclave, but is occupied on a translation of 'Daphnis and Chloe' with which I help him, in a vain attempt to learn some earlier Greek than demotic. These books at least canalise our enthusiasm which has been, up to now, dispersed over a wide area. Among sporadic translations Gideon has given me his rendering of the one poem attributed to Cleobolus of Lindos, an epitaph on Gordius, King of Phrygia. It is not bad.

> *I am a bronze girl sculptured*
> *And set up here on Midas'* [3] *monument.*
> *Believe me, so ever long as water*
> *Flows in the plains and the sunrise*
> *Delights men as the brilliant moonlight does:*
> *So ever long as rivers rush*
> *Between steep flanks, so ever long*
> *As oceans surge on beaches I*
> *Shall be seen reclining on this*
> *Old unhappy tomb to tell the passer-by*
> *'Midas lies here interred.'*

Huber places the ancient school of the orators on the little plateau near Rodini. It has the precarious look of having been created in something which any puff of smoke might dissolve. A landscape as perishable as a smoke-ring. Here, then, came Cicero to study peror-

[1] He did. The inspection was a great success, and the sangfroid of the host-pigs was much admired by his inspector, who was, it transpired, himself a teetotaller.

[2] I have completed his draft and hope one day to publish this witty and improper novel in England

Midas: hereditary title of the kings of Phrygia.

ation, adjuration and bombination. Apollonios Molon's rhetoric had seduced him when the great orator had been representing Rhodes in Rome as Envoy. After Cicero came Caesar. Sand has unearthed some notes on Rhodian oratory from the Museum. I am indebted to him for these scraps of history which make our walks more pleasureable and our arguments, if anything, less pointless.

Legend states that when Pompey visited the island he patiently heard all the resident sophists and presented each with a talent as a mark of his esteem. (Torr declares the talent to be worth £240.) Brutus and Cassius both studied rhetoric in Rhodes. Indeed the mark made by the Rhodian orators appears in every way to justify the praise of them by Tacitus. They are still, of course, great orators. Only last Sunday, at the unveiling of a plaque to commemorate some notable feat of allied arms, a certain Mr Gongorides, clad in morning-coat and sponge-bag trousers, in pince-nez and a cravat, held the floor for something under three hours, until two boy scouts fainted from the heat and the Greek garrison colonel's wife burst into floods of irrepressible tears and had to be dosed with sal volatile. Written in the classical language of the day (*katharevousa*) which is a little more intelligible than Sanscrit to the average peasant, it was an unqualified success. No wit broke the unruffled flow of those serpentine sentences. As Greek speeches go it was remarkable for the restraint of its delivery. Apart from sawing the air sideways as if he were lancing a boil Mr Gongorides employed few gestures. His pitch was uneven: for even the strongest voice cannot maintain the rapid staccato yowling note with which he began, without feeling the strain. By the time Mr Gonorides ended our throats were all sore in sympathy with him. In the Officers' Club there was much growling and swearing at the length of it—but then oratory is hardly likely to find admirers in the Army where the average officer's vocabulary is restricted to monosyllables. The waste of time was considered deplorable, and the naval lieutenant whose permanent hangover has given his face the expression of a man trying to lift a sideboard, declared that he would run Mr Gongorides to earth and dash his brains out with a bottle.

It is not clear what Theodorus of Gadara would have had to say to this speech; as Tiberius' teacher of rhetoric he would be, perhaps, the best qualified to judge it on its merits. But though Rhodes was the home of rhetoric its cause abroad was often pleaded by foreign speakers. When Artemisia occupied Rhodes it was Demosthenes himself who delivered a speech advocating Rhodian independence. Cato saved Rhodes by his speech in the Senate after the war with Perseus, and a few years later the alliance between Rhodes and Rome was the result of Tiberius Gracchus' golden eloquence. Indeed when Claudius restored to the Rhodians their much-prized independence it was in response to a speech delivered by a fattish adolescent of fifteen, who was as much admired for his learning as he was later to be execrated for his crimes—Nero.

In the great catalogue of powers which in ancient times held the sovereignty of the seas Rhodes stands sometimes fourth and sometimes fifth. For some twenty-three years about 900 B.C. the Rhodian fleet maintained a reputation for boldness and skill which could rival any other nation afloat. But the Rhodians were great colonisers as well as traders, and their ships covered the distance between Rhodes and Spain; as colonisers they perhaps gave their name to Rhodos, a town at the north-eastern corner of Spain, while legends suggest that the river Rhone took its name from another Rhodian colony founded near its mouth. In Sicily the great city of Gela was founded by them, as was the city of Apollonia in the Black Sea.

The great dockyards were maintained long after the Thallasacratia had passed from the Rhodians. And the spirit remained unimpaired until today, as anyone may judge whose daring is equal to a trip with the Kalymniot sponge-divers to Benghazi or further west. When Heraclides set fire to the dockyards in 204 B.C., thirteen sheds were burnt up and each had a three-banker in it under construction. Rhodian shipwrights built not only for themselves but for foreigners too. Herod of Judea is said to have ordered himself a Rhodian triere, while after the earthquake which overthrew the Apollo great quantities of ship-timber were among the presents sent to Rhodes by foreign kings. Torr adds that among the other presents were numbered items which suggest that other states wished to restore the shipbuilding trade in Rhodes: namely iron, lead, pitch, tar, resin, hemp, hair and sailcloth. He adds that once the Rhodian women had to cut off their hair and give it for making ropes; and that these ropes were for many years afterwards shown as curiosities to visitors. There is a story of a Rhodian captain muttering while expecting to lose his ship in a storm. 'Well, Poseidon, you must own I'm sending her down in good trim.' And they were fine swimmers. . . . When they went out to burn the siege-engines of Demetrius they simply swam home if their own vessels took fire.

From these fragments of reference and legend the picture of the Rhodian seafarer becomes clear; you will see him today, if you have eyes, sitting in the crooked taverns of the old town rolling dice and hissing through his curling moustaches: or slapping down lucky court-cards and grumbling, while his free hand gropes absently for the bottle of mastic. And when the sponge fleet puts out you will see him, a small jaunty figure, sitting loosely over his tiller, as perfectly in tune with the bucking sea as an expert rider with his horse, steering for the coasts of Africa. He hardly ever turns to look back at the dazzling white villages on the rocks of Simi or Kalymnos, or lift his hand as he passes the last cape which will hide the little dots of scarlet, white, blue, yellow and grey, which stand upon the quay and chatter like starlings.

At six these early summer mornings I rise and cross the garden barefoot to wake E by throwing a pebble at her shuttered window; and together we bathe in the cold sea before breakfast. The Mufti has taken to calling on me every morning at this hour. He has discovered that E can make real Turkish coffee. In a Rhodian Turk such behaviour is positively forward. He can have no further doubts about my suitability as a tenant. We arrive back in our bathing-costumes at seven to find him sitting on a chair under the willow-tree, resting one elbow on the little painted table. While Maria sets the table for breakfast he hums a little tune to himself, waiting for his coffee. The sunlight splashes through the rafters of the huge baobab tree which shades the house, picking up the coloured pottery, and lighting his sad preoccupied old face with a warm rosy tint reflected from the red tablecloth. Often Hoyle drops in from the hotel across the way, and all four of us settle down to breakfast in that sunny coolness. Days that begin like this cannot help carrying their perfection forward—as sums of money in a ledger are moved forward under different headings—to lighten the office-work, to persuade even the dour Manoli to sport a flower behind his ear. Idle conversations, leading nowhere except perhaps to the confirmation of a happiness as idle as this shadowy garden, with its heavy odours of flowers, coffee, and tobacco-smoke, mingled with early sunlight.

The peasant girl from Cos makes an admirable servant but she shares the superstitions of her people. It is unlucky, for example, to be the bringer of bad luck or bad news. Telegrams almost always contain bad news. Therefore rather than give me the telegram which arrived this morning she tore it up and put it down the lavatory. 'I was afraid it was bad news,' she says. When I scold her she throws her apron over her head and roars like a bull. What is one to do?

Dry friction of cicada from the palm-tree across the road. Eucalyptus leaves breaking their wrists with a small click as they begin to plane down over the tombstones. The maceration of pebbles by sea-water, mingling with the noise of coffee being ground, and the shearing noise of a pot being scoured. An inventory of sounds from a late morning walk.

Torr has some amusing facts about the little Turkish graveyard which I have come to think of as the garden of Villa Cleobolus. During the Middle Ages it was part of the Grand Master's garden. 'In 1496,' says Torr, 'an old ostrich and two young were kept with their wings clipped in a walled enclosure here. They laid their eggs in sand and hatched them by simply looking at them: they fed on iron and steel. There was also a sheep from India and various other strange animals: particularly a hound given to the Grand Master by Sultan Bajazet. It was about the size of a greyhound, mouse-coloured, with no hair at all except about the mouth, and it had claws like a bird. From this last fact comes the story that the Grand Turk had a bird that every year laid three eggs; and from two of the eggs came birds, but from the third a puppy. It was necessary to remove the puppy as soon as it broke its shell: otherwise the birds pecked it.' Not the shadow of a smile disturbs the dry exposition of the scholarly Englishman who has given us the best historical monograph on the island. But then history for Torr was a serious business. I have not been able to discover whether he visited Rhodes. Perhaps he thought it wiser to stay out of this sunlit landscape whose wine and fruit could only lead a man to laziness, procrastination and even to mendacity. From a commanding position on Exmoor he consulted 'every known authority' and pointed a long quivering finger at the bulging rhetoric of the Abbé Cutlet. We are all very much afraid of Torr. Read him and you will see why.

Rhodes, like the rest of Greece, has clung to its belief in Pan. Elsewhere he is known as the kallikanzaros and those who have been lucky enough to catch a glimpse of him have described him as a small edition of the Devil, with horns, hooves and pointed ears complete. The Orthodox Church is partial to the association, and perhaps this accounts for the name he goes under in Rhodes. He is called a *Kaous*. The word seems to be related with the verb 'kao' which means 'to burn'. Combustion, after all, is of the nature of devils, and the name suggests fire and brimstone in equal parts. But if you study the habits of the Kaous as recorded in the popular literature another association will come to mind—the creature is 'on hot bricks'. He is a troublesome visitor to the village, turning things upside down, making women miscarry and cream turn sour. He is worse still: he is a kidnapper.

The peasants believe that if a husband and wife sleep together on the 25th of March the child must be born on Christmas Eve—and this child will inevitably turn out to be a *Kaous*.

Its habits? It circulates mostly after dark croaking over and over again: 'Feathers or lead? Feathers or lead?' People who encounter a *Kaous* and give the wrong answer find themselves suddenly seized. The *Kaous* mounts them like a horse and rides them at breakneck pace across country, beating them with a stick. The annoying thing is that of the two possible responses to the question *either* can prove to be the wrong one, according to how the *Kaous* feels. A certain Basil of Kremasto was once taken for a ride in this manner. He asserts that the *Kaous* galloped him all over Anatolia for the space of a night. He arrived at the tavern exhausted at daybreak and was only able to prove the veracity of his tale by producing an apple which he had plucked from an Anatolian orchard in the course of this head-long gallop. Another man, from the village of Siana, was met by a *Kaous* on a dark road. He did not speak to it but caught it by its long pointed ears. This seemed to render it helpless. He carried it home and burnt a hole in its legs with a branding-iron. Out of the wound crawled hundreds of devilish little snakes and the *Kaous* was healed. It shuddered, came to itself and said: 'Deeply I slept, lightly I waken,' and with that it disappeared up the chimney as the first cock crowed.

Manoli the linotypist has been at it again. He has dropped into the habit of inserting small advertisements in the Greek newspaper for his friends. I do not know what they pay him for it, but it must be less than the space-rates we charge for such items. This evening I was interested to see the advertisement of one Tsirimokos, Cartomancer, Geomancer and Coffeemancer (as he described himself) offering reduced rates for fortune-telling from some obscure address in the old town. Enquiry into this item and others equally odd produced consternation at the office where my Greek editor had faithfully read final proof upon the copy before sending it down to the printing-room. Manoli had cleared himself a small corner of type by subediting an article on St Paul by the Vicar of Rhodes, and had proceeded to lino his advertisements and find room for them in the bed. We have a painful interview. Thrusting aside the basket of pomegranates which he brings with him as a peace-offering I wave the paper under his nose and ask for explanations. 'I was only helping my friends,' he says with an air of ridiculous contrition, his eyes filling with tears. 'Well, you must pay the full space-rates from your next month's salary. We can't have the paper tampered with after it is made up. What will the Brigadier say?' The Brigadier is the latest dragon. We have diligently built up his personal myth to such a point that we are quite afraid of him ourselves. The printers believe that he breathes fire, and lives on a diet of nails and broken glass like one of the Rhodian dragons of the Middle Ages. 'You won't tell the Brigadier,' says Manoli, his sense of logic overcoming his contrition all of a sudden, 'How can you? Such a mistake would reflect on you as much as on me! After all you are responsible for the paper. You should see it isn't tampered with.' I try to kick him downstairs but he is too quick for me. He returns to his linotype with a swagger. After every row with Manoli I know that we shall have twenty-four hours' first-class work from him, and this knowledge is useful. If we have to make up a special number for a feast-day or for some special calendar-date I always pick a quarrel with him the night before, in order to feel sure that he is docile and tractable when the heavy burden of an extra two pages is added to his daily task. The Levant demands a very special diplomatic approach of its own to human problems.

There is one special convention mirrored in the newspaper which is pleasing. A patient too poor to pay his doctor's fees after an illness will invariably put an advertisement in the daily paper reading as follows: 'I, George Chorakis, feel in honour bound to thank Dr Gongorides publicly for his skill in curing me during my recent dangerous illness.' It is both good advertising and good manners. Sometimes, of course, an unscrupulous doctor will use this method of congratulating himself publicly on a series of purely imaginary cures—but never in a small community like this, where he would be found out very soon.

The first autumn rains came belatedly; this warm green rain does not belong to the beginnings of winter. The Pleiades have gone below ground, daughters of Atlas and Pleione. Hoyle tells me that they are seven in number, but that we only see six because one, Sterope, hides her face on account of a misfortune that befell her; others say that her name was Electra, and she hides because of her grief at the fall of Troy. Gideon rejects their etymology from the verb 'plein' meaning 'to sail'. They were obviously called πέλιαδες in ancient times, he says, which means a flock of pigeons; and to do him justice they are known as 'the birds'[1] in demotic Greek even today. A New Year festival connected with and determined by the rising of the seven seems to have been a wide-spread custom in ancient times.

The rain cares for none of this erudition. It sweeps down among the tombstones with a dull threshing sound, blows open the window at my elbow and splashes me with its warmth. It rattles like sparrow shot in the old well, now choked with autumn leaves. The sky has become soft, melting—as if this were a premonition of spring and not of winter. But we shall have frost to follow, says the calendar, after this momentary exuberance is over and the hollow drumming of water in the runnels and drain-pipes has stopped. Sadness of the year's ending. Autumn is lengthening into winter slowly but surely. As yet there is no snow on the mountains across the channel, though

[1] Note. τα πόυλια.

the air is faintly spiced with cold. In another week we shall have to forsake the baobab tree for dinner and go indoors. 'It won't be too soon for me,' says Hoyle, who feels the cold. 'I call this embalmer's weather.' The grapes are over and the empty vineyards have turned the colour of burnt chestnuts.

Once or twice we walk out to the thermal springs of Calithes where Gideon drinks pint after pint of the sulphurous water trickling from the rock, and falls into a vein of sentimental reminiscence about Baden and Vichy in the days before the war. Hoyle is suffering from hernia, and Mills proposes to perform a minor operation on him when the weather gets colder. 'I shall have to poke a hole in your middle and let some of the sawdust out, Hoyle,' he says. Hoyle hates the idea. 'Can't I die in peace?' he says testily. 'What would happen if you didn't operate?' Mills sighs and swallows his wine. 'You would soon be going about with that tummy of yours on a tray. How would you like to hold up a tray all day?' 'I should have a servant to hold the tray,' says Hoyle with dignity.

The Rhodes we talk about so much—the marvel among cities of the ancient world—what remains of it? Nothing. Today, after lunch we walked, the four of us, up the gentle slopes of Monte Smith, past the little light-house where the Indians are quartered, and along the broad and lovely road which leads to Trianda. Beneath us the blue carpet of sea stretched away to Anatolia where, say the peasants, you may still see the claw-marks of marauding dragons graven in the mountains; stretched sinuously along the capes and faults of Marmarice to where, in the northern corners, the first faint silhouette of islands rose; like stepping stones, pointing to Cos.

Beneath us on the landward side stood the old stadium and the temple, now much-restored by the misguided Italians. In this green and sleepy hollow an old shepherd kept his flock of sheep, standing under the great oak-tree which crowns the amphitheatre. Descending the terraces slowly Sand points out all that remains of the ancient city—a few outcrops of stone-carved tombs on the crown of the promontory: and turning his finger like a compass completes the half-circle at Simbulli and Rodini. Yet the ground is still choked with red pottery and the delicate handles of lamps and oil-jars. Gideon everywhere turns them up with his stick and we wash the clay from them in the ditches, trying to assemble the fragments again, but in vain.

Down on the mossy turf of the stadium the sheep browse and tinkle, looking like so many gold and silver insects in the sunlight, while their keeper comes slowly towards us to pass the time of day. He is an old man, with a deeply wrinkled face, and black sloe-shaped eyes which seem to have had all the good humour worn out of them. He speaks the Rhodian Greek with its clipped sing-song accent and pastoral vocabulary. Sitting around him in the grass, smoking and talking, we hear the history of the last few years, of the privations endured under the Germans, and of the ugly reprisals exacted from the Italian forces which tried to rebel after the fall of Italy.

Below us in the great amphitheatre where once the white city of Hippodamnus lay, with its sacred groves and temples, its dazzling statuary and teeming dock-yards, the Crusader town lours, with its gross bastions and keeps shining through the evening mist, topped by the minarets and the turning windmills of the Turkish quarter.

How far all this is from its Greek setting, from the main current of its landscape tradition—this old swarthy peasant and his sheep on the green hill; the reclining figures of his daughters by the old well, raiding a fragrant violet-bed, and for their daily meal un-wrapping from a dirty piece of paper a dozen sour olives. Against this backcloth the towers and buttresses of the Knights rise into the sky, dark with the premonitions of an alien age, of alien ways. Yet the patient landscape has almost succeeded in domesticating the gothic north; it has sent wave after wave of tangerine-trees to assault the dark stone cliffs of the castle. It has choked the moat with almond and peach-blossom. It has coated the stern ravelins with the iridescent sheen of moss kept moist from some invisible spring seeping through the stones. . . .

After a series of protracted and laboured evolutions Gideon has at last found himself a suitable house to live in; as it is large enough for them both, he has persuaded Hoyle to join him in the bachelor venture of sharing house until the spring, when their wives will arrive in Rhodes. The Villa Mondolfo lies some way from the town on the Trianda road, and for the whole of the last four days the two of them have been away there, spending a long week-end wrestling with the domestic problems which face them. This afternoon I received a note from Gideon with a characteristic postscript in Hoyle's minute handwriting.

'The days of bargaining are over. I am rather sorry. We sat on a slab of marble outside the front door for nearly six hours, drinking excellent wine under a fine mulberry. The present caretakers run the adjacent farm. Their livestock swarm in our courtyard. A turret of blue pigeons make their warbling narguileh-like sound. Partridges reared in coops are as tame as the hens which scribble everywhere. Our host is out of Hesiod—a portrait done bristly on pig-skin. Reddish pigment face, pig snout, somewhat plethoric—but with wonderful curling hair like the waves in a statue. This isn't very good English. His wife is more pug than pig, but lovely and very fat. Two small children: one voice dactyl, one voice spondee. But apart from this fifty pear-trees, seventy apple, ten plum, ten fig, and two hundred rows of wine. . . . My dear boy, a property of size.

'Hoyle has moved in with Croker and a shelf of Latin classics. Can you see how we are going to live? Royally, nobly. We have bought a lot of wood and today, in the first soft providential autumn rain (like catkins), we set up a crackling fire. Stone floors full of nice echoes. You call in a friend to supper: shout to the wife to roast some kidney-beans and lay out some figs and perhaps a bit of hare or partridge: the children are sent to bed: you call in the old man from the field—for he cannot strip vines any more in the rainy dusk: he comes, wrinkling up his eyes to the fire, his dusty old cheek printed with rain-drops: he takes up a glass of wine in that cavernous hand: presently we dine with fruit, salads and chestnuts from our own land. . . . The red Kalavarda wine is strong and coarse. . . . I must leave room for Hoyle who wants to add a word. *Come and visit us.*'

Hoyle's postscript says: 'Gideon must be mad. We *could* live like that a year from now. At present we are living on Spam, sleeping on camp beds, and are tormented by fleas and bugs. Horrible mess.'

CHAPTER VI

The Three Lost Cities

The function of history in all this is a small but precise one: as in some renaissance painting where the hermit occupies the foreground, seated in his drab ochre-coloured cell, but where, over his shoulder, set like a jewel in the rock, his only window gives on to a limitless panorama of smiling country, exact and glittering in its perspectives, symbol of the enamel landscape on which he has turned his back. So here I would like our own idle history of conversations to open like a sally-port, and throw into relief the many-coloured background of the island's own history. Only in this way can one nourish the other, so that the landscape may be evoked from both, before the eyes of a reader who is not free to touch the living grass of Cameirus with his own hands, or to feel the waves of sunlight beating upon the rocks of Lindos. What, now, of the three ancient cities which once dominated the politics and government of the island before the foundation of Rhodes, the capital? Of Ialysos alas! little remains, but their situation has preserved the two others, while the hundred or so miles of modern motor-road which encircles the island places them within easy reach of the present capital, their child. They lie, too at roughly the same distance from the tip of Rhodes, one upon the northern shore, the other upon the southern. While they are easily reached by road, however, that is not the best way to see them.

I am thinking now of that fine August afternoon when Gideon and I set out on foot to explore the ancient cities, fortified by the knowledge that a long week-end lay before us. Our plan of march was an ingenious one, for we had arranged that Hoyle and Mills should run out by car and meet us at the end of each day's march to share the pleasures of camping out. Time and distance did not permit us to walk the whole way, so we planned to walk to Cameirus in two stages and thence to travel by car over the eastern end of the island to Lindos where we would spend our last night.

Leaving the town we chose the upper road because, if I remember rightly, there was some site whose location Gideon wanted to identify among the rock tombs which cluster round the nape of Monte Smith; but the sun was hot, and the steep hill was enough to set him puffing and blowing by the time we reached the crest overlooking Rhodes. Below us the sea sat perfectly still, cold as jelly; the old grey fort, its walls stitched and cobbled, resembled the pelt of an aged elephant. Neohori (Newtown) by contrast glittered softly in its plaster walls and red roofs. (At one time, says an ancient writer, it was known to the vulgar as Keratohori or Cuckoldville owing to the questionable morals of its inhabitants.) We sat for a while in one of those little rock-tombs where the temperature of the stone, as Gideon observed, made one think that the occupant had just left it for a stroll by the sea; and then, shouldering our packs, climbed up past the last villas and the dismantled battery where dark-skinned Indians lay about in the grass chattering, and took the high road which runs over the crown of the hill and along the glittering cliffs. It was cool here and windy. Westward along the shingle beaches around Trianda the sea was laying down its successive washes of prussian blue and violet, and thinning them out as they touched sand to green and citrons and the innocent yellows you can see on the ripening skins of tangerines. Here too we sat to get our breath and to watch, directly below us, the traffic moving along the main road. Mills emerged suddenly at the wheel of his car, bowling along to some urgent appointment, trailing a puff of dust behind him like a cherub's cloud, and skilfully negotiating the long caravans of mules moving in the opposite direction, carrying produce for the Rhodes market. Here, too then my companion's attention was taken up for a while with the professional appraisal of some sheep. Since his appointment as agricultural officer, he had developed a ridiculously proprietary air whenever any livestock came within his field of vision. 'Now, that's a fine cow,' he would say, or 'There. How's that for a sheep? Fattened up by the Gideon method.' So now, while I sat under a pine-tree and drank some wine, he took himself off to discuss a flock of sheep with a ragged shepherd-boy who was guarding them. He came back looking rather gloomy and took a savage pull at the wine-bottle. 'Their bowels are out of order,' he said at last. 'I hope to God it's not contagious enteritis.'

We set off across the plain with some caution, for the ever-present danger of mines was a constant preoccupation, and no detailed map of existing mine-fields had been published. Indeed the Italians during the earlier part of the war had mislaid their own defence plans, so that when the Germans moved into Rhodes they were forced to re-mine many areas. Maps of the latter fortunately were in our hands. But there were still large mined areas of the island unaccounted for, and Gideon had more than once been in danger of his life as he was forced to tip-toe on to an apparently 'live' field to rescue Homer, his dog, whose curiosity was always leading him into undesirable places. A maze of dry paths led us across the valley, through silvery groves of olives, and pastures richly scented with thyme and myrtle bruised by the hooves of goats. The little cottages here were encircled with walls of hibiscus and oleander, and we stopped once or twice to knock at a strange door and ask if the area was mined. But nobody seemed to be sure. One old lady in a red handkerchief assured us that there were no mine-fields here, but that the other side of the main road 'among the archaics' there was a large field. Gideon groaned. 'This incredible talent the Germans have,' he said, 'for choosing valuable antiquities as gun-sites—such vandalism.' But it is really only Teutonic military logic. What commander could choose a better defensive position than an acropolis?

We were fortunate in not having to carry provisions, for a message had been sent to Peter, the warden of Phileremo, to expect us; and from what little I knew of Peter's habits and temperament—he combined the trades of poacher, guide and family man with perfect harmony—what I knew of him led me to expect nothing less than a whole lamb on the spit. I told Gideon so. 'Lamb?' he said irritably, 'He mustn't kill lambs. We've forbidden that by proclamation.' 'Wait till you taste it—the sage and garlic, Gideon, the sauce.'

Gideon cannot resist licking his lips, but he wags his head reproach-fully at the idea and strikes an olive-tree in passing with the flat of his hand—as if to chastise the forbidden thought.

The village of Trianda stands on the level ground at the end of the fine valley which bears its name; the houses stand off the main road which passes through it, for the most part hidden in groves of olive, fig and orange. They are the summer-houses of the wealthier Rhodians, and the ambition of every man of men is to have a little house at Trianda where he can sit in the cool shade of his own fig-tree during August and September, when Rhodes is hot. It was here, I am reminded, that Lady Hester Stanhope lived during her short and dramatic stay in the island—in one of these small blind-looking Turkish houses with its barred windows and shadowy interior, with its grove of orange and cherry-trees shutting out the view of the sea: it was here that she took to trousers—or the Turkish equivalent of trousers.[1] Here we set our backs to the sea and the village, and our faces to the bulk of Phileremo, the flat-topped mountain which was Ialysos once, and which has offered a first-class defensive site to a hundred armies, Greek, Frankish, Roman, Turkish, German. It is little wonder that no traces of the ancient Acropolis remain. To our right in the valley, as we reach the first upward curve of the road, we see the 'archaics' which the old woman spoke of; a series of trenches and parapets cut in the red soil of the valley to form a square.

How much is archaeology and how much military workings we are unable to gauge until we break the back of the mountain ahead of us, following the sinuous road which now leads through a dense forest of young pine. Here on a shoulder of hill Gideon called a truce to the pace I was setting and we sat for a while to look down over the valley which now lay spread beneath us, its squares and oblongs of cultivation picked out in russet browns and green until the whole prospect looked like some fine old tweed plaid, much darned. The sun was sinking behind Tilos, and the mountains across the way had become wine-dark and bony. A light wind siphoned up the water in the shallows beyond the town and kicked up spray around a caieque heading south. Trianda drowses among its silver-grey olive-trees. Directly beneath we can see the slight tump of excavated ground

<hr>

[1] I am wrong. It was at Lindos or perhaps Malona.

where the city of Ialysos once stood, and can even discern among its scarred furrows traces of ancient wall. Of the minefield, however, there is no discernible trace from this range. Westward the torn gun-emplacement of Mount Paradiso (an almost exact replica of Phileremo) flares for a moment as the sun picks up fragments of glass and metal to play upon. We shall, I calculate, have about half an hour of light in which to potter about the ruins on the crown of the hill. We turn away from the prospect and climb the long steep road to the summit. The air has become colder, and spicy from the pine-forest which surrounds us. From time to time we shout Peter's name aloud, and the echo of our voices plays back upon us from several sides at once. But there is no answering call. He must be up at the monastery, waiting for us.

But then his laugh came out of nowhere and startled us. It was as if the trees laughed. Homer barked. We turned about, looking now here, now there, like characters in the Tempest, while Peter's tittering laughter sped from tree to tree, from rock to rock. Finally he had pity on us, and climbed down from the branches where he had been hiding. Brushing the dust and bark from the battle-dress of which he was so proud he came towards us, a short stocky man, with yellowish eyes, a snub nose, and an irresistibly comic expression on his round face. 'Did you think I was a *kaous?*' he asked. We shook hands and he expressed himself honoured to meet Gideon of whom he had many favours to ask. Together the three of us left the road and followed a narrow turning path to the summit, walking deep in anemones across the shadowy glades and mossy brakes which crown Phileremo. 'First,' said Peter, 'I shall explain all the archaics to you without any charge, and then we will go to my house where I have a splendid dinner for you.' Gideon grunts.

'I suppose you have a sheep?' he said in an off-hand way, torn between duty and a hunger which Timocreon would have sympathised with.

'A sheep?' Peter sounds outraged. 'For six people, not including my family? I have two sheep.'

The others are supposed to be coming on to join us later in the evening, and to be bringing blankets and mattresses for Gideon and me.

There is precious little to explain about Phileremo today; the monastery has been thoroughly bombed, and the image of the Virgin, which was the object of so much veneration in the time of the Crusaders, has long since vanished. Once more, however, we found ourselves walking among shattered field-guns and a metal harvest of cannon-shells, for Phileremo had been the site of fierce action between Italian and German troops shortly after the fall of Italy. The Italians, though they outnumbered the Germans by six to one, and held the crown of the hill, only lasted out a week of Stuka bombardment. They left behind them mounds of live ammunition and a small pyramid of tin helmets. The little monastery is a ruin. In the garden a few fragments of Byzantine and Hellenic stone lie forlornly about. But the view is incomparable from the little monk's walk, tree-lined and shady, which has been contrived to cross the summit from end to end. From here you can stare down landwards at the gutted aerodrome of Maritza, now dotted with abandoned aircraft, some wingless, which lie about among the fields like charred moths under a lamp. Beyond that green bowl the hills rise again and lead away to the green-spires of Monte Profeta.

'In old times,' says Peter, 'the image of the Panaghia was the patron saint of the island. In moments of trouble it was carried in a solemn procession to Rhodes, and all round the town. Even before the last siege of the Turks they did this, but it had no effect.'

'Where do you get your information from?' asks Gideon.

'There is an old monk in the village who told me.'

'How does he know?'

'Books,' said Peter, 'he has many books. Before, there were many relics in the island, but now none.' He is right there; Torr has preserved a list of them which for sheer variety takes some beating. I quote: 'Chief among the many relics preserved at Rhodes were the right hand of John the Baptist: one of the three bronze crosses made by the Empress Helena from the basin in which Christ washed the Apostles' feet: a cross made from the True Cross: a fragment of the Crown of Thorns, which budded yearly on Good Friday: and one of the thirty pieces of silver; wax impressions of which, if made by the priest in Passion Week, were efficacious in travail of child-birth and in peril by sea.'

While Gideon and I went to make a further exploration of the hillside, Peter sat down under a tree to wait for the rest of the party. As we returned we heard voices among the trees. Mills, to the alarm of his wife, was already busy collecting souvenirs from among the cannon-shells that littered the paths. Hoyle sat in Sand's old German car, quizzing the view through his glasses, while Sand himself and E were climbing the staircase to the monastery tower with Peter. After a good deal of ferocious banter from Hoyle and Mills, Gideon was permitted to announce himself more than ready for dinner, and the cavalcade started off down the hill to Peter's house, Hoyle taking his little rests every fifty yards with the punctuality of a Swiss clock, and Mills singing at the top of his voice.

The house of Peter the guide lies off the main road some two hundred yards before it breaks up through the pine-forest and reaches the crown of the hill. It is built in a cutting sheer against the mountain-side. Its forecourt is shaded by an enormous plane-tree, while a stream runs thickly out of the side of the hill, so that the air under the great tree is a perpetual mixture of shadow and spray. To the noise of cold running water the children shout and play all day, the seven cages of canaries slowly swing in the arbour under the terrace, while their occupants chirp to the note of the water. To live so close to a powerful stream is as good as living by the sea; the noise of it—black water squirting down upon stone—provides a background, a momentum for one's life. The air vibrates and wavers round one as if from the hum of a great dynamo. Even when you enter the house, and the noise of the water is stilled, you have, as if within the canals of the middle ear, a deep echo.

Peter's house boasted a precarious balcony overlooking the valley —an extremely dangerous-looking wooden arrangement built along the first floor. The feeling of height, the great expanse of country below one, and the fear that at any moment one might fall through those crazy planks of wood into the valley, gave a strange character to that first dinner-party in Phileremo. Hoyle said that he felt he was up in a balloon. Peter's own feeling for metaphor was not far behind Hoyle's as he added proudly: 'Sitting here you know what the bird feels when you hang its cage in a tree.'

The house abounded in livestock and small black-eyed children.

Visitors to the table included a tiny and immaculate lamb, with a coat as soft as moss, and an eye like a live coal. It drank wine from a saucer with the utmost concentration, its chevril ears crumpled upon its flat and woolly skull. Two tortoises walked about with a blameless clockwork air; and Gideon was kept busy buying up cicadas from the smaller children and setting them free. The peasant children have a nasty habit of catching a cicada and tying it to a piece of string. It makes an admirable bull-roarer, for if you swing it round and round your head it lets out a dull creaking sort of protest. Needless to say this is a habit which Gideon dislikes intensely, and no sooner does he see a cicada trussed up in this way but he must buy it and set it free. 'Let me see,' I remember him saying, 'Six children, six cicadas at five lirettas a head. . . . Philanthropy is an expensive game, Hoyle. Don't have anything to do with it.' But Hoyle, who was carving the lamb with an infectious air of approval, was too occupied to give much thought to this animadversion. 'I was afraid,' he said, 'it was going to be a *leetle* bit tough but,' putting a segment in his mouth, 'praise be to our Lady of Phileremo, it isn't.' It wasn't.

Lamps had been lit by now and perched on nails. They cast a frail radiance over the balcony so that, seen from the ground-floor, where Peter's wife was still busy cooking a dish of octopus in a metal cauldron, the balcony looked like some lighted ship sailing upon a canal perhaps, or the unruffled waters of some great lake. A comparison I thought poetical enough to express to Mills, who had come down with me to inspect the octopus. 'Yes,' he said, standing beside me and gazing up at the scene. 'And Gideon is lifting his glass to his mouth with the regularity of a Varsity oarsman, rowing.' Gideon, indeed, had become as ruddy as a lamp himself. He glowed. His monocle was misty with good cheer. The fourth bottle of wine had brought its customary loosening of tongues. The octopus when it appeared looking like a boiled motor-tyre was greeted with shouts of applause. Gideon proposed a toast to it. The octopus was in no condition to reply to these courtesies. It lay bubbling in a rich red sauce flavoured with garlic and peppercorns. Hoyle once more constituted himself taster and repeated 'I was afraid it was going to be a *leetle* bit tough but,' putting a piece of the sucker in his mouth, 'praise be it isn't.' It wasn't.

Mills slipped down to the car and brought up his guitar. The wooden house proved an extraordinary sound-box, mellowing the note of the strings, and making it louder, more resonant and authoritative. Voices too had a curious ebbing volume over that blue valley with its darkened border of sea. We sang for the most part the traditional Greek folk-songs, tasting once more their extraordinary purity of line, and the marriage of words and music in dance-measure which is their supreme quality. Later Peter felt emboldened enough to sing us some of his Anatolian songs, with their sharp quarter-tones and strange lapses from key to key. In order to achieve this kind of singing you must put your head back and let the voice become pliant, soft, almost undirected. Peter's voice bubbled in his throat like rose-water in the bowl of a narguileh as he followed the windings of these old melodies with their intricate cross-references of rhythm and accent. It is the singing of a bird, apparently haphazard and undisciplined, but demanding far greater voice-control than European singing does. The songs, too, though they resembled those of Crete and of Macedonia, had a hint of something else in them—the flavour of Arabia, of Persia. Their melancholy was not wild and savage as the Greek mountain melancholy is: it was softer, more quaintly flavoured.

Gideon by now was asleep with his head upon the table. Hoyle, whose capacity was normally a minim of wine per meal, had poured himself a whole glass and was sunk, I could see, in his own memories of the East, the songs he had heard in Beirut and Damascus before the last war. E sat with her black eyes fixed upon the singer's face following every supple turning, every sour change of tone and key. By her side Chloe petted the lamb and tried to interest it in a slice of octopus. Mills and Sand were cracking walnuts in the palms of their hands, expressing an over-exaggerated solicitude whenever the noise seemed to border upon rudeness to Peter. But the singer himself was lost. He held the guitar lightly between his knees, his blunt fingers folded about it with the repose that comes from long familiarity: and as I hold this picture for a moment in my mind I see him singing with his black eyes fixed on the darkness of the valley below us, his sleeves rolled back, his collar open, and the sound of his voice wobbling in his throat like a second pulse.

From there to the roaring of cars, the loud good-nights, and the yellow swathes of headlight cutting the pines, and diminishing with the noise of engines in the valley—from there the transition is immediate. Yet it must have been late. We were left with the roaring of the mountain spring and first whoop of owls. We settled down to sleep in flea-bags on the balcony, Gideon and I. 'We must be up at cock-crow,' he cried once, indistinctly, in the voice of one leading a charge against hopeless odds—and then fell asleep with his head buried upon his arm. I blew out the lights and lay for a long time, listening to the wind stirring the pines, and the faint noise of cars crossing the valley below us. The children were long since in bed, and only Peter sat upon the deserted balcony, drinking a last glass of mastika before turning in.

On the landward side of Phileremo, no doubt, the early moon had risen above the horizon and set. Meanwhile without ceasing the stream flowed on from the heart of the mountain, its water ringing steadily upon the stone still of the fountain before it disappeared among the mosses and cresses of its underground track again. But already our ears had become so accustomed to it that we should not have recognised the silence that might follow if it should suddenly stop.

It was already dawn when I awoke. Gideon had rolled out of his flea-bag and was lying on his back snoring like a clockwork toy, his face smoothed out and juvenile, the round circle of his eye scored out by his eyeglass gleaming white as a scar.

In order to reach the privy at the back of the house one had to pass through a ground-floor room whose furniture would have delighted a surrealist. There, standing upon the earthen floor, without any attempt at premeditated arrangement, I saw a sewing-machine, several Louis Quinze pieces, a Sheraton sideboard, desk, a type-writer, and a very handsome grand piano. The piano had been white-washed. The reason for this accumulation of treasures is a simple one; during the period of acute starvation in Rhodes the peasants refused to trade their vegetables for money because they were afraid of fluctuations in value, or even of the Italian liretta being recalled in exchange for some valueless occupation currency. They would accept articles of value, however, in exchange for vegetables; so it was that one saw caravans of carts setting off from the town every morning for the interior loaded with furniture, pictures, typewriters, plate, linen, etc. In the remote villages these objects were freely exchanged, and now the peasant houses are crammed with them. And the whitewashed piano? Peter's explanation has a certain nobility about it. 'Of course we whitewashed it,' he said, 'You know as well as I do that black is the colour of mourning. We did not wish to attract a death to the house. So we painted the piano white.'

The air was sweet with the damps of night as we set off, and we walked steadily until we reached Kremasto, where we explored the church with its holy well and immense cypresses; and where the vicar, who looked like a dispossessed earwig, conducted us from ikon to ikon with great circumstance and a wealth of pointless detail. Afterwards we took a glass of sticky liqueur with him in the sunlit courtyard whose floor was paved in pure white sea-pebbles, dusted spotless by the brooms of two old women who seemed to be nuns. Kremasto is the scene of the greatest festival of the year, held on Assumption Day, and on the ninth day after that date, in honour of the Panaghia. Here, as in Tenos, the holy ikon performs its yearly miracle of healing, and here come crowds of foreign visitors from Turkey and the islands round about. Along four sides of the monastery are the cells in which they are accommodated during the festival. Despite the prevailing dislocation of traffic with the mainland a good crowd of suppliants is expected, says the old man. During the war years everything was at a standstill, the narrow straits were mined, everyone was starving. Now . . . peace is here. He leaned forward and took one of Gideon's hands, pressing it warmly between his own. 'England has brought us white bread,' he said, nodding that rusty old head on his shoulders.

We moved off in good order down the sunny main street of the town which was lined with barrows full of bright vegetables, for Kremasto is the nearest market-town to Rhodes, and it is here that the peasant unloads his stocks if he does not feel like travelling to the capital in search of a buyer. Needless to say, keeping a vegetable stall is one of those occupations which do not take up all one's time; there is plenty of time to drink, to gossip and play cards—and these seem to be the major occupations of the stall-owners, who sit in the little cafés lining the main street and while away the hours in this manner. Here we bought some apples, not without difficulty, for the owner of the stall was engaged in a game of backgammon and sent us a message with a friend to say that he was indisposed; he was sitting in full view at the time, his big coarse face bent over the board, his coffee cup beside him. We entered the café and after a long argument prevailed upon him to serve us. He did so with hauteur.

We made good time in the direction of Villa Neuova along the broad motor-road for it was early as yet. Gideon chatted amicably as we walked, pausing from time to time to cross the hedge and peer anxiously into the features of a goat or a cow. By the early afternoon we had reached a hollow in a hillside beyond the town of Villa Neuova where a number of sources broke from the mossy banks of a hill and created a shady pleasaunce—I do not know how else to describe it—encircled by some tall plane-trees, forming a sort of pavilion around the little whitewashed tavern where we proposed to halt and eat. The sunshine was, by this time, fierce enough to have turned Gideon's thoughts in the direction of a siesta. There was no food to be had beyond a boiled egg or two, so we were glad of what we had brought with us. There was, however, plenty of good red wine, served in generous tin cans which had originally been intended as measures for oil. The tavern-keeper was a tiny emaciated man in the last stages of consumption. He served us deftly and quietly, and paused with pride to indicate the superb view from the little earth-terrace upon which we sat. It was indeed worth looking at—that sloping foreground of mulberry-trees, thinning away to the bold blue of sea and the violet-cloud of mountains opposite. But it was not a view that one 'saw' in the strict sense; it radiated over one, dancing in that brown heat, pouring into the eyes and spreading within the five senses—as light enters the pin-hole of a camera's lens but floods the whole gelatine surface of the negative; so that we sat in a kind of dark inebriation, tasting the sweat and wine mixing in our mouths, and breathing in the whole landscape with every breath we drew like a perfume.

The wine was ice-cold, for the pitcher had been hanging down the well all morning on the end of a rope. Our host came timidly to the table and sat down with us to watch us eat and to ask the inevitable questions. He accepted some bread and lamb with a dignified air, stretching out his thin talons in a way that reminded one of something fastidious and small—a cat, perhaps: and this impression was strengthened by his thin black moustache which grew limply enough, but whose ends were waxed and turned up like a cat's whiskers. He was called Panayotis Porphyrogennis. 'But,' he added modestly, 'they call me Pipi here.'

You have guessed it? The inevitable happened. Gideon, animated by his own excellent conversation and the weather, drank more than three glasses of wine, which turned him the colour of brickdust, and sapped his stamina as a walker. There was nothing for it but take a short nap on the mossy bank under the planes until the sun had westered a bit. This we did, and it was not until four that we mustered up enough energy to strike the road again. 'We shall never make Cameirus,' groaned Gideon, as he stumped along. 'We shall be picked up by Mills and he will jeer at me, I know it. He always swore we should never reach Cameirus if we found a tavern on the way.'

We did however manage to get a tidy way across the Kalavarda valley with its long flat grape-orchards, and its hundreds of metal windmills imported by the Italians to draw up water from the artesian wells. Despite the fact that each of these rather crude contrivances bore the legend MADE IN CHICAGO they looked very poetical in the greenish afternoon light, slowly turning their metal flukes in the north-wind. The roads were shaded too and everywhere there sounded the noise of water flowing out along the irrigation channels on to the parched red soil. Storks had built their crazy muddled nests in some of the water-wheels and we heard their cracked voices as we passed, mingled with the bubbling of water, and the swish of wind in the silver-grey olives that stretched away in clumps towards the receding hills.

We passed through one or two dirty and dilapidated villages— Gideon religiously averting his face whenever we were confronted with the word 'Kapheneion' written on a wall or lettered out on some crude signpost. By the time Mills' little hornet of a car came whizzing up we had good enough reason to be pleased with ourselves, for we had covered a good part of the way to Kalavarda. To Gideon's surprise and relief Mills was full of admiration for our prowess. He had collected the mattresses and flea-bags and proposed to go on ahead to Cameirus. As there was no room for us in that tiny car—which barely accommodated Chloe and himself on two seats shaped like egg-cups—he roared off again along the dusty road, and left us sitting in a dry river-bed among a clump of vivid oleanders to wait for Hoyle and E. Gideon was much relieved at Mills' respect for his day's walk, and felt disposed to boast a bit, and he was still in this vein when Hoyle's old German Mercedes came into sight. Hoyle, however, seemed surprised to see us so soon. 'What?' he said, 'I thought you people told me you were going to walk?' He commented briefly on Gideon's partiality to tavern life, adding dark asides about the lower nature of man, until Gideon was quite out of humour, and pretended that a sprained ankle had prevented him from walking as far as he might have done.

We climbed into the car, and swept down the long straight road into Kalavarda. Here the country changed abruptly, very much as it does when one enters the valley of Epidaurus, and the change was like a premonition, a quickening of something inside one which only the sight of Cameirus itself could satisfy. The hills were low here, and the road ran along the sea-shore. A sense of something definite and pre-arranged, as in the landscapes contrived by those ancient Chinese gardeners for the rulers of old China. Or, as Hoyle put it, 'Limestone formations, with a thinnish topcrust of green. Look here, Gideon, holm-oak and juniper.' Gideon was still disposed to be testy. 'My dear Hoyle, that's not holm-oak, it's barbed wire from a gun-post.' At last we came to a fountain set in a circle of young plane trees, and here we found Chloe washing great bunches of grapes against dinner, while Mills, who had run his car off the road under the pines, was lovingly tinkering about in its entrails with the air of a surgeon performing a delicate operation.

Leaving them to fill the water-jar, we climbed the tree-lined way which leads up the hill to Cameirus, the car groaning and panting in second gear at the steepness of the slope. Beyond the swaying tips of the pines somewhere lay the city, and in ancient times this gracious tree-lined approach to it from the little harbour of Mylantia was made more lovely by the population of statues that stood beside the road to welcome the newcomer. Now the fleshy scalp of the hillside

showed the ugly workings of anti-tank gun sites. This had been part
of the defensive system manned by the Italians. We deduced this from
their refuse which always contained a high percentage of empty hairoil bottles and discarded clothing. The road wound higher and still
higher, passing the ugly cemetery for German troops (pitched with
such vandalistic accuracy slap in the glade below the town) and
breasting the green hummock which cuts Cameirus from the world.

You arrive in the centre of the ancient town almost before you
know it; it is as sudden as a descent from a balloon. The whole thing
assembles itself before your eyes like a picture thrown upon a
cinema-screen. It lies there in the honey-gold afternoon light listening to the melodious ringing of water in its own cisterns, and the
faint whipping of wind in the noble pines which crown the amphitheatre. The light here has a peculiar density as if the blue of the sea
had stained it with some of its own troubled dyes. The long sloping
main-street is littered with chipped inscriptions. One can make out
the names of city fathers long since dead, of priests and suppliants;
they rise in a long progress up the chalky pathways of the town to
the red earth wall beyond which the archaeologist has not trespassed,
to the rather over-poetic votive column which, one can guess without being told, is part of the most recent Italian restoration work.
Nevertheless Cameirus is beautiful in a way that persuades mere
ugliness to conform to its grace of air and situation; even the curator's
Nissen hut, now crammed with verminous filth, smashed bottles,
shed equipment, and bandages—even this cannot intrude upon the
singing beauty of this ancient town uncovered by the spade of the
archaeologist. If such a city, you find yourself thinking, if such a
landscape-out-of-time was not able to strike the right chord in the
human heart by its appeals to clemency, truth, and intellectual order
of life, what chance have we with our unburied cities to do so? And
when you see the grave-stones from the little necropolis of Cameirus
stacked up in our museums (it is inevitable that the treasures of
towns like these are hoarded up in Museums) it is the so-often repeated
single word—the anonymous Χαῖρε—which attracts you by its
simple; obsessive message to the living. It is not the names of the rich
or the worthy, not the votive reliefs and the sepulchral epigrams,
but this single word, 'Be Happy', 'Be Happy', serving both as a fare-

well and admonition, that goes to your heart with the whole impact
of the Greek style of mind, the Greek orientation to life and death:
so that you are shamed into regarding your life, and realising with
bitterness how little you have fulfilled of the principle behind a
thought so simple yet so pregnant, and how even your native
vocabulary lacks a word whose brevity and grace could paint upon
the darkness of death the fading colours of such gaiety, love and
truth as *Xαῖρε* does upon these modest gravestones.

The party was not nearly as riotous as the one we had enjoyed the
previous night. Cameirus, glimmering whitely below us, was perhaps the reason. Its silence and its utter self-possession forced themselves between our sentences like the blade of a knife, separating
thought from contemplation, and filling one with self-consciousness
by their volume. So it was that for the most part we ate silently,
staring out from the dim circle of wavering yellow light to where the
late moon had quicksilvered the marbles of the old town, and picked
up the three small promontories which jutted into the sea below
Cameirus, one of which contained, in ancient times, a temple to
Pan. But if our conversation was desultory it reflected in no way
upon the humour of the company; Gideon had recovered from his
fit of pique—a bottle and a half of white Kastellaneia had seen to that.
Hoyle himself was disposed to be complimentary about our walk;
he was always slow to reach what he himself called 'a considered
opinion', and perhaps by now he had realised that Gideon's annoyance at his teasing was genuine and not simulated.

Mills and I walked about the ancient town for a while before
turning in. The moon was all but gone, yet the light brimmed the
whole amphitheatre, casting a surface of glittering aluminium over
the white houses, and blocking in great masses of shadow on the
seaward side. Despite the light frost, and the thick nap of dew which
had fallen over everything, we were only mildly cold; a few moments
of walking about, and we found ourselves warm again. In the silence
we could hear the water gurgling somewhere down there, below the
earth.[1] An owl whistled once, twice, and we heard its creaking flight

[1] The bat-infested underground water-conduits of Cameirus I never had the
courage to explore until one memorable day when Paddy and Xan and the Corn
Goddess shamed me into following them down its dark tunnels.

from one tree to another, like the rustle of a linen skirt. I suddenly remembered other moments of time spent in this landscape, time printed upon silence with all its real colours up: the faint burring of honey-bees in Agamemnon's tomb: one glittering spring day, the noise of snow melting among the meadows at Nemea: a bird singing stiffly at noon like a voice on stilts from the bushes where we had slept: the crash of a falling orange in an island: all isolated moments existing in a peculiar dense medium of their own which was like time but not of it. Each moment to itself entire, populating a whole continuum of feeling. Coming over the ridge into Sparta, bursting through a cloud to see the lime-green Eurotas gushing into the valley carrying with it a multitude of tinkling spots of ice. . . . And these separate moments, quite loose, not stitched together except by their parentage in the same quality of feeling, suddenly added themselves to this quiet second of time spent with Mills, sitting in the frail moon-light of Cameirus, tracing an inscription on a votive stone, feeling the chisel's edge hard through the moss, spelling out Χαῖρε. 'Be Happy,' 'Be Happy.' Then the owl whistled once again from a different quarter, and someone struck a match up there under the trees. We rose by mutual consent and walked back up the long main-street of the town.

Next morning I awoke with a start to see Mills on his knees pumping the Primus stove. The sun had risen, but was still behind the hill. Its warmth, however, penetrated the crust of the island, warming the statues back to life, drying the dew from the houses of Cameirus, and offering us the auguries for another lovely day. A green lizard had crawled up to a favourite stone, and was warming itself in the indirect light of the sun. Its satin throat quivered as if with song.

Today we intended to complete the circuit of the island, and spend the night at Lindos—a journey which would put us within striking distance of Rhodes for the morning following; when we were due back at our respective establishments. We started off together, but the sedateness of Hoyle's driving soon wore out Mills' patience, he passed us on a corner and disappeared across the valley in a cloud of dust. 'It'll be a case of physician heal thyself one of these days,' remarked Hoyle sadly. His own driving technique, while accurate enough, would perhaps have been more suited to a landau. It was as

if he had carried over his tendency to have 'little rests' into his driving
—or else as if he had infected the engine of the Mercedes with some
of his own heart-trouble. At any rate, when a new idea struck him,
it was his habit to slam on the brakes, stop the car, and sit awhile to
consider it from every angle.

The sun was up now. I sat behind with E while Hoyle and Gideon
shared the front. We ate grapes and watched the valley unroll itself
before us. Hoyle and Gideon were still deep in the subject of vampires,
I remember, a subject which sounded more than ever fantastic in that
clear air. The road from Cameirus runs along the flat sea-line,
dotted with beaches. Shallow hills like green tumuli stretch away
landwards, studded with bushes of myrtle and thyme—a haunt for
the red-legged partridges and the rock-dove. The road is a bad one,
so that we were quite surprised to catch Mills up by the time we
reached the little harbour of Cameiro Skala. As we lumbered up
across the plain we saw why he had stopped. Three yellow fishing-
boats had just put in and were piling up their catch. In the middle of
a chaffering crowd of Symiot fishermen Mills was standing, blond
and stocky, bargaining for half a dozen red mullet. Gideon's re-
sourceful eye had already noticed a tavern by the roadside, and here
we waited for the deal to be closed, drinking a mastika that tasted
like horse-embrocation and listening to the squibbling of a clarinet
played by a fisherboy. Here, too, we met the inevitable American
Greek who made the inevitable comparison between Detroit and
this 'lousy country', and complimented us on speaking our mother-
tongue as well as we did. Gideon flew into a temper with him: 'You
stinking empty-headed son-of-a-bitch', he said, with an excellent
imitation of a New York accent, 'why the hell do you come back
here and poison the air of your mother-country with your cheap
snarls and your passion for Coca Cola?' The man recoiled as if he had
received a push in the chest. Hoyle clicked his tongue against his
teeth. 'Really Gideon,' he said. 'An officer and a gentleman simply
doesn't, you know.' Gideon adjusted his eyeglass. 'Perhaps he doesn't,'
he said mildly. 'But I do, old man. I definitely do. The cheek of these
people.' Mills by this time had concluded his business and stowed the
fish in the tool-box of his car. We set off pursued by the cries of
'Good journey' 'Come back soon'. Greeks adore partings.

The road winds steeply uphill, past the old Frankish fort called Castello today, and then turns abruptly inland: and rising out of the cluster of hills before us, we saw the frowning crags of Atabyron, the chief mountain of the island. Its massifs of shining black towered up into the sky from a green vegetation-line marking the site of Embona. Atabyron in that lucid morning air looked more like some invention of man than a natural phenomenon, it was as if some prodigious rough model for a statue had been abandoned here. The wind and rain had eroded it. The winter snows had polished its slippery black surface until it glinted with a bluish light, as charcoal does. It lay with all the massive pregnancy of a liner at anchor among the lesser hills, and as we climbed towards it the air became thinner, and bluer, while the mountain-villages glittered in its rareness like clusters of lump-sugar.

Up there on the final crag, from which one could faintly see the mountains of Crete, had once stood the little temple to Zeus where the great sacred bull had uttered its oracles. There is evidence to suggest that the sacred bull cult had not concerned itself with the worship of a live animal but with a gigantic bronze representation of it, in which the bodies of human beings had been placed, to roast over a fire. Their cries and groans, it is suggested, may have been taken for prophecies.

Tasting the blue refinements of that air, and watching the geological structure change to granite, we felt the first pangs of hunger steal upon us, though we were far from our objective—Monolithos. We stopped in an orange-grove outside Embona and nibbled some bread and fruit, while Gideon cracked a bottle of wine. He had got into the habit of 'fining' himself for little errors of taste or judgement. 'Damn,' he would say, 'I fine myself two glasses of red.' Or else 'I simply can't let that pass without fining myself a glass of white.' Needless to say he derived a certain pleasure from this odd method of self-punishment. Now he fined himself for his rudeness to the American Greek of Cameiro Skala while Hoyle watched him with all the weight of his unexpressed distaste apparent in his expression. 'Your liver will have to pay up in the end,' he remarked sourly.

We passed the road to Embona and turned right, to circle the great charred butt of Atabyron, whose stony ramps of black rock made

it seem more than ever medieval—like some old black-letter bible
rotting away in a Museum. . . . Gideon showed some disposition to
try and climb it but we shouted him down. Monolithos lay ahead,
and we pushed on across this razor-back landscape of rock and thistle,
punctuated everywhere by springs gushing out of the side of the
mountain, and giant walnut-trees, Artamiti . . . Saint Isidore (whoever he may be). The air was thickly scented with pines now, for we
were descending gradually.

To reach Monolithos you must crash over the brow of a hill and
think that you are falling into the sea. Miraculously, however, you
see that the dirt road continues, and the great hump of rock stabs at
you, rising out of the sea like a pointing finger. You crawl down
almost to sea-level before you reach the pine-glade lying at the foot
of the castle. 'How Mills ever got down here without breaking his
neck I don't know,' mutters Hoyle as he eases the big Mercedes into
the hollow with circumspection. But Mills is sitting in a cleft of stone
at the very top of the castle, tossing pine-cones into the sea, and singing at the top of his voice.

There was everything to be said for singing. In that dry clement
sunlight we climbed the grassy staircases to the summit. Everywhere
there were tiny dells dense with anemone and daisies. Chloe had flung
herself down between two knuckles of rock, and when she sat up to
welcome us we saw that she was covered with bright yellow pollen.
The summit of Monolithos is like some great sculptured lion's paw;
between the claws thick mossy carpets have grown up, fed by some
underground spring, no doubt, and here you may lie down in beds
of flowers for all the world as if you were still in the lowland glades
around Rodini. It was in one of these that we had lunch and talked,
idly watching the kestrels dip in the blue gulfs beneath us, and the
little coloured lizards scrabble about among the crannies of the rock.

Afterwards Mills and I went off together and climbed the tower
of the Byzantine chapel to see if one could spit directly into the sea
from this vantage-point. Mills was of a distinctly competitive turn of
mind. He was always thinking up feats of this kind to test his native
skill. Spitting over bridges, playing ducks-and-drakes upon a calm
sea, diving for pennies—there was nothing that he would not do
for the sheer pleasure of doing something active and, if possible,

slightly irresponsible. In the intervals of spitting over the cliff he said: 'I say, have you ever looked at Gideon's monocle ? I picked it up yesterday while he was asleep, to see how weak his eye was. Do you know what?'

'No. What?'

'It's made of ordinary glass.'

'But what's the point of that?' Mills sighed and dusted his blue pea-jacket with his hands. 'Humanity is so constructed that when it wants to hide something it is forced to accentuate it, to throw it into relief: I doubt if you'd notice Gideon's glass eye at all if the poor old thing hadn't drawn attention to it by wearing that monocle.' I had not noticed any signs of shyness about Gideon, I must say, and the idea came as rather a surprise to me. 'But Gideon could carry a couple of glass eyes and a pair of wooden legs with ease,' I exclaimed. 'He bluffs his way through life like a tenth century man-at-arms.' Mills jumped down from the rock and began picking flowers. 'Have you never heard Gideon's own definition of an Englishman?' he asked. 'It fits him perfectly. An Englishman may be defined as a soft-centred creature with a tough and horny shell, through which two sensitive antennae (humour and prejudice) explore the world around him.'

The journey down into the flat and featureless valley to Cattavia was uneventful. Gideon discovered Hoyle's copy of the Abbé Cutlet in a pocket of the car and regaled us with quotations in an exaggeratedly correct French accent. '*Après Lindos, Cattavia,*' he intoned, '*paysage plus riant.*' It wasn't really 'riant'—simply a stretch of alluvial marshland, poorly cultivated, and lying at the back of the eroded mountain we had crossed. After an hour or so we hit the nondescript, flattish, amorphous coastal belt, with a few villages fast asleep in their flea-tormented isolation. Here sunlight was a drug.

Nearing Lindos, however, it all changed abruptly and rose up into a gnarled rock-hewn landscape—a coast bitten out in huge mouthfuls of metamorphic rock, gleaming dully with mica, and shot through with the colours of iron and trap. It was as if a storm at sea had suddenly been solidified and compressed into these frowning capes and fastnesses of coloured rock. The sea boomed upon the sand of the long beaches, while everywhere the rusty wire and the skull with its legend 'Achtung Minen' spoke Prussian to us. To the east tiny figures knelt in a frieze along the thundering coastline, as if engaged in some obscure rite. They were lifting mines. Even from this great range one could see the tense preoccupation that convulsed them, kneeling there within the sound of the sea, burrowing in the sand with their nervous fingers. Later at a bend in the coast-road we saw the little island where Lady Hester Stanhope was washed up. It is called 'the biscuit'[1] on the charts today.

Doubling back a quarter of a mile before Calato you come upon Lindos through a narrow gulley of rock. It is as if you had been leaning against a door leading to a poem when suddenly it swung open letting you stumble directly into the heart of it. The road bores through a blank wall of rock and turns sharply to the right, running down an inclined plane. Lindos with its harbour lies below you—as if at the bottom of a pie-dish. The configurations of the promontory, upon which the town is built suggest something like the talons of the crab. The little harbour is all but land-locked and the blue of it drenches you like spray. The beach-shallows are picked out in lime-green and yellow, against the reddish, deckle-edged surfaces of stone. In the air above it rides the acropolis. It does not insist. It can afford not to presume, so certain of the impact which it must make on everyone who comes upon it through the gulley in the rock. Is not Lindos the official beauty-spot of Rhodes? The contrast with Cameirus is remarkable—for where Cameirus is refined, turned in upon itself in sunny contemplation, Lindos is bold, strident. Cameirus has all the stillness of an amphora in a Museum, with its frieze of dancers caught in a timeless dancing; Lindos, under the sweetness of its decoration, is like a trumpet-call, beaten out in gold-leaf and vibrating across the blue airs of time.

The little modern town which lies at the foot of the acropolis is perhaps a quarter of the size of ancient Lindos. Its beauty is of a scrupulous Aegean order, and perfect in its kind. The narrow streets which rise and fall like music are paved with clean sea-pebbles, and criss-crossed with little inter-communicating alleys. Their width is enough to accommodate two mules abreast, but no car can enter them. Everything is painted white, a dazzling glitter of plaster and white-

[1] Paximadi.

wash, so that if you half closed your eyes you might imagine that Lindos reflected back the snowy reflections of a passing cloud.

We had intended to sleep on the summit of the acropolis, but the women declared that they would prefer beds, so we accordingly did what all travellers in Greece must sooner or later learn to do if they explore areas where there are no hotels. In the sunny tavern of Lindos we asked for the mayor of the town, and when he arrived, introduced ourselves and set him down to drink a glass of wine with us. He was eager enough to help, and without much difficulty managed to find rooms for us. The nature of Greek hospitality is such that no traveller who flings himself upon the mercies of a village 'demarchos' will ever go bedless.

The sun was low, but there was still time to admire the little Greek church, inspect samples of the famous Lindos ware in some private villas, and admire the four or five Crusader houses which were still standing, and in excellent repair. All the latter were inhabited by Greek families who offered us cups of coffee and the polite possibility of a political discussion. Mills did his 'Florence Nightingale act' as he called it, and visited the sick. By the time he came back to the tavern we had sorted the baggage and prepared such food as we had to carry up the acropolis. The sun was westering rapidly as we walked up the winding paths of the Acropolis behind Markos, the guardian of the site. He was a slow-spoken, lazy-looking man, with a fine head set well back on broad shoulders: his broken nose gave him a slanting quizzical expression. He had been a commercial traveller and regretted that we spoke Greek, for he would dearly have loved to conduct the party in French, which he said he knew well. He was as breathless as we were, however, by the time we reached the carved rock-relief of the ship which marks the entry to the fort, and which had been executed in ancient times as a trophy—perhaps even to celebrate the long Thallassoocratia of the Rhodians, which endured some twenty-three years of naval competition about 900 B.C. Markos sat him down on a stone and waited for his breath to come back as he rubbed his hands along the stone bows of the vessel. He accepted a cigarette from Mills who had completed the ascent at record speed, and who betrayed no signs of strain. 'You're too healthy,' said Gideon.

Hoyle had been left miles behind, resting on a convenient rock and staring down into that blue circle of sea whose outer end is marked by a stone tomb rising out of the sea which, say some authorities, is where Cleobolus is buried. I walked back to accompany him. As we toiled up the hill, he chatted knowledgeably about Athene Lindia who had been worshipped in Ancient Lindos with 'flameless sacrifices'. It was at the remains of the temple of Athene that we found the others. They were lying on their stomachs and gazing down six hundred feet into the eye of the sea—that peacock-green twilight eye, glimmering with caverns and deeps where only enough light penetrated to print the diffuse markings of rock and seaweed. Markos, the guide, was in full flight. 'This is Athene Lindia's temple. There.' He picked up a pebble and threw it. 'There the temple of Zeus Policus.' Nobody, I am sorry to say, was listening to him. Down there on that darkening water lay a tiny fishing-boat like a model. 'Listen,' said E. In the silence, like the voice of an insect, came the thin strains of a fisherman singing. The sound slanted up at us through the canyons of coloured rock. We stared down it, watching the curdled greens and reds of the seaweed wavering under it. From this height we could see fish moving under the boat which were invisible to fishermen, travelling in little phosphorescent sparks of light. 'Athene Lindia' I was repeating to myself, like an incantation. Somewhere there had been a grove of sacred olives dedicated to her. Pindar's great ode on Diagoras of Ialysos had been graven on tablets and placed in the temple. In the height of her glory strangers had sent her offerings from Syria and Egypt.

The sun had been sucked down into the sea; dazzling spokes of silver spread out for a moment on the blue, as if from some great lighthouse. Then the uniform dusk. 'Cleobolus was a remarkable old thing,' Hoyle was saying, for the stream of classical evocations which had seemed to dwindle away had suddenly come to life again. The fisherman was out of sight, his singing out of sound. 'Tell us about him, Markos.' Markos took a deep breath and fired out his knowledge in demotic. 'He travelled in Egypt, was very beautiful, and wrote thousands of lovely acrostics, distichs, and other verse. He was one of the Wise Men, and a close personal friend of Solon. He lived to be seventy years old. His famous epigram 'Nothing in excess' is one which the Greeks have treasured to this day.'

'But haven't lived up to,' said Gideon dryly. Markos avoided his eye and pretended that he had not heard the interruption. 'He was, with Pythagoras, one of the first to admit women into the circle of knowledge,' he said amiably baring his teeth at E. 'His daughter Cleobulina was also a writer and left many beautiful poems.'

It was getting chilly. We made a leisurely circuit of the battlements, peering down into the little inlet where, says popular tradition, St Paul was shipwrecked on one of his many voyages. Out at sea the light was fading upon four little islands which Markos pointed out to us: the fourth was a mere shaving of rock awash when the sea was rough. 'Look,' said the guide, 'those islands they call Tetrapolis.'

'Who does?'

'Everybody. The people of Lindos. In ancient times, they say, four cities were there, and all of them sank in a great earthquake.' Gideon was getting restive. He preferred sharper lines of demarcation between legend and attested fact. 'Who says this?' he demanded— and to do him justice you will not find the story of Tetrapolis in any of the authenticated histories.

'Since before my grandfather they say so.'

'But who says so?'

Markos became a trifle impatient. He waved his arm like a wand over the dusky village beneath us. 'Everyone,' he said with a trace of sulkiness. 'Is it true?' said Gideon. Markos nodded vigorously. 'Once,' he said, 'the truth was proved to me by sponge-divers. Every summer they worked this coast and every day I drank with them in the tavern. They had seen columns of marble and statues under the sea when they dived for sponges. Once they gave me some coins which they had brought up and I sold them to a German for bread.'

We slept well that night at the tavern, and next morning did the run to Rhodes in good style, wheeling up through the rock-face where the road turns at right angles to run down to the green plains by Calato. The jagged ruin of Pheraclyea lay on the coast to our right, but Gideon had assured us from an earlier visit that nothing remained of the fort but rubble, and that extensive minefields there-abouts made it hazardous for tourists.

We lumbered through Malona and past the sunburnt farms which the Italian government had subsidised and settled with Sienese farmers—one of the richest agricultural areas in Rhodes. Here Gideon stopped for a brief chat with his Italian overseer. Many of the families had stayed on to wait for a passage to Italy, and they still worked the fields as they had always done, singing and smiling.

The road curls around the shaft of the mountain called Tsambika and through a pass, so that the entry to this second valley is nearly as sudden as the entry upon Lindos.

But at last we ran out along the final spine of the island and saw, at a turn of the road, the spires and turrets of the capital come into view. Here there was time for a final cup of coffee before separating about our various business. We took it under an olive-tree, on dry grass already waking up to the drumming of cicadas.

My heart sinks as I think of the mass of proofs, of correspondence, of files, which await me.

Mills starts up his car and gets into it slowly. 'We have a little while yet,' he says. 'Before they scatter us all over the world.'

The dust rises on the road as the cavalcade sets off.

CHAPTER VII

The Age of the Knights

XV mile the See brode is
From Turky to the Ile of Rodez
At the begynning of this Ile
Wit in but a litell while
Is a thorp that hight Newtoun:
And on a hull there alle alonen,
Is a Castell stiff, and strong,
That some tyme was a cite strong.
The Castell hight men saie soo
Sancta Maria de Fulmaro . . .[1]

A strong toun Rodez hit is,
The Castell is strong and fair I wis.
MATTHEW PARIS: *Purchas His Pilgrimes*

W hen in the sweltering July heat of the year 1099 the city of Jerusalem fell at long last to the Crusaders, the Rhodians might have claimed a share in the victory, though they played no part in the appalling massacres that followed it—when some seventy thousand human beings were butchered in the streets, and when the Crusaders who had despatched them, knelt upon the blood-stained cobbles of the Redeemer's shrine, 'weeping from excess of joy', to give thanks for their victory. The sea-transports of Rhodes had helped to provision the besiegers. But even before this the island had sent out supplies to the Crusaders when their forces were encamped about Antioch. In this they exercised a religious rather than a political preference, though it is hard to distinguish between the two in the affairs of this age.

[1] The present Phileremo.

133

Yet the direct connection between the Knights of St John and Rhodes can only be treated tentatively, episodically, because it is only a small part of a larger story which clean overlaps the boundaries of time and place. For a long time Rhodes itself lay, so to speak, in the back areas of that enormous battlefield. Its importance only began to grow when the Knights were expelled from Jerusalem and retired to Cyprus in 1291. At this time, though nominally a dependancy of the Emperor of Constantinople the island was in fact very much at the mercy of the Genoese who administered it, and who, as allies of the Byzantines, exercise a sort of pirate's licence over its harbours and coves when they fitted out their galleys for expeditions against the rich commercial traffic of Venice in the Mediterranean.

High in the catalogue of these rogues, who dignified themselves with the title of Admiral, stands Vignolo de' Vignoli. It was he who first suggested to the Grand Master of the Knights of St John the idea of an attack on Rhodes and the surrounding islands. The island was his base of operations against Cyprus, and it is possible that he had become increasingly conscious of the Knights as a power lying across the path of these predatory raids. More than this, the Turks themselves were a constant nuisance, operating from the creeks and inlets of what is now Anatolia. They had virtually despoiled all the islands off the mainland. They disturbed Vignoli's whole-hearted concentration on the exercise of his craft. Every time he returned from a raid on the Venetians it was only to hear how, in his absence, the Turks had made an incursion, fired a town, destroyed some galleys, deforested an island. . . . Why not, thought Vignoli at a single blow perform a triple feat of skill: neutralize the Knights in Cyprus by an alliance with them: persuade them to consolidate the Dodecanese islands against the Turks: and leave himself free to operate as he pleased?

Fulk de Villaret, the Grand Master of the Knights Hospitallers, was a grave and cautious man, deeply conscious of his order and of the faith in which it was founded; Vignoli was both bold and persuasive. The strategic value of the plan itself was obvious—for the Dodecanese islands, as they are now called, offered something like a deep second-line of defence to the Crusaders, who were no doubt already aware of having over-stretched their lines of communication with the Europe on which they depended. With Jerusalem lost, Cyprus was like some precarious stepping stone around which the water was already lapping. While they sternly maintained their charge it must have been obvious to them that it could not be held indefinitely against the rising tide of barbarism. It was not as if the sea itself was safe; marauding privateers of every colour were abroad. The Knights were like castaways, adrift on the stone rafts of their fortresses, in a sea alive with sharks; these precarious religious enclaves they had founded—each castle which even today seems clenched like a mailed fist—depended on blood and stones for their maintenance.

They moved across this enchanting landscape, dedicated to impulse, like strange automata, these iron men: bringing purpose and direction to places where only appetite and disorder had reigned: sustaining themselves on the iron rations of a discipline and a moral purpose which awoke something like a half-hearted admiration even in the breasts of their enemies. They burned with a self-dedication which could withstand every temptation—save at last the languorous airs of the Levantine landscape they dominated for so long.

But Vignoli's plan offered something new; a string of island fortresses from which the whole variegated coastline of Anatolia could be surveyed and ravaged; a string of stepping stones pointing north to Constantinople. Yet Fulk de Villaret was worldly enough to demand precise and determined articles of the voluble and friendly pirate. The success of their joint attack would give each what he wanted most: to the Knights a defensive barrier, and to Vignoli that treasured peace of mind which was so necessary for the exercise of his talents. The plan was as follows:

Rhodes was to go to the Knights except for two villages which were to be held by Vignoli. Leros and Cos, which the pirate already held under the terms perhaps of some Golden Bull, he was prepared to cede to his allies. One third of the revenue of such other islands of the group as might be conquered was to be payable to Vignoli, and two thirds to the Knights. Vignoli reserved the right to be vicar of all the islands save Rhodes itself.

It is perhaps not without significance that one of the witnesses to this document was a member of the great Florentine banking house of Peruzzi. There were after all perquisites to be thought of in an expedition of this kind, for trade followed the Order as in later times it was to follow the Union Jack.

The Grand Master fitted out two great war-galleys and four smaller vessels for the expedition. He embarked thirty-five chosen Knights and a force of infantry, and on the 22nd of June the convoy set off in a freshening wind for this new adventure. They watered at Castel Rosso for a month while Vignoli went ahead on a reconnaissance. On his return the fleet set sail for the Gulf of Makri where it waited upon a plan of Vignoli's, who nourished some hopes of a speedy and bloodless conquest of Rhodes. Two Genoese galleys were ordered to enter the harbour and surprise the Byzantines holding the city, but they bungled their work. Their captains were arrested by the authorities, and only managed to escape by a feat of prodigious lying which puzzled their captors. On their return Fulk de Villaret gave the general order for the attack with the whole force. It was not after all going to be as easy as Vignoli had promised.

The city was attacked by both land and sea, yet by the end of September only Pheraclea, that mountain of useless rubble, had fallen to the Knights. Phileremo was surprised early in November: a Greek servant of the commandant, to revenge himself for a flogging, showed the invaders an unguarded postern. Here a disgraceful massacre of three hundred Turkish mercenaries took place. The Byzantines themselves claimed sanctuary in the chapel on the mount.

But by now the winter was setting in. The first light falls of snow whitened the grim butt of Atabyros and swelled the mountain torrents. The north-wind drummed day and night upon the north-eastern flanks of the island. It became obvious to Fulk de Villaret that his resources were inadequate for the task of reducing Rhodes. His infantry had been badly mauled in the campaign and many of his Knights wounded. Now they had made what shift they could to bivouac on the windy slopes of Phileremo, but watching them shivering round the flapping pine-fires they had kindled the Grand Master knew them inadequate for the task ahead. Spring came and summer. The stalemate dragged on. But the Knights had learned the lessons that only long campaigns can teach: patience, tenacity. Their numbers had been increased, it is true, after the bitter fighting around Phileremo, by a fresh body of Knights summoned in haste from Cyprus. But even their present forces were not enough. Worse still, the coffers of the Order were empty.

The delay was to last two years during which time Fulk de Villaret tried to strengthen his arm, first by an appeal to the Emperor of Constantinople to grant him the island and accept his Knights as vassals on the tenure of military service to be performed by three hundred of their number. This appeal met with point blank refusal. Then he had been forced to turn to the Pope for further aid which was only forthcoming after de Villaret himself had made two summer journeys northward in order to kiss hands and plead his case in person. By the spring of 1309 however he had gathered a large body of troops under his command and could muster twelve galleys, all in his pay. But by now the long wait had sapped the morale of the Byzantines, and when a Genoese transport bound for the garrison with corn and arms, was captured, Fulk de Villaret told its captain to go to Rhodes and open negotiations for the surrender of the island. He was fairly sure they would treat, and he was right.

On demanding and receiving suitable guarantees the defenders of the island surrendered on the 15 August 1309. The Knights soon acquired a number of other islands, Chalce, Simi, Telos, Nisyros, Cos, Calymnos and Leros in the north and north-west. Castel Rosso also fell to them, and while they made some tentatives against Casos and Carpathos, they quickly withdrew when the Venetians intervened, not wanting any trouble from that quarter.

Historians have remarked on the gradual change in the character of the Order after it had conquered Rhodes, and had also succeeded to the vast estates left it by the defunct Templars. The accumulation of vast material wealth, say some, was gradually sapping the moral structure of the organisation. Secular interests had begun to compete with the spiritual.

At any rate Fulk de Villaret put on one side all the old statutes which had determined the limits of his powers as Grand Master and after the conquest of Rhodes began to act for all the world as if he were a sovereign. Nor were his Knights slow to resent this and already in 1317 there was an abortive attempt to seize him while he was travelling in the interior of the island. For a while he was besieged in the fortress of Lindos and his deposition was decreed; yet the matter was somehow compromised for his successors continued to exercise much the same power in Rhodes as the Doges themselves.

Meanwhile however the Rhodians gained immensely by the presence of the Order in the island. The Turks did not dare to attack them as of old; justice prevailed in the law courts; commerce boomed. The harbours of the island offered safe anchorage to merchant ships. The Order found little difficulty now in raising substantial loans abroad—among the great banking houses with which they dealt was, of course, the house of Peruzzi. The frequent forays against the Turkish vessels plying in the Levant brought them immense booty which more than offset any budgetary deficits incurred in fortifying the islands. Rhodes basked in this transitory peace and plenty. Vignoli went about his unlawful business with a quiet mind—loading his privateers to the gunwales with gold and silver, precious stones and silks which he captured from the Turks, and sailing home with whatever would float behind attacked to his blameless rudder. Were *they* not infidels? Was *he* not a Christian?

The Knights were hardly less sure of themselves in this context, and took every opportunity of slaughtering the captured infidel. Some horrible massacres are recorded to their credit—or discredit: depending on one's angle of judgement. But a history of these early years is too thickly planted with detail for us to do more than skim it.

Irregularities began to grow up within the walled garden of the Order of the Knights Hospitallers. By constitution the member Knights were supposed only to live for the service of the poor and the defence of the true faith. They were supposed to live under the three vows of chastity, poverty and obedience. But by now the Order itself was by repute as rich as all the rest of the Church put together while many of the Knights owned immense estates in their own right. They had began to dress with the utmost luxury, to spend improvidently on gold and silver plate, on rich hangings and carpets bought from the traders of the mainland. They kept strings of richly caparisoned horses. They hawked the island. They neglected the poor. It is true that sumptuary laws were afterwards passed from time to time but it is clear that the rich living no less than the delicious airs of Rhodes had begun to etiolate their characters. How else is one to account for the stories, vague enough perhaps, but for which evidence could be produced, of the Knights themselves indulging in piracies? There were stories, for instance, of Knights disguising themselves and their men as Turks in order to plunder the passing Venetian traffic; while only a few years before the siege of 1522 it was charged that one of the captains serving under a Spanish sea-robber who haunted the coasts of Corfu, was a knight.

Nevertheless these moral lapses had not as yet impaired their fighting powers, as the two great sieges testify; and doubtless viewed through the average townsman's eyes the Order was still what it always had been—a tower of disciplined strength rising steeply out of a raging sea. It is indeed said that, so great were the dangers and hardships of the life they had chosen, hardly one in twenty of them lived to reach the age of fifty. The youthfulness of many of the Knights was remarkable. One could be admitted to the Order at the age of fourteen, and enjoy the privilege of residing in the fortress and wearing the full dress of the Order, though the admission to full privilege in arms could not be conferred before the age of eighteen. The sons of the nobility and the gentry, however, could gain admission into the Order as students and undergo instruction in the science of war.

The civil dress of the Order was black with the eight-pointed white cross, instituted before their sad expulsion from Palestine. Their battle dress was red with a square white cross, as shown in so many of the old paintings. In the sombre surroundings of their forts these uniforms in their simplicity must have glowed with all the warmth of Christian reassurance in the eyes of their patients who crowded the great hospitals for treatment. The semi-monastic nature of the Order impressed the Orthodox islanders very much, for military discipline was never at any period lax. The Castle itself was stringently guarded by night and day. Even during times of general relaxation, as during Carnival, nobody in a mask was permitted entry to the fortress on Rhodes. Generally speaking the Knights themselves were not permitted to enter the town unless on horseback or walking two by two. In the case of the Hospital in Rhodes the warehouses facing the Sea Gate formed the endowment of the prior and chaplain. The physicians were bound by order to visit their patients not less than twice a day. Two surgeons were standing by under their orders to perform whatever operations were found necessary. A large store of herbs and drugs was maintained as part of the charges of the establishment, while the patients were fed upon all kinds of nourishing food. But dicing, chess, and the reading of chronicles, histories, romances or other light fiction of the kind was strictly forbidden.

The dead were carried out into the town for burial by four men wearing black robes which were set aside specially for that purpose. The townsmen watched them come through St Catherine's gate, their faces solemn in the flapping yellow torch-light, their solemn strides measured perhaps by a single kettle-drum, walking symbols of a faith which took death as sombrely as it took life on earth. Watching such a procession the peasant crossed himself and sighed as he watched these iron men, torn between admiration for their humanity and discipline and distaste for the rigidity and excessive formalism of their lives. Ah! for the good old Byzantine days when everyone had his own opinion—provided he owned a dagger with which to enforce it!

The Order itself was composed of tongues, eight in all, and the defence of the fortress was parcelled out to the various nationalities with due regard to their numbers and prowess. At first the Hospitallers had been mainly French; for the Knights of Provence and of Auvergne were as thoroughly French as the Knights of France were. But in 1376 a Spaniard was elected Grand Master. His tenure of office lasted twenty years, and both his successors were Spaniards. The lattter of these took the step of increasing Spanish influence by expanding the tongue of Spain into the tongues of Castile and of Aragon. This was an important step, as voting in the Councils was based not upon the number of Knights but upon the number of nations represented.

This, then was the organisation which made itself responsible for the safety of Rhodes and its inhabitants. Chronicles and studies of this packed and ample age abound, and while the sour Torr in his notes on the bibliography of this period, finds this chronicler wanting in taste, that in judgement, and all a little wanting in 'factual veracity', nevertheless for my own purposes more than enough material is available to the student; there is no need for the brief and popular account so much in fashion today to bridge the gap between the joyous pages of Bosio and any of a dozen studies published since.

The two great sieges by the Turks which occupy the central panel of the medieval picture are no less marvellous than the siege of Demetrius; but so much rich and confused colouring is available with which to paint them that it would be cruel to devote less than a whole book to them. And that must wait. Suffice it to say here that the Order, which for so long withstood not only the genius of the landscape but the momentum of history itself, at length succumbed. In December 1522, after bitter fighting in which 3,000 of the garrison and 230 of the Knights perished, Rhodes surrendered to the infidel.

The terms of the capitulation were not unduly onerous. The Knights were free to take their arms and property and to depart: the Sultan himself would provision their ships. Any civilian might leave Rhodes if he wished at any time during the next three years, with all his possessions. Those who stayed would be exempt from all tribute for the next five years; their children too would be forever exempt from conscription as janizaries. Freedom of Christian worship would be guaranteed.

So, on New Year's Day, 1523, the Knights entered their battered fleet, and set sail once more for Cyprus.

Little enough remains now save the chain of ruined forts, and the names of famous battles petrifying slowly in the history-books. The culture to which the Knights were heirs took shallow roots which barely outlived their departure. It never penetrated to the heart of the Mediterranean way-of-life—that mixture of superstition, impulse and myth which so quickly grows up around whatever is imported, seeking to domesticate it. The landscape puts her nymphs arms about human habits, beliefs, styles of mind so that imperceptibly they are overgrown by the fine net of her caresses—paths choked with weeds, wells blocked by a fallen coping-stone, fortresses silvered over with moss. Decay superimposes its own chaos, so that standing on some heap of stones today, watching a shepherd milk his goats, hearing the drizzle of milk in the cans chimed by the whizz of the gnats which hover round him, you wonder whether this mauled assembly of stone is Frankish or Mycenean, Byzantine or Saracen. Often enough the answer is: all of these. But only the eye of a specialist can read it like a palimpsest, text imposed on text, each dedicated to its peculiar folly or poetry.

As for the Crusaders, you must hunt for them today in the folk-songs, in the superstitions. Here and there, too, you may find gleams reflected from their chivalry in the border-ballads of the country; or their influence in the workmanship of old weapons—styles borrowed by the smiths of Constantinople and adapted to their own style. Pottery, too. In the pottery-styles of some periods you may see the influence brought to bear by heart-sick Turkish or Persian prisoners, who solaced themselves in their exile by painting plates which even today give back an echo of their oriental homesickness.

Even this garden of the Villa Cleobolus where I write these lines. . . . Though it still lies on the site of the Grand Master's garden, its appearance must have changed at least a dozen times since those days. Nevertheless the little groups of tombs like sentry-boxes, the marble gravestones with their flowing Arabic inscriptions, make a not ineffective monument to that lost epoch; even though to the eye of an initiate they are of a later period—the graves of Turkish civil servants who died of boredom and over-eating in small consular posts, or of political exiles who wore out their hearts waiting for an amnesty. The grove of eucalyptus trees towers over them all, the drifts of autumn leaves rain down on them. Each year they have to be dug out afresh from the mounds of leaf-mould, to be renovated. And even now as I write these dry sickle-shaped leaves are breaking off and planing down, spinning like propellers as they fall upon the blue table.

CHAPTER VIII

Lesser Visitations

Hoyle has been seriously ill after his operation and poor Mills has been almost beside himself with anxiety. However after a relapse and a blood transfusion Hoyle has rallied and is now permitted visitors. He lies in the dazzling white room he chose for himself at the Hospital, his hands folded on the red counterpane, staring out at the cypresses and the sea. I am touched by the pathos of his glance, by the magical composure of his face. The room is full of violets gathered by Chloe and dressed in green china bowls made for Hoyle by Huber. Here he lies like a mandarin with a few choice dictionaries beside his bed.

'As you get old,' he says, 'it gets harder to grab hold of life. This time my fingers nearly slipped.'

He is still rather weak and we take it in turns to read to him. 'Thank God it's you this afternoon. I am beginning to hate Gideon. Yesterday he ate all my grapes and insisted on reading a book I didn't want to read at all—just because he was in the middle of it himself. He gave me such a muddled synopsis of it, too, that I could hardly make head or tail of it. Then he borrowed my Turkish dictionary and brought it back full of breadcrumbs and grease marks. What is one to do with the fellow?'

We read or chat away the afternoons.

Deep-scented groves of Profeta with those magical carpets of peonies; and everywhere in the dense tree-scapes of the mountain the breathless promise of deer. The deer you see on the vases, perhaps, with the liquid melting almond-shaped eyes. Great bundles of conglomerate rise out of the green glades. Rock and grass. But the Germans killed all the deer when they were starving.

Manoli told me a story today which I jotted down in my notebook. It is too good, in a sense, ever to make material for a short-story writer. Sometimes life itself borrows the forms of art, and the sort of story told by life is only fit to transcribe raw: without premeditation.

St Pantaleimon is a tiny village buried so deeply among the foothills around Taegetus that for weeks its inhabitants did not know that the Germans had over-run Greece. The occasional aircraft they saw only made them wonder what celebrations were going forward in Athens. Had Greek troops entered Rome? The village consisted entirely of grey-beards except for three small boys aged about ten who kept the flocks. The oldest of these was Niko, a spade-bearded patriarch of eighty, tough as holm-oak. Well, one day the news came (Manoli talking), and Niko summoned a conference. Apparently Greece had fallen and they were surrounded by Germans. Doubtless these would soon appear. It was up to St Pantaleimon to resist them. Accordingly all the old men furbished up their flintlocks, and looked to their ammunition. There was little enough of it. Enough for one good volley, perhaps, but they were determined that the Germans should have it. Weeks passed and nothing happened. Then a runner came up from the valley to say that a German patrol was on its way.

The village elders took up ambush positions at the mouth of a defile—the only entry to the village. They heard noises. Presently a strong patrol of Germans came in sight—but alas! They were driving before them the whole flock of sheep and the three young shepherds whom they had captured on the hill. In a flash Niko saw what was going to happen. He drew a deep breath and hesitated. The ambushed Germans were unaware of the rifles pointing at them. Then Niko commended his soul to God and standing up roared 'Fire'. The children fell with the rest.

The 'evil eye' is a well-known Mediterranean superstition. Most children, all valuable beasts of burden—and by extension all motor-cars, wear the familiar blue beads which can avert the malediction of anyone who has what Ovid calls 'the double pupil of the eye'. This week there was rather an amusing crisis involving this deeply-rooted belief. The seven refurbished taxis of Rhodes had just been licensed to circulate and great was the rejoicing when it was announced that from Tuesday next the taxi-rank on the pier would contain seven road-worthy vehicles. On Tuesday however nothing happened. It seems that there were no blue beads to tie on the radiators. The vehicles were in hourly danger of being blighted by the evil eye if they should circulate without this precaution. Moreover there seemed none available for sale in the town. The Administration was nonplussed. The Brigadier sent for me: 'Is it true,' he said, 'that these bloody lunatics won't circulate without lucky charms tied to their bloody bonnets?' I explained what I knew of the terrible powers of the evil eye, of how in the past innocent taxis had been struck dead in their tracks by the power of a witch: had developed carburettor trouble or the pitiful state of wasting away known as 'slow puncture'. He was not impressed by this. 'Honestly,' he said, 'they really drive one crazy. I can't think what you see in them. Now the Swahili. . . .' When he had finished telling me how superior the Swahili were he said: 'Well, I suppose we'll have to signal Cairo for some blue beads. They'll think I've gone out of my mind. Sometimes I think it won't be long before I do.'

The situation, however, was saved by Martin, the young South African who is virtually mayor of Rhodes. He came into the room at this moment and said 'It's all right, sir. I've issued them with saints.' The Brigadier threw up his hands. 'You've done *what?*'

'I got them an issue of saints from the Archbishop. They're quite happy now.'

It was a happy stroke, Martin had prevailed upon the clergy to provide seven 'assorted saints' as he called them—those little tin medallions with a coloured saint on them. These they had happily tacked on to the dashboard of their taxis.

If you should happen to admire a pretty child or a beautiful animal in the presence of the mother or owner, it is only common politeness, as well as firmly established custom, to turn your head aside, spit thrice, and mutter the charm να μην ἀβασκαθῇ ('may it not be blighted'). This is not merely a nostrum against the evil eye, though it serves its purpose in this context as well. Huber tells me that this is a custom of the greatest antiquity: in fact the πτύειν εἰς κολπον of the ancient Greeks, who warded off the vengeance of Nemesis in this fashion. Conversely if you see someone afflicted by some terrible illness you can guard yourself and your own family against it by the same charm. Gideon has contracted the habit in the course of his cattle-appraising and spits with great abandon whenever he stops to discuss a prize hog or pat a peasant's child. Perhaps the old English custom of spitting on a silver coin before pocketing it is a remnant of the same belief.

Mills has been away in the south of the island with Chloe, who combines the roles of wife and nurse with equal skill. It is his habit to scribble me a few lines from time to time, asking me to convey messages to his hospital, or to arrange for drugs to be motored out to him. Here is a typical passage from a letter: 'I was called out some days ago to a village near Siana, unpronounceable name. A farmer's pregnant ass had been gored by a bull. It had aborted, poor thing, and stood in the middle of the field beside the dead foal with its intestines hanging down to the ground through a wound eight inches long. An attempt had been made by the villagers to sew up the rent with silk but it had broken down at once. I gave the patient 3 grains of morphia and had it lifted off its feet on to its side. Chloe and I then bathed its guts in salt water to clean out the dirt. We popped them back into the abdomen with plenty of sulphonamide and did a complete surgical repair to the laceration. This took over two hours, terribly exhausting. At the end of it the donkey got to its feet and took some water out of a pail. I ordered it water and milk for a day and then a normal diet. The farmer's pent-up emotions were now free to devote to the bull. He chased it round and round the field hammering its behind with a huge rock taken from the wall of the field, swearing marvellously as he ran. As I did not want to perform the same sort of operation on him (the bull showed signs of annoyance) I thought it better to retreat, which we were allowed to do when everybody had had a chance to kiss our cheeks or our hands.

'The ass did quite well for a day or two. Then, alas, its abdomen began to swell—inevitable peritonitis—and to our great grief it died. The farmer cried, and all the villagers; and Chloe cried, and I was hard put to it not to do the same. It was not the personality of the ass that made it seem so heartbreaking. When you realise how these people live and what a beast of burden means to them the loss is far graver than the loss of a pet. It is a setback in the battle against starvation.

'Today the farmer has sent us a beautifully worked goatskin knapsack, fit for a baby Pan.'

Omens of our impending departure are in the air. There seems a fair chance of the Peace Conference coming to a decision which will involve the fate of the islands. The Greeks have appointed a Governor designate who will for the time hold a watching-brief with a small military mission. Gideon's delight is marked when he hears that this exalted functionary is to be the redoubtable Colonel Gigantes,[1] an old friend of his. We meet the little party at the airstrip near Calato and soon the two monocled soldiers are shaking hands with each. 'Gideon, you rogue,' growls Gigantes grasping him by the hand. They go off together arm in arm, their conversation punctuated by roars of laughter.

That evening we celebrate a new addition to our ranks, and the conversation takes on an added animation, an Athenian zest. The General brings with him a pungent whiff of politics and warfare from the north to enliven the *taedium vitae* of a territory where sobriety and firm government have allowed little free play to the typical Greek character with its talent for political intrigues.

The war completely destroyed the livestock, and thus stopped the manufacture of raw materials for clothes. Long before this, however, the influence of western dress had driven the peasant in the direction of the shapeless cloth cap, the trousers and open shirts which so many of them wear today. On feast days, perhaps, the elder men would open their oak chests and lay out the traditional eagle-winged bolero, the blue Turkish trousers and the sashes in which they carried their silver-knuckled pistols or daggers. The craft has not died, but the materials are sadly lacking today which would enable the wife of the family to trick out her man's costume and her own with delicate gold embroidery and scarlet piping. Nevertheless while no new costumes are being made the old have been carefully preserved, and at festivals the women once more emerge from their everyday

[1] Of the Greek Sacred Legion.

clothes and dance in full costume. This is something worth watching. The best dancers of the island are the girls of Embona, the village which lies at the foot of Atabyron; after them those of Soroni.

General Gigantes before settling in has decided to make a royal progress through the islands with the Brigadier, to show their respective flags. Gideon says that his privately confessed intention is to leave no wine untasted in the fourteen islands—and from what I know of the Brigadier he will fall in with this plan without demur. Gideon, needless to say, has succeeded in getting himself invited. 'As chief of Agriculture,' he says, 'I am more or less responsible for the wine and food. Besides, old Gigantes can teach us all a thing or two.'

The new proclamation on censorship has vested the responsibility in me; but the wording of the text runs: 'All printed material must be submitted to the Information Office before issue,' and the Rhodians have taken it all too literally. My office is crowded now with a variety of people asking me to frank beer-bottle labels, cartons, theatre-advertisements and handbills of all kinds. In this way I have increased my acquaintance a hundred-fold. It is very seldom, however, that a writer strays into my net. Nevertheless today my door flew open and standing before me was a large cadaverous individual with corn-cob teeth and curling moustaches, clad in a blood-stained smock. He turned out to be a butcher-poet from one of the outlying villages. 'Is it true,' he said with a ghastly grimace, and in a tone of such hollowness and resonance that I recognised at once the village speech-maker. 'Is it true that the *democratic* Anglo-Saxons impose censorship on works of art?' I admitted that it was true.[1] He sighed and cast his eyes to the ceiling. 'Sir,' he said, 'what a disappointment after seeing the Italians run like hares.' He produced from under his smock a wad of the ruled scrap paper that tradesmen use for their business jottings and held it out to me, saying simply. 'I am Manoli the butcher, and this is my epic.'

I cannot read the cursive hand easily, though the text was fairly written, but I was reluctant to let my visitor go without getting to know him better. 'Read me a little of it,' I said. His eye brightened

---

[1] In fact my brief was political and not artistic. Later I founded 'Techni' the first Greek literary weekly in the islands to which Manoli tried often to contribute.

and drawing himself up he launched into his epic without a trace of embarrassment. It was comical, but it was also impressive, his utter self-possession. The poem itself was a portentous piece of doggerel, written in thumping sixteen-foot lines, and entitled 'The Miseries and Trials of Rhodes under the plague of the Fascists'. I longed for Gideon to be there to enjoy it with me. Manoli the butcher was rapt. The truth was that he did not read very fluently and the monotonous cadences of the poem demanded the utmost attention if he was going to get the scansion right. He picked off each accent with a slight nod of the head. The whole performance took him about twenty minutes. The sound of all this powerful declamation attracted attention; first E tip-toed in, then the Greek editor Kostas, and finally the Baron Baedeker, clutching a handful of soiled prints. Manoli was not put out by this addition to his audience; he continued his monotonous chant, but inclined himself towards the newcomers slightly, to give them the benefit of the performance. As he came to the end of each page he allowed it to drop to the floor with a superb gesture, so that at last he stood before us empty-handed with his epic littering the floor around his feet.

Kostas humbly gathered up the pages, stifling a desire to laugh. Manoli stood there with a queer mixture of humility and pride, clasping his large hands. 'It is very remarkable,' I said. The rest of the audience muttered suitable praises. The butcher inclined his head modestly, though he obviously held himself in good conceit. 'I wish to print it,' he said, 'So that there should be some record of our sufferings.'

'Kostas,' I said solemnly, 'Hand me the rubber stamp.'

Kostas breathed on the article reverently and gave me the shadow of a wink. I gravely stamped the manuscript and handed it back to the butcher who replaced it in its hiding place under the bloody apron. 'Sir,' he said, 'I thank you,' and shaking my hand warmly he withdrew.

Later that morning when we set out in the brilliant sunshine to walk back to the hotel a breathless child ran up to us and thrust a blood-stained paper parcel into the saddle-bag I was carrying over my arm. 'It is from Manoli, sir.' he piped. For a moment I was nonplussed. There are so many Manoli's: we have three among the printers. Then I remembered. Inside the parcel were some lamb-chops, a true poet's gift.

Timachidas of Rhodes was an epic poet the loss of whose work only Gideon mourns. It was a single immense epic pregnantly entitled 'The Dinners'. Was it simply a catalogue of dinners he had enjoyed in the past—or a poem devoted to ideal dinners which he would have liked to enjoy if he had had the means? We shall never know. Parmenon of Rhodes was famous for an early cookery book which is also unhappily lost. It might have given us some help with the vexing questions raised by Lynceus of Samnos who goes out of his way to praise Rhodian delicacies among which he lists the aphye (anchovy?), the ellops (sword-fish?), the orphos (sea-perch?) and the alopex (shark?). The conjectures are not mine but Torr's.

Among an unsorted mass of crumpled notes I came upon a few lines about a visit to Calithea last week with Mills and E. A few random impressions of swimming in a dark sea under a clear and moonless sky: 'All around contorted hefts of volcanic rock snarling immobile dragon-snarls. Smell of bitter creeper and cloying jasmine. The dark water warm and salty from a day of south wind. Occasional draughts of cool air and colder currents curling in snake-like from the rock-entrances of the harbour. Hanging there in the sea as if in a web, webbed feet spread, webbed fingers parted, to look back and upwards through wet eyelashes at the star-flowered sky, huge pieces of which slide about like glassy panes, so one can reach up and knock aside the planets. A silence palpitant with quiet voices and the aberrant crunch of oars. This silence was not absolute, as if the membranes of the air, damp and sticky mucilage, were glued together with the warm sticky night, reminding one that silence, after all, is only sound in emulsion. Later in an orchard of pears above the harbour a fugitive happiness: thin sweet grapes and mastika.'

The royal party has returned rather the worse for wear. It was not however the carousing which caused the trouble—though both Gideon and the Brigadier seem a trifle chastened by their experiences. It was the tireless walking imposed on them by Gigantes who insisted on inspecting every island in detail and showed an utter disregard for distances and natural obstacles. Honour dictated that where he went the Brigadier must follow; and where the Brigadier went, Gideon must go to. 'God, what a jaunt,' said my friend. Up the dizzy crater of Nisyros, perched on barbaric eructating mules, round the crumbling coves of Patmos and Astypalea, the sinuosities of Cos and Leros—wherever there was firm ground the Greek General marched firmly, gleaming monocle in eye, pausing only to utter good-humoured taunts at their dilatoriness. Each day there was some prodigious excursion to undertake to some unvisited corner of an island where the startled peasantry (having caught sight of their visitors from distant peaks and crags) had already set out a table in the main-street and broached the best wine. And now Greek hospitality set in like a Trade wind, and glasses were clinked and emptied in response to numberless toasts—the native genius of Gigantes, like that of Gideon, lent itself to the creation of toasts. More than once they were carried back on mules from these outposts in a state of exhilarated exhaustion. Once Gideon was deposited in the sea by his mule. He suspected that Gigantes pushed him. And one of the younger liaison officers, declaring that he saw a mermaid, set off swimming after it in the direction of Asia Minor, calling upon it in eloquent terms to stay and talk. He was placed under close arrest, and was so indignant that nobody believed his story that he challenged Gideon to a duel on the sand-beaches of Cos. The Brigadier's uniform was eaten by a goat while he was bathing. . . . 'Altogether,' said Gideon, 'there is a wealth of local colour about this excursion which can only be discussed in the privacy of the club, as between officers of equal rank.' The only member of the party who was not prostrated was the indomitable Gigantes himself who declared that the excursion left him feeling 'remarkably fresh'. Among the spoils of the raid were several casks of what Gideon called 'alcoholic booty' which will enable us all to study wine-production in the islands in the detail such a subject deserves. I have agreed to give style and tone to the report which Gideon is writing, on condition that I share some of the research.

Most of the Government experimental farms will be closing down, for despite their own apparent prosperity they never formed an integral part of the island economy. Nor, unluckily enough was much learned from them by the peasant farmer who might have profited by Italian experience. For example, the Rhodian peasant has not yet learned to grow his own forage crops; yet the government farms have been growing their own stocks of vetch, lucerne, trifolium incarnatum, and so on. A knowledge of this skill would have had an important effect on the Rhodian economy in its effect, not only on the rotation of crops, but also on the fate of the heathland and forest—at present grazed promiscuously and indiscriminately. The present day village rotation is variable but in general consists of 1 to 2 years straw crop and from 2 to 4 years fallow.

Soil-erosion, too, is far advanced, though the Italians did much to preserve the top-soil of the greener areas of Rhodes. The peasant is intransigent, however. One of Gideon's problems is to persuade him that all the soil-preservation measures initiated by the Italians were not baleful infringments of Fascism upon human liberty.

By the post of England on the medieval walls—so broad that six horsemen could gallop abreast upon them—we spend the afternoon lounging. We can overlook the whole town from here, as well as the shrill private lives of a dozen families who live directly under the towering walls, in gardens picked out with palms and bushes of red hibiscus. A windmill turns, creaking, and from the invisible marketplace rises the surf of human bartering—the vibration of business. On the wall itself two armies are fighting with wooden swords—a dozen children in paper hats against half a dozen bareheaded ones. They are not Knights and Saracens, as one might think, but British and Germans. The battle sways backwards and forwards. Nobody dies or is hurt, though one of the shock-troops has started crying. Their shouts marry the thin keening of the swifts by the walls, darting against the blue. High up against the sun an eagle planes above us, watching history plagiarising itself once more upon these sunmellowed walls.

CHAPTER IX

The Saint of Soroni

'A village without an ikon: a head without an eye,' says a
proverb more comminatory than most, for the psychic life
of these small Aegean communities is healthiest where it can
be focused upon some such arbiter of fate. Lines of force radiate outwards from the shrine of a patron saint like holiness from a halo and,
none the less real for being invisible, they play their part in the
common adventures of the fisherman, herdsman and farmer, easing
the burden of his conduct—not in the narrow theological sense, but
in the sense of faith in acts.

A journey by water may be dedicated to the protection of the
saint, just as an illness may be placed, so to speak, on his knees. He is
a help against the brute adversities that face simple folk in these
islands. But it is not only in adversity that one turns to him, it is also
in joy. One's precious male child is dedicated to him. After a successful harvest, who can forget to offer the shrine a measure of oil for his
lamps? Oaths both good and bad are uttered in his name; while no
material object is too small to commend to his care—a sick child, a
sickly lamb, or a tattered fishing net. He stands at the confluence of
those two great rivers, man and the unknown, and his job is to
domesticate each for the other. He remits the temporal pains.

I am not speaking now of the more famous ones whose medicine
has become a cult, and whose sphere of influence is no longer
regionalised—located in some small tumbledown church, whose
cracking gesso backgrounds bear the half-obliterated faces of forgotten Byzantine divinities: I am not thinking of Tinos where the

little hanging offerings of crutches, bandages and paintings testify to the miracle having taken place, and remind one once again that here, as in the ruined and forsaken shrines to Aesculapius, healing and divination are one.

The little saints of local fame are those who keep the broad current of everyday life flowing in the right direction. Often they are only names without a pedigree the peasants understand; their faces are kissed with no less reverence for that. Often fragments of contemporary history have become entangled in the legend.

The Aegean saint is not an object for contemplation, of self-enquiry in the western sense. He is not remote enough for that. His role is like that of an ordinary mortal over whom he enjoys the advantages of several special faculties; he is in touch with God on the one hand and man on the other—standing between them rather as a Platonic *daimon* than as anything else. He is an extra-terrestrial being domiciled on earth as a sort of heavenly vice-consul with the powers of a chargé d'affaires. This is a status that suits him perfectly for in it he commands reverence without servility; prayers and petitions to him have a man-to-man quality. And it is right that he should wear this half-human aspect—for has he not taken up his position upon the very altars of the Greek gods he supplanted and has he not inherited some of their more human and endearing characteristics? Sometimes like them he may find himself ever so slightly disposed to accept a bribe for his services—a silver dish for his altar, a candelabrum, a taper the size of a human limb. And where is the harm in all this if the influence he exercises is over a journey which does no harm to anyone, over a marriage prejudiced by illness, over a small business deal in contraband tobacco? Somebody has to lend us a hand with these problems.

The three most venerated relics of Rhodes—the hand of St John the Baptist (cut off by Luke who found the exhumed body too large to carry off whole): the cross made from the True Cross: and the picture of Our Lady of Phileremo—were carried off to Malta, whence the last Grand Master took them in 1798 to Russia. Of these I have little doubt that the wonder-working portrait of Our Lady was the most famous. Its history, unlike that of St John's hand, is obscure; the Knights apparently found it in place on their arrival in the island

and its reputation antedated the more general publicity it enjoyed when the eyes of all Christendom turned upon the famous Order's battles against the Saracens. Phileremo, to judge by the accounts of earlier travellers, was a well-established place of pilgrimage before the time of the Knights, and the picture had doubtless served generations of petitioners before the standard of St John flew over Rhodes. In times of danger it was customary to carry it into the city, where it lay in St Mark's, a church which had been founded by the Venetians; here, during the siege of 1522 a cannon-ball burst over the altar where the picture stood, killing several people, and the Grand Master, fearing for the safety of the relic, ordered it to be placed in the chapel of St Catherine which was inside the palace. As far as I know, nearly as much mystery surrounds it as surrounded the Colossus: there does not seem to be any record of how she looked—this latter-day Artemis, nor have any details of her miracles been preserved.

The little modern chapel on the summit of Phileremo is a ruin today, its battered walls still heaped with mountains of discarded Italian ammunition, water-bottles, bayonets and grenades; a few heavy carcases of anti-tank guns lie about forlornly under the trees, already so thickly overgrown that one might believe them to be all of a piece with the few fragments of Hellenic and Byzantine stone in the once sacred precincts. The architecture of the modern church is adequate but uninspired. In the single habitable room of the monastery lives a solitary Franciscan—a strange bird-like youth who rides a borrowed motor-bike and uses a piercing hairoil. He peddles a leaflet setting forth in brief the history of the church and carrying on its cover what purports to be a representation of Our Lady of Phileremo. But the whole business smells of premeditation and of unction. One feels the long arm of the propaganda office on one's shoulder, as one does in Capri.

Nevertheless in Greece there is room for everyone; travellers have already noted that in the neighbouring village of Cremasto the church is dedicated, unusually enough, to the Panaghia Katholiki, and there seems little doubt that the great panagyri of August is a faded memorial to the powers of Our Lady of Phileremo. Our Lady *in absentia* she should be called.

Is she descended from Artemis or from Athene Lindia—who was

once the most venerated Goddess of the island? It is hard to tell. Artemis crops up quite frequently today in the folklore of the peasantry, and I am reminded as I write that not far from here, beyond the grey stone slopes of Profeta—the road winding upwards through clement forest-land carpeted with red and white cistus, anemone, and great peonies—there is still a small monastery-site called Artamiti where, to judge by an inscription found thereabouts, once stood an ancient temple. She, like Athena, was a daughter of Zeus, and the loveless puritanism of the one perfectly matches the qualities of her step-sister, the giver of the fruitful olive.

But if Rhodes has lost her Lady of Phileremo she has gained another local saint whose fame is growing daily and who is well on the way to supplanting her in the general veneration. No literature has grown up around this new figure as yet, and no critical apparatus; the Orthodox Church itself seems a little puzzled as to where he fits in—at any rate no hagiographer has come forward with an explanation as to how Saul, a footsore apostle of Paul, managed to win himself a shrine in the shallow hills around Soroni.

Saint Soulas (as he is called in demotic) is supposed to have been a member of the party which, headed by Paul, was washed up in Rhodes on the way to Palestine. (At Lindos a little cove is still pointed out to one today as the actual landfall. During his short stay in Rhodes, Paul walked for miles each day, expounding the scripture to whoever would listen. His disciples followed his example, and among them Saul, who must have been something of a walker to reach Soroni, which is by no means near to Lindos. At any rate, here he found an ancient shrine with a warm spring—though unluckily legend has not preserved the name of the original tutelary God. The neighbouring villagers seemed to him in need of testimony as they were all heathens of the darkest dye; he tried adjuration, exhortation, and peroration without any success at all. They clave to their folly. He talked till he was hoarse, but they regarded him with the unmoved scepticism that we should all feel if a small, hairy foreigner with a beard, dressed poorly, with dusty feet and a funny pronunciation, tried to undo in one afternoon what had taken centuries of pious mumbo-jumbo to create—a complex of belief, comforting, homely as a salt-lick. Saul was at his wit's end to know how to cope with these obstinate and semi-literate peasants. Much against his will he was compelled to resort to a miracle. There were a number of people with sores about. He healed one out of hand by dipping him in the spring. 'Can your God do that?' he asked. The villagers took his point and came over to the true faith in a body.

I am not happy about this story; in the first place it seems to me that peasant belief has really muddled the issue. It seems to me that St Paul himself must be the hero of this widely-held belief—for his name was Saoul, or, in its ancient Greek form, Saulos. That the warm spring was already famous for its cures there is little doubt. Even today the locality is called in Greek στοῦ ψωριάρη. Furthermore the most common kind of sore in the Aegean seems to be caused by a parasitic substance which is contained in the bag at the root of the sponge; it is a common enough affliction among sponge-divers and can be cured only by bathing the sores in some mild astringent. The spring *could* have been famous for these cures long before St Paul appeared on the scene. In this context we should perhaps remember that Heracles was the common patron of hot springs and his name is connected with Lindos from times of the remotest antiquity; according to the ancient legend he, like Paul, arrived in Lindos one day, hungry after a long journey. With him was his son Hyllos. He asked a passing husbandman for food for the latter but met with curses. He therefore helped himself to one of the oxen with which the man was ploughing and breakfasted thereon with Hyllos, while the infuriated owner watched the pair from a safe distance and cursed them. This is said to have been the origin of the strange form of Heracles worship which once prevailed at Lindos. While the actual sacrifices were offered the officiating priest heaped curses and abuse on the name of the Hero, not haphazard but according to a fixed ritualistic order. There was apparently nothing like this in the rest of Greece and the saying 'Like Lindians at their sacrifice' became proverbial for all who used profane language in sacred places. Does a tenuous thread run through these detached fragments—or is it just that history itself, conditioned by place, repeats characteristic and familiar gestures, as a friend might?

It was however something more than the spirit of disinterested enquiry which led Gideon and I to embark on an expedition to

Soroni on the day of the saint's panagyri. For one thing the whole of Rhodes town would be there, and certainly all those among our friends who were not bound by administrative preoccupations. We decided to travel in the old town bus with the staff of the printing-house, who had all booked tickets one way, intending to sleep or dance away the night under the pines.

By nine o'clock the first buses have begun to rumble off down the blue road to Trianda, each loaded to the brim with holiday-makers, laughing, gesticulating or singing songs. Three big lorries, packed with Italians who are due for repatriation to Italy next week, pass through the town with streamers flying. These are Sienese farmers from the state farms around San Benedetto and they sing beautifully as they rumble by; a sharp, poignant singing which has something almost valedictory about it. This will be their last fiesta on the island, and the buses travel so slowly that one imagines they want to draw out their last view of Rhodes, to pack their memories with its green landscapes which will continue to haunt them perhaps in their own graceful homelands. Italy is beautiful, but it lacks the wild pang of the Greek landscape; it is tamed and domesticated—an essay in humanism. It is not the cradle of tragedy.

Our departure is not until midday. In the far corner of the square behind the market-place stands the machine in which we are to travel—a package-like municipal bus which at this moment is surrounded by an extremely angry crowd. One sight of those waving arms and flying fingers, and my heart sinks. It is obvious that something is wrong. Familiar faces loom up out of the dense press. The Baron Baedeker stands in his severe black clothes, clutching his step-ladder grimly, and shaking his head. Christ, the author, dressed in a white boater and a composition collar an inch wide is repeating something despairingly and waving a ticket. His voice cannot be heard above the hubbub. On the step of the bus, guarding the door-way, stands the conductor, viciously repelling boarders with his elbow. The crowd has clenched itself around him like a fist. At the head of it stands Manoli the linotype-setter, his eyes gleaming through his spectacles, his hands flying. He is obviously in charge of the boarding-party. Every few seconds, overcome by impatience, the crowd gives a lunge forward and he is driven like a battering ram into the conductor's side. The conductor, half-turning, fends him off with an elbow shouting 'I tell you no'. The argument is resumed until impatience sets in again and the crowd rears like a wave, only to break in vain against the sides of the dusty bus. Small eddies of violence are thrown off from inside the crowd itself—some of which have nothing to do with the main argument. For instance in one of these frantic lunges a man with a guitar has got himself entangled with his neighbour's coat-buttons; these have wrapped themselves round the guitar strings which are in danger of being broken. The press is so great however that the men cannot disengage and at every lunge they are carried forward in unison, one crying 'My guitar' in tones of anguish and other crying 'You fool'.

Reluctant to get caught up in this battle-scene we hang about on the outskirts of the crowd trying to get a clue as to the nature of the argument. It seems hopeless, so great is the noise and so continuous the flood of invention and rhetoric. Occasional snatches rise above the general uproar. 'I tell you I *have* got.' 'Everybody knows what it....' 'You should ... police would soon....' Another heave forward and another shuddering impact against the bus. A melancholy long-withdrawing roar of 'I tell you no' from the conductor.

Kostas, the Greek editor, comes staggering out of the mêlée to greet us breathlessly. 'The usual has happened', he says, when he can get his breath. 'There are forty people with tickets and only twenty seats. The bus company is always doing this.' At this a little man, quite beside himself with rage, comes up and shakes his fist at the boy, shouting: 'I tell you that is not true. I am in charge of the tickets. I can tell you that we only issued twenty. Here is my own.' He thrusts a soiled ticket under my nose. Kostas raises his shapely hands deprecatingly. 'Have you no shame,' he says, 'to shout so before foreigners?' The little man swallows and turns purple. 'They must hear the truth,' he splutters.

Christ has been edging his way towards us from the opposite corner of the crowd. He beckons to me, holding his straw boater in his hand. There is something he wishes to confide in me. We move to one side and put our faces together under his hat. In all that swelling hubbub we are like people trying to light a cigarette in a high wind; his voice is grave and troubled. 'May I tell you something in complete confidence?' It seems an unlikely place for an exchange of confidences but there is little to do except to agree. 'Manoli,' he says, 'is responsible for the trouble. You know we print the tickets for the bus company in books of five hundred? Before dispersing the type last week he took the serial numbers of the tickets and printed twenty extra for himself and his friends. He is taking a large party with him to Soroni and they are all travelling free—perhaps he has told them that he bought the tickets for them as a present: but it is more likely,' and here Christ's voice sank to a dark and diabolical register, 'it is more likely that he made them pay *him*.' His dark eyes dilated as he watched my face for reactions. 'If,' he goes on, 'you wish to prove it you will see that he has printed his own tickets on different paper—the coarse Italian newsprint. The bus tickets are on the imported paper.' Having delivered himself of this vital piece of information he replaces his hat and retreats to a far corner of the crowd to see what will happen—like a man who has lit a fuse and wishes to keep a safe distance from the explosion.

Gideon groans when I pass on this piece of information. 'It would be Manoli again. I suppose it's up to you to quell him.'

The problem is how to get at him through the press, for the argument has reached renewed heights of violence. Manoli's grandmother has appeared, a whiskered old lady who brandishes a rolled umbrella over his shoulder at the conductor, and who is backed up by a couple of old beldams—nuns from the convent, carrying baskets. Things are getting lively. The conductor is getting rattled too, and shows some disposition to make use of the starting-handle of the bus which lies behind him on the step. I take a deep breath and wade into the crowd pushing and scrambling breathlessly forward inch by inch until with my outstretched fingers I can just grab the sleeve of Manoli. He shakes me off impatiently once or twice until he realises who I am. Then he grins and turns sheepishly towards me and enables me to shout: 'You have forged the tickets. All is known.' A momentary flicker of astonished anger flits across his face and is almost immediately replaced by an expression of desperation. The crowd heaves once more and we are swept apart, Manoli to plunge into the midriff of the bus-conductor, I to be sucked back into that sea of vociferous holiday-makers. Manoli faces a terrible dilemma now, for if his friends find that he has sold them non-existent places on the bus they will most likely dismember him; on the other hand it must be clear that if he persists in his folly Gideon and I will either expose him or call a policeman. For a moment or two he marks time as he thinks over these alternatives, plunging forward with every push from the crowd behind, and shouting just as vigorously. Then the situation is saved as if by a miracle by the appearance of a completely empty bus which draws up alongside with a shriek, while a tousled head leans out and a voice shouts the equivalent of 'Any more for the Skylark'?

This is a bus which has been taken off the road for repairs; but the festival of St Soulas has proved too tempting for the solitary mechanic to whom the repairs have been entrusted. Half way through the morning he has decided to defer the work and to visit Soroni on his own. But a natural generosity of spirit, plus the fact that he has been drinking, caused him, on seeing the surging crowd round our bus, to stop and offer a lift to those who could not find places. Manoli is overcome with relief and joy and loses not a moment to save his face and his pocket. 'This way,' he shouts, and grabbing his grand-mother hustles her in the direction of the empty bus, while his rumpled party of guests follow suit with all despatch. We mount our bus now with comparative ease and sink breathlessly into our seats, to watch Manoli's party swept gesticulating and shouting out of sight. Our conductor expresses his relief by crossing himself. 'Another moment,' he says, 'and I should have had to hit him.'

So we set out. After a perilous journey (for Paul the driver is known for his competitive spirit), we approach Soroni. One by one the lorries rumble forward throwing up a wave of dust on either side. Countless walkers are met and passed on this strip of the road, for the most part peasants bearing baskets of fresh fruit to sell at the fair. Merrily honk the horns. Despite the choking clouds of dust the shouting and banter between those in the lorries and those on foot is continuous. We pass a dilapidated old cart in the back of which Manoli the fisherman lies at ease, surrounded by his family and a few select friends. At one point we are pelted with flowers by a dozen young girls. At another an elderly peasant, with a crate full of turtle-doves on his head, flings a handful of sweets in through the window, one of which cracks a lens in the Baron Baedeker's spectacles. He is most provoked, and for a moment one has the feeling that he is going to say something peculiarly offensive and to the point. He restrains himself however and says: 'What people. What people,' in sad and reproving tones as he turns the damaged spectacles over and over in his fingers.

We bowl over the crown of the last hillock and there before us lies the site of the shrine; the ground slopes away on all sides in a series of thinly-forested hillocks, leaving a level space of perhaps four acres. Here the villagers of Soroni have performed their usual task in digging a dozen large pits which will be filled with glowing charcoal and over which sheep and oxen will be roasted. At strategic points, too, huge bundles of dry brushwood lie piled, waiting for the night. Lofty pine-trees give a good deal of shade, and here out-door cafés have sprung up all round the shrine, which looks something like a small provincial bus-station. Paul jockeys us out of the line of lorries and we bump across the dusty soil toward the cover of the trees where he draws up with a triumphant smile. Everybody piles out of the bus into the sunny afternoon light, eager to see what is going on.

The sky above the eastern hollows is suffused with clouds of pinkish dust kicked up by the heels of mules; apparently some of the races have already started, as one can discern the gesticulating figures who ride them, with coloured scarves tied round their heads. The course itself has been squared out neatly with tent-pegs, and in one corner, on a wooden dais, sit the Brigadier and senior members of his staff, half choked with dust, and busily trying to memorise speeches in demotic which they will have to deliver at the prizegiving. To the westward, under the pines, stand groups of black-coated figures—each looking for all the world like a spiny black hedgehog in the shadow; this must be a cluster of choirs from various parts of the island. The low grumble of their chanting can be dimly heard above the prodigious hubbub of the crowd which fills the middle distance. They too have a dais from which prizes will be distributed, gaily decked with Greek and English flags stencilled all over it in water-paint. Overhead is a roof of plaited palm-leaves which contributes a faintly central-African flavour to the scene.

Around the shrine itself (which resembles an ant-hill) streets have begun to improvise themselves as if a boom-town were suddenly growing up under one's very eyes. Yet the streets are lined, not with houses, but with stalls packed to the sky with sweetmeats, lemonade, almonds, cheese. There is hardly an unfamiliar face here, for every itinerant pedlar of Rhodes has made the pilgrimage on foot. Here for example is the old one-armed man who trundles a barrow about the town, loaded with chestnuts which he roasts on a brazier; I have often watched the skill with which he fills the little paper bags, shouting all the time in a deep croaky voice, 'Chestnuts . . . Chestnuts.' Next to him stand several of the itinerant fresh-water sellers, each with his little white municipal cart shaded by a cluster of green. Next again come the sweet-meat sellers, shouting as if their hearts were broken 'Sweeeeets. . . . Sweeeeets.' There is chocolate, nougat, almond paste, marzipan, pistachio nougat as well as those heavier confections like *galactobouriko* and *baklava,* which Gideon claims are made from waste blotting paper and honey. At intervals too stand the *loukumades* experts, their long spoons at the ready to seize the roasted doughnut when it is fried brown and crisp, and then to duck it in honeyed sauce. Small children stand round these stalls breathing in the flowery scent of the ovens with appreciation, each holding a slip of paper on his small brown palm, waiting for the hot sweetmeat to be plumped into it. Here too pine-nuts are being roasted, and there spools of mastic (the Aegean chewing-gum) are being wound out and pressed into shapes, or being merely loaded into spoons and dropped into glasses of water.

At one end of this gallery of smells and sound is a section inhabited by a number of ferociously unshaven gentlemen, each stripped to the buff and liberally coated with soot. They dwell in an absolute forest of entrails out of which they stick their heads from time to time in order to utter a shriek before they return to their work at the spits; all round them on biscuit tins loaded with fine charcoal roast the entrails of Gideon's luckless sheep and lambs. Every sort of offal is here accorded expert treatment; tripe is wound round and round a giant spit, plugged with clove, nutmeg and garlic, and is roasted slowly; sheep's entrails receive horizontal roasting, being basted quickly with fat and lemon juice as they turn. Testicles, hearts and livers are all given an exacting professional attention and distinctive treatment on spits of various kinds. The cooks themselves carry long knives between their lips which gives them a terrifying look, and they dart from side to side of their stalls, now shaving off a tiny piece of beef to see if it tastes right, now banging a whole cluster of kebab off a spit on to a tin plate. They seem never to stop shouting for a moment, even when their knives are between their teeth. The attitudes they strike are magnificent, gladiatorial. Pools of hot dripping fall in the deep dust beneath the stalls, and here whole colonies of cats and dogs lounge, waiting for tit-bits. The pandemonium which reigns the whole length of this street is indescribable; but set back twenty yards on either side of it, the cafés are less noisy. Chairs and tables have sprung up like mushrooms everywhere, and here the peasant families have seated themselves in bright semicircles to drink and eat. Here and there, too, small bevies of musicians are tuning up their accordions, guitars and violins, standing back to back to play a few stray phrases from time to time. Somewhere a big drum is banging, slow and paunch-like, which suggests that already a dance has begun, but I cannot see where; meanwhile the upper air is hoarse with the sickening braying of asses and the fever-shrill bleating of sacrificial lambs.

On the high ground where the green grass is thickest and where the line of myrtle and arbutus begins, lorries are slowly straying, like lost camels, looking for good camping-sites. Here whole families have unpacked their belongings, spread coloured rugs and pillows, and have settled down with no intention of moving before to-morrow. Stately peasant matrons are unpacking their squamous litters of small children, and their saddle bags full of bottles and cans and immense loaves of home-made bread. I wander in this forest of human beings with the loving detachment of a child in a familiar countryside, drinking it all in—even the savour of the harsh reddish dust which coats the air and dries the throat: all the weird mixture of smells which together compose the anthology of a Greek holiday under the pines—petrol, garlic, wine and goat.

For a while I sit myself down under a tree, the better to study this crowded canvas, in every corner of which simultaneous and totally disconnected scenes are being played. Mehmet Bey, who has obviously succeeded in running a good cargo into Trianda bay, is busy unloading an enormous chest into the gaping suitcases of the dozen or so pedlars who are doubtless his agents; beads, mirrors, rings, combs, cards of Turkish embroidery, and various childish confections in celluloid, like small propellers mounted on sticks. (Waved from side to side, the propellers revolve with a satisfactory furry noise.) The children have thrown themselves upon the cart like dogs at a bear. They are beaten off. They return. Mehmet Bey pulls off his gaucho's hat and makes ineffectual sweeps at them as he tries to calculate with one half of his mind how much stock he is giving to each pedlar. A little to the left some children are pelting with crusts a lunatic, who is doubtless attached to one of the café's as a luck-bringer: or perhaps he has come to he healed by the Saint. To the west, I observe the Baron Baedeker working like a beaver. Business is evidently booming. Everyone wants his or her photograph taken. The Baron has set up his headquarters against the whitewashed side of a dais—which makes an admirable reflector. On to it he has put up his only backcloth which is, I must say, most suitable to the time and place. It is a garish picture of an aeroplane with holes cut in the canvas in which the sitter or sitters can insert their heads, and so be photographed in flight, as it were. The peasants are delighted by this fantasy and argue furiously with each other about whose turn it is next. The aeroplane itself is of a very improbable kind: I doubt whether Bleriot would have dared to cross the channel in it. Nevertheless the whole conception is most successful and attracts admiring smiles from everyone.

The Mufti is wandering gravely in the crowd clad in a new turban and his elastic-sided boots; beside him I notice Hoyle and General Gigantes. They have been buying *kolouria*—bread cooked in circlets[1]—and each wears two or three of them on his wrist like bangles. Hoyle is discoursing with waves of his unencumbered hand, his spotted bow tie behind his ear, his coat flapping loose. If I am any judge of character I should say that he was hunting for the roast-pits over which by now a dozen sheep are sizzling, and more than one whole ox. They lie beyond his field of vision, however, on the slope at my back. Here the heat has burnt a great shimmering hole in the atmosphere, for the charcoal is red hot. I am pleased to see that

[1] Stuck with sesame seed.

among the turnspits are some of the members of the printing-house staff, stripped to the waist. They kneel about the pits, talking gravely, and from time to time making minor adjustments of height or speed to the spit. There are about a dozen of these pits scattered about in a rough semicircle. Two have oxen roasting on them fixed upon enormous cast-iron bits which are turned by an old-fashioned spring-winding device such as one sees sometimes in old English farms. These spits revolve with a slow dry clicking sound until the spring runs down—a process lasting perhaps three hours. In this little corner there is not noise—or comparatively little; a heavy air of professional preoccupation hangs over the scene. The turnspits all wear piratical handkerchiefs round their heads, and lounge about outside the range of the heat, talking gravely to the sound of the ticking spits. Occasionally a volunteer approaches a pit, shielding his face, and cuts a slice of meat from the animal; this is gravely eaten by the jury of ruffians who sit around, shaking their heads, and offering ripe comment and advice. Once in a while the oxen are basted, when a terrific hissing is heard and a column of charcoal dust rises into the air, rich with the scent of fat and blood. 'Ah!' cries everyone with satisfaction.

Prolonged cheering and clapping to the east now suggests that the mule-races are over, and through the clouds of dust vague figures can be seen to mount the dais and bow as they accept something from the hands of the Brigadier. It is too far to hear the speeches and the toasts. Gideon emerges from the press, panting, with a celluloid propellor whirring in each hand. He sinks down beside me to mop his brow and to grope in his pockets for some nougat. 'Not bad, is it?' he says. 'There must be fifteen thousand people here. Kostas says that Manoli's bus ran into a tree and they all had to walk.'

There is, after all, some justice in the world, to catch up with the wicked. Luckily, however, nobody seems to have been hurt—at any rate Manoli at this moment is having his photograph taken, with a baby on each knee.

Two more big drums have begun to beat with punctual emphasis and one circle of dancers is beginning to form below me on the slope. They are gathered round a cluster of music-makers, drummer, violinist, clarinettist and guitarist, who stand back to back, heads inclined towards one another. The dances always unfold like this from the centre, in a flower-like pattern. For a moment or so the participants stand in a semi-circle about the musicians, listening with lowered heads and nodding to establish the time: then they begin, slowly, hesitantly, to dance, the subtle meshes of their footwork calculated, deliberate, matching itself to the scribbling of the strings. Then, one by one, they appear to catch fire; their heads rise on their shoulders, their tip-tilted chins begin to carry upwards from the very ankles the smiles of recognition which light their faces. As the circle moves slowly about its centre—the little statuary group of musicians—it begins to establish the authority of the rhythm, rising, you feel, as much from the warm dust of the earth as from the music that is being made. In a little while too, the musicians begin to feel the established circuit, and raise their heads with a sort of pleased relief; they relinquish the melody to its own created momentum and allow it to be carried away on the tide of the dancing feet. Meanwhile the circle itself is growing as new dancers break into the circumference at every point, taking up the rhythms from the twinkling feet of their neighbours', smoothly as candles taking a light from one other. Soon the whole organism has developed its own life and swallowed up the individuality of each of its members, accepting it into the rhythm of the whole, which now moves round and round the live hollow centre of music with the queer archaic peristaltic movements of the *kalamatiano*—the most graceful and earth-coaxing of all Greek dances. From where I sit I cannot hear the highly syncopated jabber of the violins with any clarity: but the spicy afternoon air begins to tremble at the thump of the big drum which marks the end of each bar with a cavernous wallop. The circle wheels and sways, ever-widening as new dancers surrender to its magical appeal.

I am about to go down and get a closer view of the dancing when my attention is distracted by a new development. It is apparently time for the litany to be read at the shrine, for across the dry brown sward from the direction of the trees comes a small straggling procession of villagers, some holding aloft ikons painted on banners. They are headed by the dark figures in clerical robes and tall hats. Ten paces before them walks a small boy, diligently tapping a triangle. The priests are perhaps chanting, for their lips move; but so great is the hum of the crowd that the remain as yet beyond ear-shot.

This little procession advances in measured fashion towards the shrine, at the door of which a dense crowd has gathered—like the shapeless clotting of bees at the entrance to a hive. From time to time it is shaken by internal convulsions which throw up the figures of those (either the most curious, or the most in need of the Saint's magic) who wish to station themselves before the iron grille which marks the entrance to the grotto. But by the time the priests approach a pathway clears itself in the dark mass of bodies and a hoarse murmur rises. The doors open and the procession descends; and I am close enough to them now to hear the hollow resonance of voices echoing in the cave, amplified by the hollowness and the presence of water. Candle-light flickers warmly where there was lately nothing but a dark hole; and the sour spiral chanting of the monks begins in a lower key. Question and response, separated by a semitone. Draughts of incense sweep up through the gloom, over the water. A shiver runs through the crowd. Lips move in prayer. Everyone makes the sign of the cross. With a bitter struggle I succeed in elbowing my way as far as the iron grille. From here I can gaze down the steps into the grotto. The incense clouds rising from the water gives one the impression that it has issued, boiling, from the earth. Yet two or three elderly women, clad in white shifts, are standing dispiritedly in it, and beyond them I catch a glimpse of a mongoloid youth being held by two old crones dressed like nuns. They form a strange bedraggled group as they stand thigh-deep in the concrete basin, the candle-light flicker-ing on the whites of their eyes. The chanting goes on punctuated by a series of respectful groans and sighs from the crowd—though whether they express religious emotion or annoyance at the heat I cannot tell.

I feel a touch on my arm. It is Mills, who has fought his way into the crowd to see the saint at work. 'All my patients,' he says in a whisper, 'I want to see if the old man can do better than I can.' 'Materialist,' I whisper back. The immersions have begun within the grotto. The swishing of water almost drowns the chanting of the priests. The mongol is making some semi-articulate protests but the two old nuns have him fast in their talons; all three subside in a scrambling heap in one corner of the bath.

'I do not know why we are standing here,' says a hoarse voice, 'The miracles take place two days after the service, you all know—never on the spot.' I recognise the butcher-poet who once read me his epic in my office. He has a bunch of spring onions in one hand and a propeller in the other; he seems a trifle intoxicated. 'At least,' he continues, baring his teeth in a grin, 'so the priests would have us believe.' Several people turn their heads and hiss for silence. He eats an onion loudly and puts on an air of scornful scepticism. For villagers today this attitude (so far from what they really believe or feel) represents, so they think, intellectual emancipation. It has come down to them through the village schoolmaster and lawyer, those heirs to the vague radicalism and agnosticism which is poisoning the whole source of our culture. In the butcher-poet I recognise the kind of sceptic who, while he is busy telling you that God does not exist, nevertheless is the first to cross himself if someone would mention the death of an acquaintance.... And yet, as Mills says, the real trouble with both reason and mumbo-jumbo is that they are equally suspect. They are both fogged mirrors, badly in need of cleaning. But the ignorant man can get nothing from either—not even a reflection of his own stupidity.

The suppliants have emerged from the pool now, and are drying themselves briskly with towels, their faces still turned in the direction of the altar from which the sounds of prayer still issue, accompanied by great draughts of incense. No miracle appears to have taken place, yet as my butcher-poet says, the effects of the service are often not felt for a day or two afterwards. It is as if the saint needed perhaps time to think things over—to convince himself of the validity of the claims made upon him.

Outside the shrine the shades of evening have begun to fall. The sun is westering behind the mountains, plunging slowly down into the sea beyond Tilos. The sky is beginning to take, softly, wash by wash, the subdued violet tones of evening which slant across the leaves of the trees, and begin to fill out the shadows of objects with darker volume. A light breeze springs up, scattering the dust raised by the brown feet of the dancers and tilting the smoke which rises from the pyres of roasting flesh. We make our way slowly across the violet slopes, so plump and rosy now from the encroaching night, both of us consumed by conflicting curiosities. The dancing-competitions have begun in earnest now. Three hissing carbide lamps fling down a chalky blaze of light upon the brown earth floor where the champion dancers are to compete. A dense crowd has formed a semi-circle, almost engulfing the raised wooden dais upon which we can see the long-suffering face of the Brigadier, flanked by various mayors, dignitaries and churchmen. Other dancing circles have sprung up all over the valley now, but this is the central one; and as we reach it we can hear the heralds shouting aloud the name 'Embona', which raises a great hail of clapping and cheering—for the Embona dancers are reputed to be the finest in Rhodes.

They plunge out of the shadow of the trees with a queer jigging movement—a long line of brightly dressed girls like circus ponies, tossing their heads. Each holds the girdle of the one before her. The line is led by a tall and graceful young man, clad in a white shirt and in tapering trousers, cut something like our riding-breeches, who shuffles a tambourine. The girls wear high boots of calf-skin, and their dark blue pleated dresses are picked out with concentric rings of brighter colour which throw into relief the white shirts they wear and the vivid looped head-scarves. The long line flows out into the arena with this curious loping shuffle to the jingle of the tambourine. Then it halts and dresses itself by the right. The young man steps forward, holding the hand of the endmost dancer and raising the tambourine above his head, pauses, watchful, tense. Then he cuts the air downward with vivid emphasis and the music bursts into life. The dancers drink in two bars before they follow it, each springing forward and backward with the queer see-sawing movement of the dance called 'the cradle'. It is taken at top-speed by these practised village-girls and is something out of the ordinary—though perhaps not the most graceful of the Greek dances I have seen: it has strange elliptical figures which fill in the main structure of its form—a swaying, cradle-like jig, and the formation they adopt is that of a half-moon. This, it is true, gives them a certain mobility and enables the chain to break the measure and flow from side to side of the floor with small shuffling steps, to take up the dance-position in a new corner. But always at the head of the line, capering like a satyr and jingling his tambourine, dances the young man in his soft jackboots.

The dust, too, has begun to rise in clouds from the hard floor of baked earth, so that the crescent of dancers seen from the shadows beyond the plane-trees look like some coloured planet whirring on its course, and surrounded by its own dense atmosphere. 'Come,' says Mills, 'Let's go and see what old Gideon's doing. I've seen the *susta* often enough.' But it is easier said than done, for the dark press of faces behind us offer no hope of an easy egress. We are walled in by the bodies of the crowd. The critics follow the dancers with a passionate intentness, some beating time with their heads. The whole dance-floor has become one swelling cloud of reddish dust by now in the centre of which (their faces preoccupied and remote) ride the dancers, their flower-like bodies carried forward on the music like river-narcissus. The warm dust-cloud has risen to the height of their top-boots, giving them the ghostly appearance of goddesses being born from the earth itself, and aided only by their struggles, and the unearthly music of the fiddles which torment them. The young dance-leader alone raises his feet above the dust-cloud, capering and shaking his tambourine, proudly showing his twinkling heels. His goat-like eyes glitter.

I am reminded, as so often in Greece, that dancing is never a performance so much as a communal rite—the transmission of an enigmatic knowledge which the musician has summoned up from below the earth. It flows outward through the dancing feet which are building the dusty circle, stitch by stitch, like a fabric being woven: step by step like a city being built: and the darker circle outside, the lookers-on, gradually absorb the rhythm which triumphs over them by sheer repetition—being laid down on the consciousness like successive coats of a thrilling colour. One can watch the crowd being drawn into such a dance man by man, impelled by something like that gravitational law which decrees that autumn windfalls should plunge towards the centre of the earth when they are ripe. The vivid circle of the dancers is the centre towards which the audience leans, its blood quickened by the notation of the music—itself (who knows?) a transcription in terms of cat-gut and wind of profounder melodies which the musician has quarried from his native disenchantments and the earth.

But while we have been watching, the darkness has fallen in

earnest; westward the pines still describe themselves against the sky, but very faintly. To those lucky couples who lie about on the grassy slopes it must seem as if they were looking up at the heavens from the bottom of an inkwell, so deep is the blue darkness, yet striped here and there like a leopard's skin with the sulphurous patches of yellow fire from the great bundles of dry gorse and twigs which have now been set alight all along the circumference of this sunken valley. We walk across that dark hinterland, Mills and I, stopping from time to time to watch other teams of dancers in action, some dancing in the eerie light of lanterns, some by these crackling furnaces of thorn and light brush. Everywhere the light scoops out rosy pools in which the dancers swim, as if in an element lighter than air, while the pink puffs of dust which flow upwards seem as light as foam beneath their feet. And everywhere the thumping of the drums only underlines the sullen vibrations of the earth itself under so many moving feet. Everywhere outside lie pastures of ink, where movement is small, individual, owing nothing to the group hypnosis of these dancing circles. Candles flicker in the bushes where the peasant families are making their arrangements for the night; some of the children, after being put to bed, have escaped again into the magical darkness to join some rapt circle of dance critics. Their mothers' plaintive voices can be heard calling 'Spiro! . . . Pavlos! . . . where are you?'

Once we blunder into an untethered mule, and once Mills trips over a prostrate body which groans and curses in accents jocund with garlic and mastika. The light is better in the long main-street of the boom-town, which by now resembles an oriental bazaar lit by pressure-lamps which have the same ghastly brilliance as old-fashioned gas-lighting. Here Mehmet is busy haranguing people from a stall covered with carded embroidery. Business is still brisk, but it is chiefly the old people who are still busy arguing, assessing and buying goods. The young have been drawn off by the dancing. Christ is busy before a pastry-cook's stall, buying some sweet cakes for his old mother who is sitting at a table on the slope peering into the gloom eagerly with those cataract-covered eyes which somehow look abnormally keen and clear-sighted.

On one of the dance-floors Sergeant Croker is in action, dancing with a comical stiffness, but with faultless accuracy, cheered on by an appreciative crowd. I have heard that he is engaged to a Greek girl now and has learned the language passably well. His fellow-dancers are a queer mixture; some are tradesmen from Rhodes town, and some villagers from one of the remoter villages. Croker's cap has fallen off. Prolonged shouts and cheers. 'I've never seen old Croker dance,' says Mills with admiration. 'He must be as tight as a drum.' It is true that as the Sergeant swings round into the light one notices a distinct glassiness of expression, but this may be accounted for by the intricacy of the evolutions he is performing. They need some con-centration. Hoyle suddenly appears at my elbow, gnome-like, pant-ing, delighted. 'I've been looking for you everywhere,' he says. 'This crowd is rather far gone. Isn't Croker wonderful? When he went on to dance people began to jeer and shout at him. All of a sudden a Herculean figure bounded into the ring—Gigantes. He took Croker's arm and they danced together for a while, and of course the jeers changed to cheers for the General. Don't you think that was a graceful and delightful thing to do—typically *Gigantesque?*' Croker is by now having his full meed of cheers. He looks as if he could go on until morning. The General, by showing him public favour, has endeared him to everyone. 'Where the devil is Gideon?' says Mills irritably. Hoyle has lost track of him. 'He said he was going to get his fortune told. Which means that he was going to hunt for a good wine.'

So we turn our steps towards the cafés under the trees, and it is not long before we run Gideon to earth in one of them. There is not very much light up here, but our friends seem to know where we are; within a few minutes of our arrival little gifts of food begin to arrive for us. They are handed to the waiter in the darkness outside and he places them before us, whispering in our ears the names of the donors as he does so. Mehmet sends us a platter of black olives and some paprika which has been steeped in vinegar—a favourite appetiser of Hoyle's. Christ sends us a noggin of black wine and some white roses, while Manoli unexpectedly appears in person bearing a wooden bowl piled with crystallised fruit and green apples. 'What a country,' says Gideon. 'One only has to look hungry, to sit around for a while, and people just send you things.'

After a while we are joined by Sand and the Baron Baedeker, who converge upon us from opposite directions. Sand is his usual taciturn self, but the Baron is a man transformed; he has a very weak head, and has been given a glass of wine by one of his clients. He will normally only speak English when his courage is at meridian. Now he refuses to speak anything else. 'Ah, if I had *flesh*,' he keeps repeating, 'If I had *flesh* I could take a picture of you all . . . piff.' It is too dark, alas, for his camera, though he climbs his step-ladder rather unsteadily and peers at us through a finder-lens once, just to be sure. His grave and gentle face bears an expression of unwonted animation. He accepts a small glass of wine with a simper and says to Hoyle: 'I have my circumcision in Turkish town tomorrow—you wish to see?'

We are well into the second can of retsina when a messenger comes panting into the circle of light with a message from the General. We are urgently bidden to the village banquet which is being given in honour of the representatives of Greece by the mayor and alder-men of Soroni. Gideon and Hoyle gaze at one another with some misgiving, for a banquet means toasts and probably speeches; however, if Gigantes has sent for them, go they must. For my part I am loth to be tied down by any one entertainment on a night like this; I prefer to remain free to wander. And Mills makes some excuse which must be truthful, for he gets up and disappears into the darkness.

After parting from the others, and wandering round for a while, I stumble upon a little group of figures whose immobility in the midst of all that noise and movement is almost shocking. I am drawn by something like as sense of impending danger towards the little construction of reeds and plane-leaves—a makeshift shelter—inside which, posed as if for the crude Nativity of some medieval painter crouches a group of peasants. A horn-lantern with one feeble candle alight in it stands upon the ground, throwing its waxen light upon a half-circle of faces whose blank uncomprehending anguish, devoid of recognition, seems trained downwards, as if eternally fixed, upon the figure of a small child lying upon a dirty peasant blanket which is drawn back over his knees. He is dressed in a shirt of vivid white-ness open at the throat, and he gazes out beyond the circle of faces at the sky with some of that gentle vagueness which the human face wears at the approach of death. At the fringes of that puddle of sallow light crouch the patient sleeping forms of goats and a rough-coated sheep-dog. To the left a kneeling woman with her bright scarf drawn across her face and her head bent. But dominating the foreground is a figure I recognise, clad in much-patched blue trousers and a dark open jacket which is barred across the chest by the heavy woollen vest of the fisherman. It is the other Manoli—the old sailor whom I visit every day on my way to work. Those toil-swollen fingers are resting on his knees as if to spare his rheumatic joints some of the strain of kneeling on the hard ground. I say that I recognise him, but the truth is that the figure I know to be his, bears to the Manoli I know the resemblance of a plaster effigy.

His features seem to have been stripped of all meaning—the gesture, mobility, or repose, which alone give an accidental significance to the inert structure of flesh and bone, and which carry on them the index of the human personality, its masks. He crouches there like a figure stamped on some old leaden seal; and while my own startled senses clearly interpret his physical attitude as one of pain and misgiving, to someone else casually passing, he might seem to be like a man who has just been deafened by an explosion which has scattered the whole sum of human expressions by which his face might register some idea of its magnitude. The very earth seems deaf around the little group, fixed in the attitudes of a forgotten tableau around the flickering lantern. As I come nearer I understand the meaning of this graven immobility. They are holding their breath for the child, trying to stare out of countenance the death that they can seen on his face; which rises noiselessly within him like a column of water rising in a well. A little circle of villagers have closed in about the actors, forming a web of human heads, a circle of compassionate helpless witnesses. All are silent. The whole scene has the veridic fixity of an old master—though the figures breathe, and though one recognises the brush which has so thoughtfully, so masterfully painted them in as the brush of pain itself. Some of the men have the faces of those whom shock has somewhat sobered; one holds a mattress, one a bottle of wine, and even these objects so listlessly held in hands whose very pose suggests the uselessness of all action, seem somehow lost to common context. They are like the wreckage left behind after an invasion of the senses by all the armies of the unknown.

The child himself wears a cold original chalky bloom; he breathes, but there are long spaces between each breath, during which he gazes with an expression of almost voluptuous detachment and purity at the outer night, giving little visible sign that it is exactly here—in the spaces between breaths, that the intrusion of something so unforseen as death is to be feared. Yet each sip of the spicy air is drawn to his lungs with a languorous burden—a deep sigh, hanging like a bead of water to the lips of a pitcher: it trembles and falls; and after a long wait another is drawn from the inexhaustible treasury of the darkness, to fill his veins with oxygen. It is scarcely visible, this process. He breathes as a flower is said to breathe. I can see the white tip of a pointed ear above his collar. His hair has been cropped close, like that of all village children in summer, to guard him against ringworm. The two dark eyes—one cannot say that they are expressionless: it is rather that their range of focus, the depth of their experience, has suddenly widened to include a new horizon, a wealth of new preoccupations based in a magical stillness, a terrific but unstudied world-weariness.

In the earlier darkness and confusion which reigned during the setting up of the outer encampments on the slope a lorry had swerved aside and passed over him as he lay asleep. The little fringe of faces moves slowly, heavily from side to side—like the movement of a shelf of seaweed in some submarine calm. In the face of that terrible considered breathing the breath of these frightened peasants has itself become shortened—too precious to waste on the usual whispers or lamentations. As for the child, he seems already to be entering that class of material objects whose context has been torn from them by the force of the tragedy—all these bottles held half-empty in still fingers, the idle propellor of celluloid which his brother still holds in a thoughtless fist, the burning candle-stump. His mother repeats his name from time to time under her breath but without conviction— as if she were trying it for the first time. Though she crouches with lowered head most of the time there are moments when she will straighten her back and, as if to knock the memory forever into her reason, as one would drive a nail into an oak, she bangs upon her forehead twice with the knuckles of a clenched fist, uttering a hoarse cry of pathetic incomprehensibility, which fades out into the deafness of that death-divining circle of faces as soon as it is uttered.

It is strange how passion held in restraint burst, so to speak, upwards into the very musculature of the human body, as if it must at all costs exteriorise itself. The heavy rope-like muscles of Manoli's body, already swollen and contorted by rheumatism, have further tightened under the pressure of unexpressed feeling and of shock. It is as if in some old house, ruined by damp, the arterial system—the plumbing—had been revealed by a fallen wall, or by the incursions of damp or snow. Yet he crouches limply, hands unclenched, gazing with a dumb and sightless longing at the boy stretched under the blanket. It is as if someone had drawn a wet sponge across everything else in the world leaving only this circle of fading light and the characters which peopled it as the whole content of his thoughts.

All this, which takes so long to describe in words, is seen and apprehended in the space of a few seconds—for in a dozen short paces I have reached the crowd, which has the curious (sour earthbound) smell that I recognise as the smell of human beings suffering from anxiety. Mills is already there; but he is crouching on his knees and is hidden by the onlookers. Those quick sensitive fingers have already explored his subject with the tact and deftness that is their special gift. He kneels for a second to watch the child, his chin on his hand, his face puzzled. Then he rises to his feet and turning catches sight of me. He clears his throat and shoulders his way through the crowd to me, to take my arm and lead me into the darkness beyond the tableau, saying: 'Good. You can help.' We were already hurrying down the slope when he adds: 'Someone's gone to phone for an ambulance, but I don't trust them. Or the phone may be locked. It may take ages. Will you take the car and go up to the Hospital and see that they get the message? I think the kid's had it.' He stops in surprise for we are suddenly bathed in the moonlight, which has brimmed over and is filling the dark bowl of the valley, dredging up solid objects and giving them shape—as if some great lake of darkness were being slowly drained: cars, shining bicycles, tents and hoardings are being reclaimed one by one. 'I needn't come any further. You can see the car under the trees there. Take the keys.'

The wheel of the little racing-car is slippery with dew, but she starts readily enough. In a moment I am bumping and chattering down the coast road towards the sea, which swims up towards me in the moonlight, glittering and peaceful. The hills begin to skim away on every side now, taking up new positions to the north and south, until at last I clear them and reach the coast road which turns sharply right and runs along through the mulberry-groves and sleeping villages towards Rhodes. On the long road leading to Trianda I catch sight of a white floating object out there on the coast road, flickering between the hedges as if recorded on a strip of old moving-film. It is the ambulance. I draw across the road and hear the sweet tinkle of its bell gradually becoming louder as it approaches through the trees. It flutters towards me like a great white moth and stops. The driver and the duty-nurse are perched up in the front seat waiting for me. The message got through. I tell them as briefly as I can what they are to expect and they nod curtly. The driver crosses himself. Then I stand back and the ambulance plunges off down the road to Soroni, its sweet cloying bell ringing it away into the distance like a messenger from the stern world of duties and penalties let loose upon this elegaic God-befuddled landscape.

Between Trianda and Mixi the road reaches the sea for the first time, and here the beaches have been swept by the moon until the floor of pebbles and sand glitters as if it were slippery with the mucus of frogspawn. It is warm and there is not a soul about. In a moment I have shed my clothes and am swimming out across the golden bars of moonlight, feeling the soft foamy commotion of water drumming on my sides—the peerless warmth of that summer sea. The light filters down a full fathom or more to where, on the dark blackboard of weed, broken here and there by dazzling areas of milk-white sand, the fish float as if dazed by their own violet shadows which follow them back and forth, sprawling across the sea's floor. Or perhaps it is the blinding shimmer of phosphorus which outlines my own swimming body as it plunges towards them throwing out sparks. I swim for a moment or two and then turn on my back to watch the sky through wet eyelashes and lying there, arms behind my head, on that resilient tideless meadow of water, I see in my mind's eye the whole panorama of our Rhodian life, made up of a thousand different scenes and ages, all turning before me now as if on the slow turntable of the four seasons.

In Rhodes we have been the willing bondsmen of the marine

Venus—the figure that sits up there alone in the Museum, disre-
garded, sightless; yet somehow we have learned to share that timeless,
exact musical contemplation—the secret of her self-sufficiency—
which has helped her to outlive the savage noise of wars and change,
to maintain unbroken the fine thread of her thoughts through the
centuries past. Yes, and through her we have learned to see Greece
with the inner eyes—not as a collection of battered vestiges left over
from cultures long since abandoned—but as something ever-present
and ever-renewed: the symbol married to the object prime—so that a
cypress tree, a mask, an orange, a plough were extended beyond
themselves into an eternality they enjoyed only with the furniture
of all good poetry. In the blithe air of Rhodes she has provided us
with a vicarious sense of continuity not only with the past—but also
with the future—for surely history's evaluations are wrong in speaking of civilized and barbaric ages succeeding or preceding one another,
surely they have always co-existed—for one is the measure of the
other? Everywhere the dualism of the human personality has
created side by side profanity and piety, truth and falsehood, hate and
love. Time is always aspiring to a dance-measure which will entangle
the two in a dance, a dialogue, a duet: dissolve their opposition. The
radiance of that worn stone figure carries the message to us so
clearly. . . .

Arriving back in Rhodes, I leave the little car in its usual place
under the plane-trees and walk slowly down the hill towards the
Villa Cleobolus. In a field a horse stands asleep, its coat aglitter with
dew. As I reach the esplanade I see that there is a light on in the duty-
room. This is unusual except when, for one reason or another, the
Cairo plane is delayed, and the mail is sorted at night. I climb the
staircase and push open the door to the duty-office. Sitting at a table,
facing one another, sit the two Sergeants Manners and Kirkbride,
puffing pipes and playing Rummy. They are inseparable friends, and
by consequence always elect to share tiresome guard duties together;
also as elderly married men they prefer a quiet life to the more
meretricious joys of festivals and balls, so that one usually finds them
on duty late at night or when the whole administration has had to
turn out for some function or other. 'It's come, sir,' says Manners,
taking his pipe out for a second and making a sort of token gesture of

standing up before he subsides again. Kirkbride, who has some of the middle-aged, matronly spread of a natural beer-drinker, copies his fellow and adds: 'Just come off the wireless room, sir. Order to pack up. I sent the signal clerk up to the Brig's villa.'

So it has come at last. The islands are to be handed back to Greece. I am delighted as I picture the beaming figure of General Gigantes when he hears the news. But my happiness is touched with regret, for this means yet another separation from a country which I have come to recognise as my second home.

I turn and go slowly downstairs and by the narrow gate into the heavy darkness of the Mufti's courtyard—so dark that I must grope my way past the tomb of Hacmet: the goat awakes in alarm and swings out on the end of its cord, scattering droppings with its hooves. In the silent garden the leaves are still dropping. They are not inclined to wait for autumn this year. My thoughts turn to E and I walk across the garden to the hotel to see if there is a light in her room. The shutters are open but the room is dark.

In my familiar room at the Villa Cleobolus I strike a match and the Turkish lovers leap off the counterpane towards me—as if they had been asleep. Yet the serenade has not ceased for an instant. The viol has been playing all the time in the darkness, touched by those long saintly fingers: she has been smiling idly up at him: the bird in the branches above their heads has been on duty all the time, singing as if its heart were broken. The two white vases filled with lilac raise their long graceful throats above the fireplace. I remember so vividly the thump of the clay on the wheel, and the gradual emergence of their fine stems under the broad thumbs of Egon Huber as he said 'Something for you two', trimming them with a fine knife as they turned: and then moving them off the wheel still wet, to the shadowy pottery where they would be given their glaze. They had stood there for two years now, fronting the shelf of sea-stained books and indifferent water colours, the rolled tent, the tinned food, the anchor. I think I have never loved a room so much. Here I have spent all my spare time—a whole winter—working on a play which is never destined to be published or played, stopping from time to time to pitch a resin-scented log on the fire, or look up a reference in a book. 'Here too I have been visited by friends who dropped in like swallows from the sky—Paddy and Xan: the Corn Goddess: John Craxton: Patrick Reilly—all bringing with them the flavour of the outside world: Romney Summers, Tricoglou and Jim Richards, who stayed and remembered: Mary Mollo and Katy P. who nearly died here. And Boris who thought I should get a job with Unesco and said that "This cult for islands was becoming deplorable".'

I sit for a while thinking about it all before undressing. I am half asleep when I notice something pinned to the counterpane. It is a signal adressed to my office. On a corner of the sheet of paper in E's tall handwriting is a message. 'Here it is at last.' The signal reads: 'The date for the handover is to be announced on Saturday. You will complete preparations for winding-up and report to Cairo by the first of next month, liquidating all our press responsibilities in the islands.'

I get into bed and settle down to sleep; but the waning moon has moved over and peers in at me from an unshuttered window, so that after perhaps two hours I am awake again. So radiant is the night, and so rich with the scent of flowers and creepers that I am reluctant to waste it in sleep. The news of our impending departure has made me miserly. I dress and walk rapidly across the little town to the hospital. The white ambulance is parked outside in the drive and a sleepy duty-nurse dozes under a weak yellowish bulb in the ugly stone entrance hall. I leave him asleep and climb to the first floor, tip-toeing through the long sleeping-wards in the direction of Mills's private room, which lies at an angle to the operating-theatre, on the shadowed side of the building. I open the door and make my way through the darkened room to the terrace. It is empty, but turning to my right, I can see shadowy figures seated around a table two terraces away. Very little moonlight penetrates the dense clump of pines which grows out of the side of the hill and all but hides the sky.

I retrace my steps into the lighted corridor and meet my friend as he is about to enter a door. He looks pale and weary, and is stripping his hands of their rubber gloves. 'He's no right to be alive but he is,' he whispers with the ghost of a smile, untying the tapes which meet across his back and pulling off the little sterile mask from his mouth in one deft flowing movement born of long practice. From somewhere to our left comes the faint clink of steel on metal. I imagine that some operation must be going forward in the theatre, but taking my arm he pilots me to the end of a corridor and into a small buttery where Chloe is cutting bread and butter. 'Come in,' she whispers and I sit down on a chair by the sink.

'Manoli and his wife are on the terrace. They've been crying, but they're asleep now, both,' she says. A nurse's head appears in the doorway and Mills jumps up with a muttered apology to vanish through the door. I say: 'Chloe, our orders came through tonight. We'll be leaving in a fortnight.'

She looks up with a wistful and sleepy grace, her face full of sympathy. She looks very beautiful with her hair piled carelessly up on the top of her head, her face unmade-up, her body youthful and candid in the flowered kimono. 'So have ours,' she says at last. 'They came through last week. We are posted to Abyssinia. He wouldn't let me tell anyone before it was necessary. We didn't want to break up all this.'

'Gideon will be sorry. I can see his face so clearly when he hears the news,' she continues. 'He will soon be left with only Hoyle for company.' 'But,' I say, 'their families will come out. A new life will begin.'[1]

'It is not the same,' she says, a little wistfully.

The enamel plate is full of sandwiches now. 'Will you take the plate and go and sit with Manoli, please? I must help Ray. They will be so hungry when they wake.'

I step into a darkened room and cross it on tiptoe to the terrace, placing the plate silently on the table and sinking into the empty chair which stands between the two sleeping figures. Manoli sits in the wicker chair like a waxwork, bolt upright, only his head has fallen a little to the right and his mouth is open. His Italian wife has drawn her head under her flowered shawl, as a bird draws its head under a wing. Their breathing sounds utterly composed, utterly peaceful. Before them stand untouched glasses of cognac on the metal table.

As I sit here between them I find myself sinking into that feeling of

---

[1] Not for Gideon alas! He was accidentally killed in crossing an unmarked minefield on Nisyros, and left a gap in our lives which could never be filled.

detachment, almost of peace, which visits me when I am alone in a great crowd of people all urgently occupied with their own affairs. Or else when I am an onlooker, at some drama which is going on before my eyes but in which I am powerless to take part. At such times one's individuality seems to focus itself with greater emphasis; one overlooks the affairs of men from a new height, participating in life with a richer though a vicarious understanding of it; and yet at the same time remaining fully withdrawn from it.

Sitting between these two sleeping figures, who will wake to a new meaning of life, a new daylight, I see them as symbols more than as human beings. Italy and Greece, if you like, the lovers: the Italy of the domestic arts, the passionate feeling for husbandry and family order, the feeling of a vineyard built with the fingers, pinch by pinch, into terraces of household wine: Italy that conquers as a wife or nurse, encroaching on nature with the arts of love. Then Greece: the vertical, masculine, adventurous consciousness of the archipelago, with its mental anarchy and indiscipline touched everywhere with the taste for agnosticism and spare living: Greece born into the sexual intoxication of the light, which seems to shine upwards from inside the very earth, to illuminate these bare acres of squill and asphodel. It seems to me so clear that their arts of life are not divergent ones, but the complementaries of each other. How unlucky that here, among the humps of Aegean stone, islets dropped red hot from the trowels of the Titans, among the windmills and the springs curdled by moss-grown cisterns, the truth should not have been made plain. They both belong to this sacred territory, husband and wife, as the myrtle and olive do.

And then again, between the sleeping figures, I saw the dying child, no less a symbol—but of what? Our world perhaps. For it is always the child in man which is forced to live through these repeated tragedies of the European conscience. The child is the forfeit we pay for the whole sum of our worldly errors. Only through him shall we ever salvage these lost cultures of passion and belief.

Then my thoughts turn to complete the greater arc of this small green island, touching my sleeping friends—the sightless stone woman in her cubicle, Gideon and Hoyle snoring somewhere among the mulberry trees of Trianda, Huber tacking for a late landfall at

183

Mandraccio after a night's fishing, E in her calm bed at the hotel feeling the first faint breath of the dawn-wind from Asia Minor as it stirs the balcony curtains, the Baron Baedeker and Christ snoring under the pines at Soroni . . . all playing an unconscious part in my own inner life, and now, by this writing, made a part of it forever.

The light is growing fast and it has turned much colder; the strip of sky behind the pines has been drained of the violet moonlight and is slowly filling with the new colour of approaching sunrise. I am suddenly beginning to feel sleepy here, alone with my thoughts. When Chloe comes to find us with whatever news the new world of sunlight has to offer she will find me dozing between the two silent figures.

EPILOGUE

The Sporades are lean wolves and hunt in packs; waterless, eroded by the sun. They branch off on every side as you coast along the shores of Anatolia. Then towards afternoon the shaggy green of Cos comes up; and then, slithering out of the wintry blue the moist green flanks of Rhodes.

It is good to see places where one has been happy in the past—to see them after many years and in different circumstances. The child is asleep in its rugs: that long, much-loved, much travelled coastline breasts its way up against the liner's deck until the town fans out—each minaret like the loved worn face of an earthly friend. I am looking, as if into a well, to recapture the faces of Hoyle, Gideon, Mills—and the dark vehement grace of E.

Ahead of us the night gathers, a different night, and Rhodes begins to fall into the unresponding sea from which only memory can rescue it. The clouds hang high over Anatolia. Other islands? Other futures?

Not, I think, after one has lived with the Marine Venus. The wound she gives one must carry to the world's end.

A Short Calendar of Flowers and Saints for Rhodes[1]

JANUARY

In some parts of Greece January is called 'The Pruner' because now the husbandman trims vines and trees. An omen is drawn from the observation of the weather at Epiphany. The following saw illustrates this:

> *Dry Epiphany and pouring Easter weather*
> *Bring us happiness and plenty both together.*

The woods are starred with early anemones of a delicate purple (Mostly *Anemone coronaria* L.) Visit the lush meadows around Casa del Pini.

January 7th is the feast of St John the Baptist and there is mumming in the streets by children in masks.

Glorious pink and white flowers of the wild almond in puffs everywhere. Flowering often begins as early as mid-December (*Amygdalus communis* L.) Loveliest in the hill districts.

The shy winter crocus with its lavender-coloured flowers appears (*Crocus Sieberi* Gay).

The Japanese medlar is in bloom. Its scent is strongest just after sunset. Wistaria blooms.

The weather in this month is often fine, dry and cold (the Halcyon days).

[1] Acknowledgements are due to Dr. Theodore Stephanides for help with this calendar.

FEBRUARY

On the second falls the Feast of the Purification of the Virgin (our Candlemas), and the prevailing weather on this day is popularly supposed to last 40 days.

Anemones still at their best.

The large purple periwinkle (*Vinca Major* L.) begins to flower.

Purple-blue irises (*Iris cretensis* Janka) appear.

The deliciously scented narcissus (*Narcissus Tazetta* L.) appears, esp. in swampy places.

Wistaria still in bloom.

MARCH

The first cuckoo and the early spring winds. (Charcoal-burners dread the cuckoo's note as foretelling dry weather.) Now the first cicadas begin to welcome the sunlight, and swallows start building under the house-eaves. (Destroy their nests and you'll get freckles, says popular legend). On the 1st of the month the boys fashion a wooden swallow, adorn it with flowers and travel from house to house collecting pennies and singing a little song which varies from place to place in Greece. This custom is of the remotest antiquity.

For the first three days of March peasants think it unlucky to wash or plant vegetables. Trees planted now will wither. The March sun burns the skin: and a red and white thread on the wrist will prevent your children from getting sunburn.

Some of the orchids begin to flower, incl. the purple lax-flowered orchid (*Orchis laxiflora* Lam.) which grows in swampy places; and various species of pyramid, bee and fly orchids.

Other blue irises (*Iris attica* and *Iris florentina*) appear.

The bright yellow bog iris (*Iris Pseudacorus* L.) brightens the dykes and other swampy places with its quarantine-like flags.

Narcissi still found: anemones dying off. Periwinkle still seen.

Orange and lemon trees in full bloom.

The arborescent heath (*Erica arborea* L.) shows its masses of white flowers. It is from the roots of this plant that 'briar' (from the French *bruyère*) pipes are made.

EASTER

has been grafted on to what was probably the Lesser Eleusinia in Ancient times—the return of Persephone. It is the period of red eggs and roasted lamb on the spit today and is ushered in by the great 40 days fast of Lent. The two Sundays before Lent are known respectively as Meat Sunday and Cheese Sunday. The week between them answers to our western carnival week and is so celebrated in the cities of Greece with masquerades, black dominoes etc. . . . Scholars hint at pre-Christian survivals saying that these antics suggest the Old Cronia festivals of ancient times while Lent itself suggests a connection with the Eleusinean mysteries—commemorating Demeter's long abstinence from food during her search for her lost daughter.

March 25th, Lady Day comes when peasants hang red coloured sashes and handkerchiefs from their balconies. Eggs are dyed red, and with the first egg the mother makes the sign of the cross on the face and neck of her child, saying 'May you be as rosy as this egg and as strong as a stone.' The egg is then placed near the family ikon of the Virgin until next year.

On Good Friday do not touch vinegar. It is unlucky because on this day the Jews moistened Christ's lips with it.

On Holy Saturday do not wash your hair or you'll turn grey before your time.

The midnight Mass of Easter Sunday is the highpost of the year's festivals and no traveller should miss the impressive ceremony. In villages the gospel is read out in the churchyard under a tree. At the end the news that 'Christ is risen' is announced to the banging of gongs and the explosion of crackers; in the dark church the priest holds up his consecrated candle and calls out to the congregation 'Come and receive the light'; they light each one a taper from his candle and pass the light back into the dark body of the church to the rest of the congregation. If you are lucky enough to get your candle home without it going out you'll have good luck the coming year.

APRIL

In the uplands sheep are shorn and the air is full of the plaintive crying of lambs unable to recognise their shorn dams; about the 23rd of the month (St George's Day, the patron saint of Brigands and Englishmen) the shepherds return to the mountains with their flocks.

Orchids at their best. Irises still going strong. Narcissi ending.

The spring Asphodel (*Asphodelus microcarpus* Viv.) shows its *branched* spikes of white flowers in the olive woods.

Snake-wort (*Dracunculus vulgaris* Schott) shows its huge green, brown and purple blossoms (rather like an outsize arum lily, rare) and can often be located from a distance by its carrion-like smell.

The prickly-pear (*Opuntia Ficus-indica*) begins to show its pretty yellow flowers.

The yellow wallflower (*Cheiranthus cheiri* L.) now in flower.

Various species of cistus begin to show their pink, white and yellow flowers.

The Judas-tree (*Cercis siliquastrum* L.) sometimes begins to bloom towards the end of the month.

Gorse (*Calycotome villosa*) and broom (*Spartium junceum* L.) explode into bright yellow on the hillsides.

The golden marigold (*Crysanthemum coronarium* L.) decks the fields.

MAY

Parties are formed to go picnicking and 'fetch back the May'; the young men of the village make wreaths of flowers and hang them at their sweethearts' doors; but May is unlucky for marriages because, says the proverb, 'In May the donkeys mate.'

Cistus, wallflower, periwinkle, prickly-pear, dracunculus, still in flower.

Judas-trees at their best, in great splashes of magenta all over the countryside. Gorse and broom in full wing. Bog iris still going strong.

Orchids finishing.

The climbing clematis (*Clematis flammula* L.) shows its white flowers. The peasants call it the swallow flower—chelidonia—probably because it appears when the swallows return.

The wild thyme (*Thymbra capitata* Griseb.) begins to flower, to the delight of the bees which produce the Hymettus honey.

White acacia trees in full flower (*Robinia Pseudacacia* L.).

JUNE

In some places called 'The Harvester' because the harvest begins normally in this month. On the 24th June falls the Nativity of St John the Baptist which is celebrated by a great feast with crackling bonfires.

Nigella (love-in-a-mist, alias devil-in-a-bush) shows its delicate pale blue flowers.

The seeds of the ailantus tree (*Ailantus glandulosa* Desf.) show great masses of orange and crimson.

The squirting cucumber (*Ecballium elaterium*) shows its pale yellow flowers. Within the month it is ready for action, and then mind your eye. Active until September.

Thyme in full swing; also mint and sage.

Swamp iris, prickly-pear, still in flower.

The spineless caper (*Capparis inermis*) shows its large white flowers with their long purple stamens. In rocks by the sea-shore.

The leaves of the eryngium turn a metallic blue.

The bright vermilion flowers of the pomegranate are seen; flowers also in July.

The chaste-tree (*Vitex agnus-castus* L.) shows its purple flowers; esp. along the coasts. The Ancient Greeks believed that the scent of its leaves and flowers was an 'anti-aphrodisiac', hence the name.

JULY

In some places called 'The Thresher' presumably because the corn is threshed in this month. In Macedonia farmers make a thin wafer-like cake from newly ground corn which they crumple into wells and distribute it among the passers-by; this is called grasshopper-cake—an offering to the favourite insect of the farmer. The cicada is the insect of this month, and his orchestra fills the long afternoons with deep humming. Often at this time a distant cousin, the locust, moves in for a week or two in the flat land about Malona and causes alarm; so far however his depredations have been successfully checked. He is blown over the sea from Africa, it is surmised. On the 30th July there is a huge open-air festival at Soroni to celebrate the arrival of St Saul who was a fellow-passenger of St Paul during his ship-wreck at Lindos. (A case of transferred names and attributes—as with ancient Gods and Goddesses, one wonders?)

The violet delphinium (*Delphinium junceum* DC.) in flower. Also in August.

The golden thistle (*Scolymus hispanicus* L.) shows its yellow flowers in all uncultivated places.

The mullein (*Verbascum undulatum* Lam.) shows its yellow flowers.

Some species are used by the peasants to make fish poisons. The oleander is seen in masses of pink (occasionally white).

Prickly-pear still in flower.

The agave (aloe) rockets upwards after a flying start in May and shows its spike of yellow-green flowers. Also in September.

AUGUST

The jackdaw is the bird of the month, and August begins with the Progress of the Precious and Unifying Cross. This feast prepares one for another fast which is prelude to the Feast of the Repose of the

Virgin. On the 23rd the Feast of the Holy Merciful is celebrated; again on the 29th a feast for the Cutting Off of the Precious Head of St John the Precursor heralds more abstinence.

In general however August is the great dancing month, and panagyreias are held at Maritza on the 6th, while the big feast of the Virgin held on the 15th and 23rd at Trianda and Cremasto is the biggest event of the year, attracting islanders from Simi, Cos, Casos *et alia*, and highlanders from the brilliant hill villages like Siana whose costumes and dancing reminds one of the fastnesses of Crete.

The beautiful sand lily (*Pancratium maritimum L.*) shows its white flowers in the coastal sands.

The caper still in flower (until September).

SEPTEMBER

On the 14th there is a festival dedicated to the Cross at Callithies. Childless women make the weary pilgrimage to the top of the razorback hill called Tsambika below San Benedetto—and here, in the chapel of Our Lady, they eat a small piece of the wick from one of the lamps which will make them fruitful. If the resulting infant is not named after the Virgin it dies.

The autumn asphodel (*Scilla autumnalis L.*) shows its *unbranched* spike of white flowers in all the olive woods. The peasants make a rat poison from its huge bulb.

The grapes are gathered (beginning.)

OCTOBER

A golden month which belongs to St Demetrius; at his feast on the 26th wine-casks are unstapped and the new wine tasted. Many weddings take place in this month, and an eagerly anticipated spell of fine weather which comes around the middle month is known as The Little Summer of St Demetrius.

Grape gathering in full swing.

The crocus-like *Sternbergia sicula Tin.* shows its bright yellow blossoms after the first autumn rains.

The autumn mandrake (*Mandragora autumnalis*) shows its purple flowers at about the same time (rare).

The cyclamen have just started their lilac flood.

NOVEMBER

In many places still called 'The Sower' because seed-time is beginning; St Andrew is the most popular saint of this month and his feast falls on the last day of the month. He is the bringer of the first snow (Popular saying: 'St Andrew has washed his beard white'). The feast of the Virgin on the 21st is sometimes not celebrated in Rhodes. On the 18th also St Plato the Martyr (whom popular ignorance has transformed into St Plane-Tree, the names being very similar). The weather which prevails on the 18th will last through Advent (The Forty Days). Now the Pleiades begin to rise, and the first sea-gales drive the long-shore fisherman to his winter quarters. The melancholy of the dying year is hardly cast off by St Andrew's holiday on which everyone eats 'loucumades'—a sort of doughnut-shaped waffle.

The autumn crocus (*Crocus laevigatus*) appears. Flowers white to mauve.

The saffron crocus (*Crocus cartwrightianus*) also appears. Purple blossoms. Bulbs used to make the condiment 'saffron'.

Cyclamen in full blossom.

The fruit of the orange and tangerine begin to turn golden.

DECEMBER

The saint of the month is St Nicholas, and rightly so; the seafarer needs his patron saint most at the year's end; but there are plenty more on the index of saints.

4th December		St Barbara
5th	,,	St Savvas
6th	,,	St Nicholas
12th	,,	St Spiridion

After Spiridion's day the days grow longer by a grain—a horrible pun in Greek.

Christmas Eve—Incense is burned before supper, and those flat hot-cross buns called 'Christ's loaves' are baked in the oven. After supper the cloth is not removed from the table because it is believed that Christ will come and eat during the night. A log or an old shoe is left burning on the fire: the smoke will ward off stray 'Kallikanzari' (see 'Kaous' in the text).

New Year's Day belongs to St Basil: a cake with a silver coin in it is made and cut and luck belongs to whoever finds the coin. After supper the family plays games of divination. A slice of new year cake under a girl's pillow will do for a Greek girl what a slice of wedding-cake does for an English girl.

Twelfth Day—The curious ceremony of diving for the Cross can be seen on Rhodes harbour where a dozen shivering lads contend for the prize, and duck the winner of the reward.

Cyclamen end; anemones begin.

Almond and Japanese medlars in flower towards end of month.

Oranges and tangerines ripe.

Snow-drops come out in bloom in some parts of the island.

Peasant Remedies

A few peasant remedies are given here, quoted by permission of the author, from a paper contributed by A. Raymond Mills to the *Bulletin of the History of Medicine*, Johns Hopkins University.

ABSCESS.

1. Crushed onions with mastika are put on hot as a poultice.
2. Scoop out the centre of an onion and fill with sugar, incense, powdered dried reed, olive oil, and a little soap. Cook in the oven and apply to the abscess hot.
3. Snails are gathered, taken out of their shells, ground up, and applied.
4. Baked potatoes without their skins are mixed with oil and sugar and used as a poultice.

BALDNESS AND FALLING HAIR.

1. Mix garlic, dynamite powder, and powdered roofing tile and make a paste with water. Shave the head and apply the paste. Cover the paste with cow dung.
2. The dung beetle is powdered, mixed with alcohol and dabbed on to the bald patches.
3. Two yolks of egg are added to powdered dry fig leaves. This paste is put on to the hair. It cures baldness and dandruff.

BIRTH.

This is often performed in the sitting position, and a chair cut away in the seat is used specially for this purpose. (The squatting position is now being tried by a London hospital.) In the Cyprus Museum there is a terracotta figure of a woman giving birth and being held up by the arms in the sitting position, with a helper delivering the baby. This figure dates from 500 B.C. and shows a strong Phoenician influence.

To bring on labour pains bran (pítyron) is boiled and wrapped up in a cloth and applied to the abdomen hot. A hot tile (keramídi) is used in a similar way to apply dry heat.

Seven days after the birth of the child the midwife puts her bare foot on the vulva of the woman and pulls each hand in turn. A vaginal douche is then performed after which sexual intercourse is permitted. This treatment is supposed to replace the genital organs and its efficiency was vouched for by a woman who was the mother of fifteen children!

BURNS.

Ink is used in a similar way to tannic acid.

In the majority of cases mastika is applied liberally and a light dressing put on. Infection is said never to occur with this method.

COMMON COLD.

Crude sheep's wool is dipped into a mixture of paprika and mastika. The whole body is rubbed vigorously with the wool.

CONJUNCTIVITIS.

Wash out eye with sap of vine or tears. Or with cow's or human urine. An ophthalmologist friend of mine has seen bilateral gonococcal conjunctivitis as a result of this method. The child lost the sight of both eyes.

ERYSIPELAS.

1. Dissolve copper sulphate in mastika and massage into the area.

2. A piece of red cloth is put on top of the area of the rash. Seven pieces of resinous wood and seven small pieces of cotton wool are used. A piece of cotton wool is placed on top of the red cloth and a piece of resinous wood on top of the cotton. The wood is lighted and as soon as the cotton takes fire it is flicked off with the finger and the following words are repeated. The whole process is repeated seven times:

> 'káto stó gialó stín ámmo
> oí spanói zeygári kánoyn
> vázoyn tís psolés tón alétri
> kài t'archeídia tón zeygári.

Mi òspóros tón matiásei
míti fókio na rizósi.'

This may be translated as follows:

'Down on the beach, on the sand
the beardless ones are mating,
they use the penis like a plough
and their testicles like a pair of oxen.
Let not the Evil Eye fall on the seed (sperms)
nor the erysipelas take root.'

This is strongly suggestive of the ancient phallic ceremonies in which foul words and gestures were used to ward off evil spirits and at the same time, ensure fertility.

LACTATION.

An amber bead hung round the neck of a pregnant woman will ensure a plentiful supply of milk, as will wine and hot bathings. If the mother wishes to stop lactating, a key is hung down the back inside the clothes. Mud from flat roofs (patelía) is made into a paste and smeared on the breast to stop the flow of milk. (This is an interesting link with the Egyptian Arabs who use mud from the roof for the same purpose, the mud in this instance containing dung.) If a woman suckles her child she believes that she cannot become pregnant, during that time. I have seen children being suckled at the age of three and a half years.

PREGNANCY.

The desires of the woman for unusual foods at unusual times must be satisfied. If she does not satisfy her desire and happens to touch her body at the same time, the baby will be marked where she has touched herself. The birthmark of the child is also supposed to indicate the nature of the desire.

Indigestion during pregnancy is due to the unborn infant developing hair. The indigestion is cured by a spoonful of sesame seeds. Coffee is applied to the umbilicus of the newborn infant as an astringent and antiseptic.

A pregnant woman must not cross her legs on sitting down because the child will have the 'cord round the neck'.

SEX.

To determine the sex of an unborn child the following methods are used:

1. When the woman is seven months pregnant, a drop of breast milk is expressed into a glass of water. If the milk dissolves, the child will be a female. If the milk drop remains fibrous and upright in the water, it will be a boy. The latter is obviously a phallic symbol.

2. A knife and a pair of scissors are placed each on a seat and covered with a cushion. The expectant mother is sent out of the room while this is being done and she is called in to choose a chair. If she sits on the knife, it will be a boy; if she sits on the scissors, it will be a girl. The knife is another phallic symbol.

SMALLPOX.

The Greek name is 'evlogià'. This means 'she must be named with respect'. This is a reference to the fear of omnipotent destructive spirits. They must not be offended. Hence the respectful name. Compare with Evil Eye.

Select Bibliography

In English

Rhodes in Ancient Times	1885	Torr
Rhodes in Modern Times		
Aegean Islands	1887	Tozer
Travels and Discoveries in the Levant (2 vols.)	1865	Newton

In French

L'île de Rhodes	1881	Bileotti and Cottret
L'île de Rhodes	1856	Guerin
Description des Monuments de Rhodes	1828	Rottiers
Histoire des Chevaliers Hospital-iers	1726	Vertor

In Italian

Isola de Rodi	1688	Coronelli: Parisotti
Istoria del Sacro Militare Ordine Gerosolimitano	1602	Bosio

In Modern Greek

ΡΟΔΙΑΚΑ	1939	*ΑΝΑΣΤΑΣΙΟΥ Γ. ΒΡΟΝΤΗ*
ΡΟΔΙΤΙΚΑ ΤΡΑΓΟΥΔΙΑ	1939	*ΑΝΑΣΤΑΣΙΟΥ Γ. ΒΡΟΝΤΗ*
Ο ΑΓΙΟΣ ΣΟΥΛΑΣ	1934	*ΕΜΜ. ΚΥΡΙΑΖΗ*